VICIOUS MURDER

The mother was hysterical, crying, her clothing covered in fresh blood. She repeated over and over "Michelle did it." Her friend tried to comfort her as paramedics and police noisily milled around her in the small apartment.

Inside the bedroom it was quiet.

Sixteen-year-old Laurie Show lay faceup on the floor. Large pools of blood encircled her upper body. Small clumps of blood-saturated hair dotted the white carpet, and the closet doors were smeared with blood.

There was a five-inch knife slash across her throat.

OVERKILL

Lyn Riddle

PINNACLE BOOKS
Kensington Publishing Corp.
www.pinnaclebooks.com

PINNACLE BOOKS are published by

Kensington Publishing Corp.
850 Third Avenue
New York, NY 10022

All Kensington Titles, Imprints, and Distributed Lines are available at special quantity discounts for bulk purchases for sales promotions, premiums, fund-raising, and educational or institutional use. Special book excerpts or customized printings can also be created to fit specific needs. For details, write or phone the office of the Kensington special sales manager: Kensington Publishing Corp., 850 Third Avenue, New York, NY 10022, attn: Special Sales Department, Phone: 1-800-221-2647.

Pinnacle and the P logo Reg. U.S. Pat. & TM Off.

First Printing: February 2001
10 9 8 7 6 5 4 3 2 1

Printed in the United States of America

For my mother, Doris Howell Nabers,
and my father, Robert Franklin Nabers,
heroes, too

Part 1: The Murder

One

The sun had not yet peaked above the cutover corn-fields of Pennsylvania's Amish country when Hazel Show guided her three-year-old Ford Tempo out of the parking lot of her condominium complex. Hazel thought it was odd to be summoned to meet her daughter Laurie's high school counselor so early in the morning. But, at least she could get the ordeal over with and get on with her Christmas shopping. Only four more days until the holiday. Her house had been decorated for some time. A Christmas tree with family heirlooms—the handmade treasures Laurie made in school—stood in the corner, decorated a few days earlier by Laurie and two friends. A pine wreath hung from the center of the garland-wrapped railing outside the second-floor condominium.

Hazel wondered what the counselor wanted. Laurie had no idea. The night before, Laurie had said she had done nothing wrong. Nothing unusual had happened at Conestoga Valley High School, where Laurie was a sophomore. She seemed genuinely puzzled, Hazel thought. Surely, they were not going back to the time, some months earlier, when Laurie was hanging out with people Hazel disapproved of, when some of Hazel's jewelry mysteriously vanished. Hazel now considered Laurie's earlier problems normal teenage rebellion that had run its course. School was a priority and her friends seemed fairly stable.

Hazel Show worked as a nurse's aide at Community Hospital in Lancaster, about two miles from her condominium at the Oaks in East Lampeter Township, the heart of Amish country. She was at the hospital the day before, sterilizing instruments, when the counselor's call came into the nurses' lounge. Few people had that number, so Hazel had known before answering that it was something important, most likely from Laurie or one of Hazel's brothers.

"Mrs. Show, this is Mrs. Cooper at Conestoga Valley High School. I'm wondering if you could meet me at school tomorrow morning. I need to talk with you about a problem with Laurie."

"A problem?" Hazel had said.

"Yes, a problem with a boy and something that happened outside the gym today. I'd rather talk in person."

Hazel had agreed to meet her at 7:30 A.M.

Twenty minutes later, the lounge phone had rung again.

"Mrs. Show, this is Mrs. Cooper. I forgot I have a meeting at Conestoga Valley Junior High on Friday. Could you just meet me there, about seven?"

Hazel had agreed and gone back to work. Now, she was driving past a collection of homes, turning onto Horseshoe Road, which led to the farms of the Amish in Lancaster County, situated in Pennsylvania's southeastern corner. She had lived her whole life in the area, where the Amish and the folks they called the "English" had forged an alliance, symbiotic yet separate. The Amish kept to themselves, but everyone in one way or another relied on the tourists who flocked to see for themselves the simple life, a life of horses and buggies, farming for subsistence and for profit, no electricity.

Hazel Show pulled into the parking lot of the junior high school and walked inside. It was a few minutes before seven and the commotion of a middle school's day had not yet begun. A janitor directed her to the office to wait for Mrs. Cooper. Hazel sat down and noticed the festive Christmas decorations. Minutes passed. Mrs. Cooper did not arrive. A man delivered presents adorned in elegant Christmas wrap. A secretary came in and sat behind her desk to start her day, the last before school let out for vacation. Another secretary walked in, but no Mrs. Cooper.

Hazel looked at her watch: 7:07. Normally a patient person who would wait thirty minutes or more for someone, Hazel decided "that's it," and scratched out a hasty note for Mrs. Cooper. She headed home. Something nagged her, telling her to hurry. Driving fast, she darted easily along narrow Horseshoe Road, retracing her route of a few minutes earlier. This time, she made every one of the five traffic lights on the seven-mile route and arrived home quickly.

A neighbor met her as she alighted from the car.

"Is something wrong?" said the neighbor, an older woman, crippled by scoliosis, who always seemed to be around. She and her husband lived downstairs from the Shows in a complex of two-story apartments, four to each building.

"What do you mean?" Hazel said.

"There was a commotion upstairs," the woman said.

Hazel Show darted up the stairs, put her key in the lock, and pushed inside. The lights were on in the kitchen. Maybe Laurie had made cocoa, she thought. Hazel assumed Laurie had already left for school; her boyfriend, Brad Heisler, was supposed to pick her up. Must have been when Brad came in that the neighbor heard what she considered a commotion, Hazel thought.

But then, as she walked past the bathroom, Hazel noticed Laurie's curling iron was still plugged in. Decidedly unlike Laurie, Hazel thought. Brad and his father both served on the local volunteer fire department. That would have certainly caught his attention.

She peeked around the corner into Laurie's bedroom. It took her a moment to realize what her eyes were seeing. On the white plush carpet lay her daughter covered in blood. Arms jerking at her sides, Laurie gasped for breath, mouselike noises coming from her throat. Her eyes were open.

Hazel turned and ran to the front door, screaming to her neighbor, "Call nine-one-one. Laurie's hurt." She hurried back into her daughter's room and saw a white rope—like something used for a clothesline—tied around Laurie's neck. Hazel dropped her coat onto the floor, which was covered with blood and dirt from a potted plant that had been knocked over. She rushed into the kitchen, grabbed a paring knife from a drawer, and darted back into Laurie's bedroom.

Hazel cut the rope from Laurie's throat and Laurie's head fell back, revealing a horrible gash across her neck. Laurie's throat had been slashed to the spine. Laurie moaned. Frantically Hazel lifted her daughter, trying in an almost senseless way to keep Laurie's body together. She just wanted to stop the blood that now covered her, her daughter, and much of the rug. Hazel braced her daughter's back with her chest, holding Laurie's face close to her own.

Gasping for air, Laurie looked at her mother.

"I'm so sorry," Hazel cried. "It was a setup. Who did this?"

"Michelle. Michelle did it," Laurie wheezed. The words were barely there.

"You didn't do anything wrong," the mother said, anxious to make her words count. She feared her daughter was dying. "I love you. Daddy loves you. God will take care of you."

Laurie mouthed, "Love you."

The neighbor came into the apartment followed by another neighbor, who felt for Laurie's pulse. He told Hazel he found a weak one and then Laurie moved her leg. Hazel felt her spirit rise. Maybe Laurie will pull through. Hazel had been around hospitals and injuries long enough to know there was nothing she could do. She needed doctors, surgery. Laurie had lost so much blood.

Hazel knelt on the floor, cradling her daughter, and then she looked up mournfully into the smooth face of a paramedic, who seemed not much older than Laurie. Five others came in seconds later, and Hazel moved away. But the medics stood where they were. They looked at Hazel covered in blood, at the rope and the knife on the floor, and did not move.

Realizing they thought she was the attacker, Hazel screamed, "I didn't do it. You've got to help her."

They moved in, checking for a pulse as Hazel sat on her daughter's bed, covered with clothes Laurie had considered wearing that morning. Laurie still had on the navy blue sweatshirt with Penn State Lions embossed on the front and matching sweatpants that she usually wore to bed.

Police arrived moments later. It was 7:45 A.M., December 20, 1991.

A friend from the hospital arrived and guided Hazel Show out of the room. Sitting at the dining room table, Hazel took a glass of water from someone—she didn't even notice who—and wanted only to squeeze the glass until it broke. But she sat there wordlessly as the world seemed to spin in a most gruesome way. Her only child. Her daughter. How could this happen? She realized the medics had not transported Laurie to the hospital. No one told her, but she knew her daughter was gone.

Corporal Jan Fassnacht, the shift supervisor that morning for the East Lampeter Township Police, was first on the scene. His wife worked at the same hospital as Hazel Show, and he knew the family. He'd been a fixture within the police department as a dispatcher and as an officer for more than twenty years. Officer Robin Weaver, the policeman colleagues called "Pretty Boy" for his good looks, followed within seconds. Fassnacht approached Hazel, who was crying. "Michelle did it," she screamed as he drew close. "Brad saw it. He was here." She was crazed, sputtering words between sobs.

Weaver headed toward the bedroom. East Lampeter is a small town, just twelve thousand people, and Weaver, too, had had prior contact with Laurie. He glanced at her now lifeless body, her blue, almost hazel, eyes staring vacantly at the ceiling. Laurie's room looked so much like most every other girl's room he had ever seen. Her iron bed—a daybed—was painted white and covered in a beige and blue comforter dotted with red roses. Amish dolls hung from the walls. Two bookcases, loaded with stuffed bears, nearly touched the ceiling in a corner of the room. Weaver walked around the apartment to make sure whoever killed Laurie Show was not there still. He walked into the living room, filled with teddy bears and other stuffed animals. He noticed a sunroom at the back with a wall full of windows but no doors. Sun shone brightly in, despite the cold winter outside. Only one way in and out—the front door—and it showed no sign of forced entry. The windows were locked, he noted. Weaver looked into Hazel Show's bedroom. No one was in there.

Police and friends convinced Hazel to go downstairs to the neighbor's apartment while police began their first homicide investigation in ten years. Though reluctant to leave her daughter, Hazel complied as blood dried on her cream-colored sweater and blue jeans.

Weaver then turned to his assigned duty: to sketch the floor plan of the apartment, showing every detail, from a blood splatter on the wall in the hallway, to the body, to the telephone that had been jerked from the wall. As he moved about Laurie's bedroom, taking notes, he collected evidence. Several small clumps of hair. The blood-soaked rope. He noticed the wounds on Laurie's body. Besides the gash on her neck, she also suffered a large gash on her left leg and deep wounds to her fingers and palms. Dozens of small stab wounds. She fought hard, Weaver thought. Those wounds were clearly an act of desperation, someone trying to stem an assault, to grab a weapon.

Police were stunned by the viciousness. Many years later, Renee Schuler, then a corporal with the East Lampeter Township Police, said, "I've never seen so much blood." A tall, thin woman with carefully coiffed bleached blond hair, Schuler lived across the parking lot from the Shows. She knew Laurie and her mother only to wave as she left her apartment, usually on her way to work at the tiny one-story brick building that housed the police department, about a mile away on Old Philadelphia Pike. When she was hired in 1981, Schuler was the first woman on the force.

The morning of the Show murder, she and her husband, Jere, an officer with West Lampeter Township, a neighboring police department, were fast asleep. Fassnacht's loud banging on their front door jolted them awake shortly after 8:00 A.M.

"There's been a murder," Fassnacht told Jere Schuler as he opened the door. Renee Schuler dressed quickly in jeans and a T-shirt and headed across the pavement. She'd had only a couple of hours of sleep because she and her husband had celebrated their fourth wedding anniversary the night before. They were supposed to be off from work that day, but as it turned out, no one was off duty that day. The investigation drew in all available East Lampeter Township officers as well as others from surrounding communities such as Strasburg and West Lampeter and the state police. Renee Schuler drew the assignment to interview neighbors, looking for anyone who had seen anything suspicious.

By nine o'clock, other police officers had arrived, including Ron Savage, a detective who would lead the investigation. At 9:20 A.M., Trooper Anthony Suber of the Pennsylvania State Police arrived to take photographs. He worked in Laurie's bedroom for about fifteen minutes, the bright flash illuminating the horrid scene, recording the slaughter. By the time Suber began his work, Laurie's body lay straight out across the floor, her head near the wooden door of her closet. It had been moved by her mother and by paramedics.

Green envelopes, containing Christmas cards she was to send to friends, littered the floor near her head. A basket that had held a peace lily was now empty, tipped over against three large boxes swiped with blood. Hazel had brought the boxes home for Laurie to use for Christmas presents. The cord of Laurie's baby blue trimline telephone was wrapped around her right leg; a leather jacket she was giving her boyfriend for Christmas had been slung into a heap on the floor near the bed.

On her hand, positioned on her hip as if she were

idly standing somewhere, was her high school ring from Conestoga Valley High School. A silver bracelet her mother gave her adorned her wrist.

Police moved Laurie's body into the dining room just before 10:00 A.M. and continued collecting evidence, measuring, photographing. They picked up the wood-handled knife Hazel Show had used to get the rope from her daughter's neck. It had been partially lying under her. Sometime before noon, they eased Laurie's body, shrouded in a black body bag, down the steep steps and into a waiting ambulance for the ride to the morgue. An autopsy was scheduled for the next morning.

John Show, Laurie's father, had taken a truckload of poinsettias from a Lancaster greenhouse to the market in Philadelphia. It was a side job for him. He made farm machinery full-time, but loved to work with flowers. Laurie had helped him load the truck the night before. She had mentioned the counselor's call and told her father she hadn't done anything wrong. She was being blamed for something she didn't do.

"Mom's going, Mom will get it all straightened," Show had said of his ex-wife.

They had had dinner at Kentucky Fried Chicken—Laurie loved fried chicken—and he'd taken her back to the condominium. He'd gotten out, as usual, to hug and kiss his daughter, who was wearing her signature Penn State sweatshirt, before getting back into the Blazer to watch his daughter lope up the steps and slip inside.

Now, early Friday morning, the greenhouse owner walked over to John as he unloaded the poinsettias and said he had better get back to Lancaster; his daughter had been in an accident. John jumped into one of the trucks, but his boss insisted another worker drive. They

were told to go to General Hospital. John thought that
was odd. His father, a doctor, and Hazel, a nurse's aide,
were both affiliated with Community Hospital.

"I betcha Michelle had something to do with this,"
John Show told his coworker. They stopped at the greenhouse for John to pick up his SUV.

"Laurie's home now," a secretary called out to him.

John hurriedly drove to East Lampeter and saw ambulances parked outside. Then he saw the preacher
from the hospital—Reverend Samuel Knupp, known as
"Reverend Sam"—and the coroner.

It's bad, he thought, darting up the stairs toward the
condominium. A crowd of policemen held him back.
They wouldn't let him inside as he struggled to break
free. Reverend Sam stepped over to him and told John
Show his only child was dead.

John screamed at the police. "You should have done
something. You knew Michelle was harassing Laurie. You
should have found her."

He sat down on the steps and cried. A loud wail
shook his body. All he could think of was how he wanted
to go in and see his daughter, but police and others
wouldn't let him get inside. Hazel came outside and
yelled his name. He grabbed her in desperation and
hugged her, and they cried together for their lost child.
They held on to each other like they never had before
and cried. Finally they let go and went into the apartment of the downstairs neighbor.

Savage and Lancaster County detective Ron Barley
soon came in to talk to Hazel and John. Sitting in the
sunporch, the tall brown-haired mother was a bit more
composed now. Occasionally she wiped her eyes. Tears
would not stop, but the words came easier. She told
them her daughter's last words: "Michelle did it." Just
the night before, a policeman had come to the Shows'

apartment. Hazel was there alone; Laurie was out with her father. The policeman told Hazel they had not found Michelle Lambert, whom Laurie had filed simple assault charges against a month earlier.

"She just won't go away," Hazel Show told police as her daughter pressed the charges in November.

Lambert, Laurie claimed, had pushed her against a wall and hit her as Laurie left her job at the Deb Shop in East Towne Mall, not far from her condominium. Laurie had told police her problems with Lambert had begun several months earlier after she dated Lawrence Yunkin, a tall, handsome twenty-year-old who made rafters for a living. He was Michelle Lambert's one great love; Laurie's brief fling. Lawrence and Michelle had broken up, but then reunited ten days later when she had told Yunkin she was pregnant with his child. A week and a half had been all the contact Laurie had with Yunkin.

About 10:30 A.M.—three hours after the murder—East Lampeter police issued a press release informing the public that they were looking for a two-tone brown Mercury Monarch occupied by a white male in his late teens to early twenties, six feet tall, 190 pounds, with shoulder-length blond hair, and a white female, eighteen, brown eyes, blond hair, five feet seven inches, pregnant. No names were revealed, but in the small town, most knew who the police were looking for. One day, the hurriedly composed release would come back to haunt the tiny police department, as would so much of what they did that day.

Renee Schuler walked through the condominium complex knocking on doors. Most of the residents had already gone to work. She found one couple who lived near the road who said they saw two figures clothed in sweatshirts with hoods pulled over their heads walking out of the apartment complex shortly after the murder took place. At another apartment, a neighbor said she saw two women leaving the Show unit. That was the sum total of their witnesses. No one had really seen anything.

At Conestoga Valley High School, where Laurie should have been joyously celebrating the last day of school before the Christmas holiday, the principal, instead, announced her death. The words were launched throughout the modern brick facility over the public-address system at about 1:30 P.M. He told students they could come to the guidance department if they wanted to talk about it.

"It was quiet, very quiet," seventeen-year-old Jason Chastain told the local newspaper, the *Intelligencer Journal*. Jason knew Laurie well. A month earlier, he had been with her at a Park City Center store, where she bought him a baseball cap he had admired.

"She'd give you anything," he said.

He and his brother, David, went to the Shows' apartment after school and stood around with other onlookers as police worked inside, behind the yellow police tape that now strung across the area like a garish Christmas decoration.

Police worked in the Show apartment until after 4:00 P.M.

That afternoon Hazel Show asked a friend to take her to the morgue. She had to see her daughter. When Hazel arrived at the Lancaster facility, housed in the basement of the Conestoga View Nursing Home, her ex-husband, John, was there. She felt bad for him to have to get such a startling call—your daughter's been in a very bad accident—all but saying aloud she was dead. Hazel had never gotten a call telling her someone she loved had died. It wasn't that she hadn't lost someone she loved; it just seemed for some reason, she was always there. She had been with her grandmother when she died thirty-one years before, her mother when she died fourteen years earlier, and her dad when he died early in 1991. Now Laurie. It meant everything to her that Laurie had held on long enough to say good-bye, to tell her who had killed her.

"She fought to stay alive until I got home," Hazel told her family.

Now she looked at her daughter's sixteen-year-old body lying on a table in an austere death house, a sheet pulled to her neck. Her face had been cleaned of blood and dirt.

A smile was affixed to her face. Hazel then knew her daughter was with God.

"After what she had been through, to be able to end up with a smile on her face, that was just one more thing to let me know she was OK," Hazel said years later.

Sometime later that night, Hazel Show was driven out to her brother's house in East Earl. She and her four brothers and one sister had grown up nearby in a little wood frame house in the mountain community about twelve miles northeast of East Lampeter. Her brother was remodeling the home place, tucked into a curve on the winding road to the mountains, surrounded by cedars. She and Laurie had helped. They had torn out walls. Painted. Whatever was needed.

Laurie was to have spent the Christmas holiday there. It was the perfect place for her to get away from Michelle's interminable harassment. The thought of that now seemed like a cruel dream to Hazel. "Guarded" by Hazel, John, and her boyfriend, Brad, Laurie had not been alone in public for months. She had been killed in her own home, her own bedroom, despite all the precautions, despite the police report.

Hazel Show sat down wearily at the kitchen table, her hands propping up her head. Crusted blood clung to her sweater, her jeans. She felt numb. Hazel doesn't remember how long she sat there. Minutes, maybe an hour. Finally her sister-in-law walked over, placed her hands tenderly on Hazel's back, and said, "Honey, don't you want to get a bath?"

Hazel almost said she didn't. But she looked around at what was left of her family and realized how uncomfortable they were, how unsettling all that dried blood was. She walked into the bathroom and began removing her clothes. Layer by layer. Blood had soaked through her bra to her skin.

She ran the water until it was hot enough and stepped in.

"I didn't want to," she remembers. She stood in the tub, water dyed red flowing off her shivering body, the color stark against the white porcelain. With every beat of the water, she felt her only child drift out of her life.

At forty, Hazel Show was alone. She sat down in the tub and wept.

Two

At about the same time Hazel Show arrived at her brother's house on the night her daughter was murdered, Michelle Lambert, Lawrence Yunkin, and their friend Tabbi Buck were hanging out at the Garden Spot Bowling Alley in Strasburg, a pretty little town of narrow, tree-lined streets and two-story brick shops just south of East Lampeter. The highlight of an evening in Strasburg for tourists is a ghost walk sponsored by a local gem and jewelry store. A country-style ice cream/gift shop at the center of town offers a place to watch a steady stream of Amish families trot by in their horses and buggies. The gray-topped buggies mean Old Order Amish, the all-black that the family is of another sect. Buggies without tops are for courting couples. It is a sight that never ceases to bring wonder to fast-driving, city-dwelling tourists.

Police had been looking for Yunkin and Lambert much of the day. Yunkin was not at work at Denlinger's, a rafter manufacturer where his stepfather, Barry Yunkin, worked as well. They weren't even sure where the couple lived. They had moved someplace out in the country from an apartment in the Bridgeport section of East Lampeter months before. Police knew Yunkin frequented the Garden Spot—his mother, Jackie, worked there part-time—and they had asked a friend of his to call them if he arrived.

About 10:00 P.M., the friend called. Yunkin had arrived and Lambert was with him. Police decided to simply ask the couple to come into the police station, rather than arrest them. If Yunkin and Lambert refused, police would arrest them on two outstanding warrants. Yunkin for a noise violation; Lambert for the earlier simple assault against Laurie.

Six officers—from East Lampeter police, the state police, and other agencies—descended on the bowling alley at about 10:30. They located Yunkin's car, a Zephyr, not a Monarch as they had said in a press release earlier in the day. They had discovered their mistake from Yunkin's parents, who had gone to the police department to get information. Jackie Yunkin had heard about the murder from a customer at Weis Market, where Yunkin worked in the produce department. The news was all over television and it was the lead story in that afternoon's edition of the *Lancaster New Era*.

"Did you hear about the mother being lured away and her daughter was killed?" the girl said excitedly.

"No, who was it?" Jackie said casually.

"The girl's name is Laurie Show."

Jackie Yunkin could not have been more shocked if the girl had slapped her across the face. She knew Laurie. Her son had brought her home one afternoon, during the time he and Lambert had been apart, a time Jackie had felt hopeful for her son's future because he had finally gotten away from the girl she considered too controlling. A bad, hopeless feeling swelled inside her.

"How could he do this?" Jackie screamed. She called her husband.

"You know he didn't do it," said Barry, who had adopted Lawrence as a toddler. He was the only true

father the boy had ever known. Biology meant nothing.
Lawrence was his son. He believed in him.

"Why did he do it?" Jackie persisted. She knew where
one was, the other was. Lawrence and Michelle were
inseparable.

The Yunkins tried desperately to find their son. They
went to see Savage, the lead detective, but he would not
give them any information. It seemed to the parents
that he suspected they wanted information so they could
help their son get away. That was not so. They just
wanted to find him.

Years later, Jackie Yunkin still reeled at the way she
felt Savage treated her.

"What I'm doing is no business of yours," she recalls
him saying. She had blurted out the information that
the police were looking for the wrong car. It had been
her own way of saying the police didn't know what they
were doing.

At the bowling alley, John Duby of the Pennsylvania
Police spotted Yunkin and Lambert sitting on the floor
near a pool table. He asked them if they would come
with him to the East Lampeter Township Police headquarters. Police needed some information, he said, trying to be casual. Before they could answer, Chief Robert
Ham of the Strasburg Borough Police told them they
were under arrest and ordered them to put their hands
on a railing in front of them. They were handcuffed
and led outside to waiting patrol cars.

At the time, police did not know Tabbi Buck. She was
not a suspect. But she soon became one when police
saw a nasty scratch on her face and realized she had
come to the bowling alley with Lambert and Yunkin.
Police told her they would drive her to the police station. She could call her mother from there.

On the way out, Duby asked Lambert if she was all

right, referring indirectly to her pregnancy. She said she
was. Police did not read her or the others their rights.
Lambert settled into a car driven by Robin Weaver and
John Bowman, both East Lampeter Township police officers. Duby and Officer Kenneth Crouse of East Lampeter drove Yunkin, while Jere Schuler and Clarence
Flory of East Lampeter took Buck. Buck asked if she
could make a phone call. Schuler responded she could,
in due time. His wife, Renee, took Buck's coat and purse
with her to the police station.

At seventeen, Buck was a juvenile, meaning different
rules applied to her. Police could not question her without a parent present. At about 11:15, police called her
mother, Joanne Guier. Guier had been home from the
nursing home where she worked for a couple of hours.
She was finishing her packing for a trip she and Tabbi
were going to take over the Christmas break. They
planned to surprise Tabbi's sister in North Carolina.
Joanne switched on the television and caught a news
report about a murder in East Lampeter Township.

Oh, man, how terrible, Joanne thought as the phone
began to ring. It was East Lampeter Township Police.
They asked her to come to the police station. They
wouldn't say why, except that it had something to do
with her daughter.

"I don't even know where you're at," she said, and
got directions. She rushed to the police station from
her home west of Lancaster.

When Donald Snyder, a trooper with the Pennsylvania
Police and an experienced interrogator, entered the
traffic sergeant's office half an hour later, Buck was sitting with her mother. The room was beige, with a desk
in the center and a few family photographs displayed.
A machine to check intoxication sat in the corner.

Buck told Snyder that Yunkin and Lambert had

picked her up at the apartment she shared with her mother at about 6:20 A.M. They went to Kmart at East Towne Mall. Yunkin had dropped them off and had gone to McDonald's, but Kmart was not open yet. They had stood around outside. Yunkin had come back about ten minutes later and Buck had gotten in the back, Lambert the front. Lambert remembered she had left her purse at Kmart, Buck said, so they had circled back. Then Yunkin had noticed something wrong with a tire, so he had pulled into another McDonald's. He broke the key off in the truck lock, she told Snyder.

"These two Puerto Rican girls appeared," Buck said. "I'm not sure whether they got out of a car or how they arrived there, but they started saying things to Lawrence. They were saying 'hey you' and such like that, and then Michelle Lambert said something to them, and they started calling us whores and sluts."

One of the other girls had hit Lambert in the mouth, Buck told police.

"I told her Michelle is pregnant and that she was to knock it off and the other one hit me in the face with keys or something. That is how I got the cut on my face," Buck said. She described one girl as five feet three inches with orange hair, the other as five feet with black shoulder-length hair. Both wore baggy pants, Buck said.

Yunkin, Lambert, and Buck then had gotten back in the car and filled the tire with air at a car wash near the intersection of Rohrerstown Road and Highway 462, Buck said.

"It was one of those air pumps that you have to put quarters in," she said.

They had gotten lost, ended up on a dead-end street, and had finally gotten to Penn Manor High School, where Buck was a senior, around 9:00 A.M., an hour late.

As Buck checked in at the attendance office, the clerk had asked her about the scratches. She had told her some "Mexican" girls had scratched her at breakfast at McDonald's.

"Heck of a way to start the holidays," the clerk had said.

Buck had told several other teachers and students the same story.

Shortly after 2:00 A.M., Snyder told Buck she was free to go.

But one more thing, he said, "Laurie is dead."

Joanne Guier jumped from her chair and shouted, "What are you talking about?" Her daughter collapsed into her arms. Tabbi's thick curly brown hair covered her face as she sobbed for at least fifteen minutes.

The policeman told them about the girl and the murder as the situation came into focus for Guier. He was talking about the same vicious murder she had seen on television just a few hours before.

Again he told them they were free to go. They walked from the station and got into Joanne's dark blue Comet.

"Tab, what's going on?" her mother said.

She leaned over and put her head on her mother's shoulder.

"Mama, I don't want to talk about it. I just want to go to sleep."

They rode in silence the thirty minutes back to their Manor Township apartment. They didn't know the apartment was already under surveillance by police. It was well after three o'clock in the morning. They went to bed, silently. Joanne figured they would sort things out in the morning. It had to be some terrible mistake.

Yunkin, meanwhile, sitting in the detective's work-room a few doors down from where Buck and Lambert were, told detectives virtually the same story as Buck.

He called the girls "Spanish" girls and said they had hit Buck, insulted Lambert. He recounted it word for word. McDonald's, Kmart, tire trouble, taking Buck to Penn Manor High School. Nothing special.

In the chief's office at the front of the building, Lambert was talking to Sergeant Carl Harnish of the Pennsylvania Police. Her demeanor was as calm as a surgeon performing a heart bypass operation. Harnish told Lambert she had been arrested on the outstanding warrant for assaulting Laurie Show and read her her constitutional rights as required by the U.S. Supreme Court's ruling in the Miranda case. It was 11:20 P.M. Laurie had been dead for fifteen hours. He asked Lambert how she knew Laurie.

"My brother Lenny Lambert goes to school with Laurie Show. The first time I ever met her was at Rachel Winesickle's house this past summer. I've seen her after school for about two years or so, but I never talked to her until this summer at Rachel's house."

Lambert told Harnish that Laurie had wanted to beat up Rachel, but she told Laurie to leave Rachel alone. Lambert confided to Harnish, as one friend would to another, that she didn't like Rachel anymore, though; didn't even talk to her, in fact, because Winesickle had told Yunkin that Lambert had slept with another man. Rachel had told him that because "Laurie likes Lawrence Yunkin and Laurie slept with Lawrence four times."

Lambert said she and Yunkin had reconciled when he was convinced she had not had sex with his friend. Shortly afterward, Lambert had seen Laurie at East Towne Mall near Auntie Anne's Pretzels.

"I grabbed Laurie by the hair and pushed her into a window," she told Harnish.

Later the same month, she and Yunkin had seen Laurie's father at the same mall. Lambert told the po-

liceman Show's father had called Yunkin a "dickhead"
for breaking up with Laurie and had called Lambert a
"whore" because she was pregnant. They had yelled
back and forth and then gotten into a shoving match
before John Show strode off, angry.

Lambert said she did not see Laurie again until November.

"I pushed Laurie and she pushed me after I first
grabbed her by the hair," Lambert said. "She started
trying to kick me in the stomach and stuff."

Harnish suggested they take a ten-minute break. At
midnight, he resumed questioning. Lambert told him
virtually the same story Buck was telling Duby, and
Yunkin was telling Savage, but with some embellish-
ments. She told which stores they had driven by and
that her purse had been sitting on the cement outside
Kmart when they went back for it. They had turned left
at Anderson Pretzels. The Puerto Rican girls—one with
dark hair, the other with orange-yellow hair—had whis-
tled at Yunkin.

"I told them to shut up," Michelle said. "They called
Tabbi a whore."

They had gotten back in the car and a tire went flat.
Yunkin had gone to open the trunk but had broken the
key in the lock. Lambert went on for about thirty minutes until Harnish suggested another break. Six minutes,
this time. Picking up the story, Lambert related they
had taken Buck to school, done four loads of laundry,
gone home and watched *Little House on the Prairie,* had
eaten lunch and then watched *Matlock.* She told Harnish
she was five feet six inches and weighed 143 pounds.

"Michelle, do you understand, or do you realize, why
we have you in here and why we're talking to you?"

"I don't know. Is it about the fight with the Spanish
girls or because of the speeding fine?"

"No, Michelle. That's not right. Have you heard what has happened to Laurie Show?"

"I don't know," she responded.

"Laurie is dead."

She broke down and cried.

"Have you ever said you were going to kill Laurie Show?" Harnish asked when she regained her composure.

"The strongest thing I ever said was I was going to kick the shit out of her."

"Did you kill Laurie Show?"

"No and don't know who did," she said as she held on to a Pepsi.

Harnish stepped into the hallway to compare information with his colleagues. The three were telling the same story, almost word for word.

"Something was really wrong," Harnish would say later. "They had this story matched up so well."

Harnish went back into the chief's office. He told Lambert he didn't believe she was telling the truth.

It was about 1:30 in the morning.

"Michelle, you're facing some serious problems."

"Yes, I know," she said.

Detective Ray Solt came in to take over the interrogation.

Soon Lambert's story began to change. It changed from then on and through the ensuing years as often and as easily as a winter wind alters the snowy fields of the Amish. She sat calmly, wearing tight pants and a pink flowered top, as Detective Ray Solt said, "Laurie's dead."

"Oh my God," Lambert replied. "She's dead?" Her voice raised at the end of the question in alarm. Solt thought she was not much of an actress. She knew Laurie was dead. His colleague had just told her and he suspected she had known it before she had even gotten to the station. In fact, he believed she had killed Laurie. First Lambert said she was not at the Show house at all. Next she said she was there but she stayed outside the whole time and didn't see anything. Then she said she saw Buck attack Laurie.

"How could you have seen that from downstairs?" Solt asked.

She had moved to the top of the stairs, Lambert said, her bleached blond hair hanging over her eyes as she kept her head tilted downward. Sometimes the detective could not see her eyes.

Finally Lambert said she had been in the apartment, but she had tried to save Laurie's life. Tabbi was the killer. She had been crazed, Lambert said, striking blow after blow. All Lambert had wanted to do was talk to Laurie and perhaps humiliate her in some way, cut her hair or something. Moreover, Lambert said, Yunkin hadn't been there. He hadn't known anything about the plan. No involvement at all. He had simply driven them to the apartment.

Sometime after 4:00 A.M., Harnish went into the room Yunkin was in and said one of the girls was talking and suggested he might end up with all the blame. Yunkin opened up like a trained dolphin at feeding time, as if he had been waiting all day to tell his side of the story. He was not a killer, he told Barley and Jere Schuler. The sequence of events actually had begun the night before, he said. He had taken Michelle to the Kmart at Kendig Square. He had waited in the car, and she'd returned holding a bag. He had taken her to Buck's house, and while she was inside the house, he had looked in the bag and seen a white nylon rope and a black ski hat.

The next morning, he had woken up around 5:30

and gone with Lambert to pick up Buck at 6:30. He had driven them to The Oaks, and Michelle had told him to go wait at McDonald's for thirty minutes. Then he was to pick them up outside the complex.

Yunkin maintained he did not know what the women were going to do once they got inside with Laurie. He said he had assumed Laurie's mother would be there. He had driven by the pickup point four times, he said, waiting for them. Finally he had spotted them kneeling beside some bushes. Lambert had gotten in the front of his brown Mercury, Buck in the back. He said he had asked what happened, but they wouldn't say. Five minutes later, Buck had blurted, "The bitch scratched me."

Lambert had shown him her upper lip, which was cut, she had said, by Laurie kicking her in the face. Michelle had blood on her hand and fingers, but still, Yunkin contended he did not know Laurie was dead.

Barley needed to stretch, get some coffee. He asked Jere Schuler to sit with Yunkin while he did. It was after 6:00 A.M., an unbelievably long night, but things were wrapping up. Already they had statements admitting some degree of culpability from Lambert and Yunkin. Schuler sat down and started talking to Yunkin. They just hashed around some small talk, nothing about the Show murder. Eventually Yunkin looked at him and said simply, "There's something else I need to tell you. I don't know if it will help or not, but I know where the clothes were thrown."

Schuler opened the door to the hallway where Barley was standing talking to other officers. He told him to step back inside. Yunkin had more to say. Yunkin then told him piece by piece where he had helped Lambert throw the clothes.

Renee Schuler and John Bowman were told to go out to the trailer where Yunkin and Lambert lived to collect evidence. The couple had given their permission for a search. The police officers, in a police cruiser, followed the hilly roads to a wooded piece of property in the far southern part of Lancaster County in Conestoga Township. They walked into the aged mobile home, and Schuler felt she had walked into a nightmare. Cat and chinchilla feces covered the floor. Garbage was strewn about. Stench filled the air. They found only a pillow and a few other items that looked like they were stained with blood. They also retrieved a machete.

Police did not have enough evidence to charge the trio with Laurie Show's murder. They were close, but not completely there. They needed autopsy results and other evidence to show probable cause. But they did not want to let Lambert and Yunkin go. In Pennsylvania, police must charge someone with a crime within six hours of the arrest or they must let the suspect go. In the early morning hours of Saturday, time was running out for them. They charged Yunkin with the noise violation and Lambert with the simple assault, and sent them to the Lancaster County Prison, a redbrick fortresslike building at the edge of downtown Lancaster.

East Lampeter police felt proud that they were well on their way to solving their first murder in a decade. For most of them, it was their first homicide. They knew they had lots of legwork to do, lots of information to gather for trial. But within twenty-four hours, they had the suspects behind bars. In truth, though, the case of the *Commonwealth of Pennsylvania* v. *Lisa Michelle Lambert,* docket number 423-1992, had only just begun. The ramifications of that twenty-four-hour period would strike at the heart of their twenty-person police force for years, and would cause people to question not only their competence but their integrity as well.

Three

After police sent Lambert and Yunkin to the county jail, they still had some work to do to be ready to arraign them on the murder charges Saturday afternoon. Yunkin had told them he had helped Lambert dispose of the clothes she and Buck were wearing Friday morning. They had thrown them into a Dumpster near where they lived, he said, stashed inside a pink trash bag. The clothes had been washed. In fact, Yunkin said, he and Lambert had gone to the laundry to wash clothes shortly after they had dropped Buck off at school. Yunkin had washed the clothes from the house; Lambert the clothes from the morning.

Police discovered the Dumpster had already been emptied and called the company to tell them to hold all their trucks at the incinerator in Conoy Township in the western part of Lancaster County. Slogging through the waste, detectives pulled out a light pink trash bag, the only pink one there. It contained, as Yunkin had said, two black knit caps, one pair of black gloves, one pair of white gloves, white socks and yellow socks, Levi's jeans, black sweatpants, and a flannel shirt coat. At least part of Yunkin's story now could be verified.

By the time they got back to the station, the autopsy report was in. Enrique Penades, the Lancaster County forensic pathologist, performed the autopsy at the morgue beneath Conestoga View Nursing Home. Penades, who was born and educated in medicine in Spain, was not board certified in forensic pathology, but he had worked with well-known forensic experts, including Dr. Russell Fisher, formerly the chief pathologist in Baltimore, who had been a consultant on the autopsy of President Kennedy. Penades, who came to the United States in 1953 and Lancaster County in 1960, figured by the time he performed Laurie Show's autopsy, he had done well over four thousand autopsies.

Two police officers, a representative of the district attorney's office, and a specialist in ear, nose, and throat medicine watched as Penades and his assistant worked to discover what happened to Laurie Show in the moments before she died and what actually caused her death.

He found Show had been stabbed twice in the head and was beaten with some sort of blunt object in the head. Three stab wounds marked her back, and her leg had been cut. There were dozens of cuts on her fingers and palms, where she had apparently raised her arms to stave off the blows. None of those wounds—except perhaps one in the back—were life-threatening. The neck wound—a slashing cut made with several strokes of a butcher knife, as if someone were slicing a turkey—was the most likely cause of death, Penades found. Show had bled to death.

Meanwhile, at East Lampeter Township Police headquarters, a few of the officers went home for some sleep. They'd been awake since Friday morning. Renee Schuler stayed at the office. She knew if she went to sleep she would have trouble getting up for the arraignment, which was scheduled for 7:00 P.M. Schuler did not want to miss that. She had begun as one of the first officers on the scene and wanted to see the process through. She busied herself with the grunt work of policing: paperwork, all so necessary but all so time-consuming and tedious. She wrote up reports and filled out the evidence log. She stored the evidence the officers had collected so far. A secretary came into the office to type the official papers, guided by someone from the district attorney's office.

On Saturday morning, Joanne Guier and Tabbi Buck prepared to leave for their respective jobs—Joanne to the nursing home in Lititz, five miles to the north, and Tabbi to Weis Market in Bridgeport. Joanne would drop her off. As they stepped out of their apartment, officers approached and asked them to go back in the house. Guier realized then the officers had spent the night outside her home. It was looking less and less like this was some mistake that would be cleared up soon, as she had thought initially. They told Tabbi and her mother that Tabbi was to be arraigned that evening on a charge of murdering Laurie Show. They put Buck in a squad car and drove her to the hospital to get fingernail scrapings and a blood test. Guier followed dazed in her own car.

Officers retrieved Yunkin and Lambert from jail and took them to district justice Arden Kopp's office, where a crush of reporters, cameramen, and the just plain curious waited outside. Buck was taken there as well. One by one, in thirty-minute intervals, the trio stood before Justice Kopp. It was a simple process, one whose result was clear from the start. Bind them over for trial. No bail, Kopp said, for Lambert or Buck, both charged with first-degree murder. Buck would stand trial as an adult. Yunkin was charged with hindering apprehension or prosecution. Kopp set his bail at $1 million, an impossibly high figure for his parents—simple working people—to come up with.

Buck left the court first, walking through the glare of television camera spotlights into the Pennsylvania night chill, to a waiting police car. She was taken to Lancaster County Prison.

As she did so, Heather Furnia, a friend of hers from school, turned to her father, William, and said, "That was definitely Tabbi. Oh, goodness."

Heather and Tabbi had been friends the year before when they both had attended Conestoga Valley High. They both had been new that year and had sort of clung to each other as they had made their way in an unfamiliar environment. They had been in some of the same classes and had eaten lunch together. Buck had never seemed violent to her.

"Just a normal kid," Heather said years later.

Yunkin went next. Detective Savage told the court Yunkin had admitted driving the women to the Show house and helping them get rid of bloody clothing. He also helped them establish a story about where they had been that morning. They were to say they were at McDonald's and Buck got into a fight with some Mexican girls.

As Yunkin, wearing a blue prison jumpsuit, shackles on his ankles, handcuffs on his wrists, turned to leave the courtroom, he met his mother face-to-face.

"How in the hell could you have let this happen?" she raged. "How could you do this? Why did you do it?"

The muscular, tall young man with deep-set eyes and a chiseled profile, which could readily become steely, looked at his mother and started crying.

"I'm sorry I let you and Dad down," he said. He told his parents he believed Hazel Show would have been at the house and that she would have protected her daughter. He thought Lambert just wanted to cut Laurie's hair.

Jackie Yunkin watched sadly as her only child walked to a police cruiser for the ride back to county prison. She felt so much anger, but beneath that lay immense sadness. How did they find themselves in this position?

Bystanders sent out loud hoots as Yunkin got into the car.

Lambert went last. Spectators crowding the sidewalk could barely see her face as she walked in, head down, bleached blond hair hanging down. She was wearing prison garb. Savage told the court Lambert confessed to holding Laurie Show's feet while Buck stabbed her.

Leaving the justice's office, Renee Schuler pushed through the crowd, leading Lambert to a waiting police car. As the police driver prepared to leave, a late-model sedan, carrying a man and a woman, sped into the parking lot. Lambert's mother, Judy, jumped out of the car and ran to her daughter's window. "My baby, my baby," Judy Lambert shouted.

"Mommy, Mommy," the teen responded as an officer held her back, away from her mother.

The two had not spoken in months. Lambert wept as the car pulled out, heading for the hospital to get scrapings from under her fingernails and a blood sample. Police took Lambert to the station to fingerprint her.

Finally they took Lambert to county prison. Her baby was due in two months.

Four

Hazel Show woke to the quiet of a mountain morning on Saturday. Sheer solitude reigned that morning in her brother's home, near the place she grew to be a teenager, where she and her siblings and parents packed into a shotgun house beside a curve in the road. Hazel had been not much older than her daughter when she left that home for the big city—Lancaster, about thirty minutes to the west. Now her daughter was dead and she would plan her funeral this day. The others in the house knew to leave her alone. Let her ease into her day as she saw fit.

Hazel got up and prepared to go to Groff-High-Eckenroth Funeral Home, or High's as New Holland folks knew it. New Holland, in the eastern part of Lancaster County, was where Hazel worked her first job, at a hardware store at sixteen. Later she had worked at a drugstore and then at Sperry New Holland, making farm machinery, where she had met her now-ex-husband, Laurie's dad, John Show. New Holland was also where Hazel and Laurie had gone to the fair every year.

Needing to fill some time before the appointment at the funeral home, Hazel Show went with her older brother, George, to their family home, about two miles away, to look at the remodeling work. It was coming along well. Soon George and his wife, Elaine, would move in. Before long, Hazel rode with George and Elaine to High's. They met John and his then-girlfriend there. High's is not a big place, yet its brick facade holds a place of prominence on the main street of New Holland. The Shows decided to have the funeral there at 2:00 P.M. Monday. They would greet friends beginning at noon. It was convenient for Hazel's older aunts, a better choice than Bridgeville Church, where her parents had gotten married and in whose cemetery they were buried, and where she and her ex-husband would bury Laurie. The plot was to the rear of the cemetery, off the road, in the center of a long line of graves holding the remains of members of Hazel's family, the Haases.

Laurie would be buried in a football jersey from the Penn State Lions, her favorite team. She had wanted a real jersey for some time, and John had bought her one for Christmas. Hazel and John decided Laurie would have wanted to be buried in it. Navy blue sweatpants and a blue turtleneck underneath the jersey would complete the outfit. She would wear Penn State earrings as well.

Hazel wanted to tuck teddy bears in the casket with her daughter—the special ones Laurie so loved, ones she had gotten when Laurie and her mother worked together at The Bear Shop, a specialty store near their home. She also wanted to include one a friend of Hazel's had made. She thought of five others she'd like to get from Laurie's room. Hazel knew she'd have to go back there that night to get the bears. Back into Laurie's special place, filled with white furniture and stuffed animals, where the morning sun filtered in, where wine-colored dark stains now covered the floor.

She put the image from her mind. They had to choose a casket. Fred Groff, the funeral director, moved to show them to the rear of the building, but Hazel Show balked.

"I can't go back there," she said, weeping. A doctor had given her some pills—she didn't know what—yet the pain was still there, full and throbbing. She could not pick a casket for her daughter to be buried in. John and George went without her.

"Get something pink," she told George, referring to the inside lining.

They picked an elegant mahogany with yellow lining.

"They don't have anything pink," George tenderly told his sister. "John has picked out a nice one."

"If George likes it, it's OK," she replied.

Renee Schuler was sitting on the steps as Hazel Show drove up to her condominium Saturday night. Schuler had the key and was there to preserve the scene, the evidence. Hazel needed to get the bears for Laurie's casket and a dress to wear to the funeral. She pulled her bloody clothes from the Tempo's trunk and handed them to Schuler.

"My brother wanted to throw these away, but I thought you might need them for evidence," Show told the corporal.

Hazel mechanically swept through the house, retrieving the items she needed. She took the teal dress from her closet, her sole dress. She wore scrubs at work and casual clothes most of the time. She collected the teddy bears and Laurie's clothes and jewelry, and then handed the key back to Schuler. Hazel Show was subdued, but didn't break down.

Hazel does not remember much about Sunday. Time seemed to slip away like a far-off fog. The *Sunday News* carried but one story about the murder, a straightforward summary of the arraignments the day before. The headline proclaimed: MICHELLE DID IT: DYING TEEN'S LAST

WORDS WERE SPOKEN TO HER MOTHER; THREE YOUTHS ARE CHARGED.

The community was more than stunned. It was outraged. They asked the inevitable questions, the ones without answers: why and how. Why did this happen to a lovely young girl whom everyone considered "nice," and how could three young people who had never been in trouble before suddenly become caught up in such a vicious crime? None of them were from the so-called bad homes. "Senseless" was the word most often heard. Like everyone in every town where a murder beyond understanding occurs, they thought such tragedy only happened someplace else.

Sunday night was reserved for the family to view Laurie's body. They were joined at the funeral home by some members of the extended families who could not attend the service the next day. John Show's father, Dr. Whitlaw Show, extended his hand to Hazel and said, "Do you know who I am?" Hazel had not seen her ex-father-in-law in some time and had never had much of a relationship with him, but she found his question unusual. Grief works on people in varying ways, creating behavior that can seem odd. Sometimes emotions teeter, almost inexplicably, between tears and laughter.

Hazel Show was pleased with the way her daughter looked, except there was something about her hair that just didn't seem right. It looked off-kilter, but she said nothing. They probably just didn't know how to fix her hair exactly right. Years later, during Lambert's trial, Show learned it wasn't the funeral home's hairdresser's fault. Laurie's hair had been chopped with the knife that killed her, testimony showed.

Hazel and John decided to keep the casket open, the norm for their families and their community. The turtleneck covered the neck wound. Hazel felt it was important for friends and family to see Laurie one last time. The good-bye would not be complete without that. And even more important, Hazel said, she knew friends and family would find solace in Laurie's smile, just as she did in the morgue when she saw her daughter's face.

On Monday, the family gathered at High's sometime before noon. Misty rain fell through the cold air, sending chills right through heavy winter coats. A line of solemn well-wishers wove through the funeral home and spilled out onto the street for more than a block. It would remain like that for hours, as some seven hundred people waited to offer condolences to the Shows. Girls with faces too young to be grieving. Boys in awkward stances, trying to look brave. Old people and couples. Singles. Amish farmers. Doctors who worked with Hazel and those who worked with her ex-father-in-law, the longtime coroner of Lancaster County. The turnout stunned everyone and showed the family their community was made of caring folks who went out of their way to reach out to those in need.

Hazel, in the teal dress, and John, in a gray suit, and his parents stood beside the casket and greeted every one of them, hugging them, crying with them. Hazel was particularly supportive of Laurie's friends, many of whom enjoyed being at Laurie's house for her mother's company as much as for hers. She tried to say something positive to each, to bolster their spirits even as hers were sagging. A teacher stood nearby and moved to comfort teens who were particularly upset at seeing Laurie lying in the casket.

Several friends slipped pink roses into the casket. Dozens of floral arrangements lined the walls, some sent by people the Shows did not know.

John Show was especially struck by the large number

of Conestoga Valley teenagers who told him Laurie had helped them with schoolwork.

"I didn't know that," he told more than one person.

Groff, the funeral director, decided to let the visitation go on for as long as people kept coming. At 2:00 P.M., when the service was to begin, the line stretched far beyond the funeral home's doors, and people were still arriving.

"The family needs the support," he said.

Sometime after 4:00 P.M., the family sat down in the small chapel with about 150 friends who stayed for the service. Hazel Show had left the contents and form of the service to the two ministers she asked to perform it: the Reverend Samuel Knupp, the chaplain at the hospital she worked in, and the Reverend Benjamin Fenninger, the retired pastor of Cedar Lane Chapel, the nondenominational church she had attended as a child.

Fenninger began: "Sometimes it seems, especially today, that our world has fallen apart. We need you to pray for the family, for her mother, in these particular days of stress."

He told them he knew they felt bitterness and hate, but God had the answer to turn that around.

Knupp looked out into the faces of the mourners and said, "This is a time that defies words and understanding. It is a death that makes no sense and makes us angry. As I was driving over here today, I was really struck by the fact that I've run out of words. Nothing I seem to be able to say or do seems to take away any of the pain and hurt and sense of loss."

He said he, like they, felt pain, bewilderment, anger, outrage, and he simply did not know what to do with those feelings. He did not understand why events unfold as they do, why children are killed, but he found some-

thing in the crowd that afternoon as he walked the line
of the grieving.

"It was a line of hope," he said. "It is people responding to people, people comforting one another. Let the
legacy of Laurie's life be the fact that you and I can
care more deeply and share more intimately, because
there is no other answer to this tragedy, these angers,
these fears, and this loss."

Knupp asked if anyone wanted to share a special story
or memory of Laurie.

Hazel Show stood up, turned to her friends with tears
flowing down her cheeks, and said simply, "Laurie was
the best daughter. She was my whole world. She was a
good person. And she's never going to be forgotten."

No one else stood or said anything. That was all there
was to say.

They traveled in procession to the cemetery. A silver
Buick hearse bore the teen's body to Bridgeville Cemetery. Darkness had fallen. The Goodville Fire Company
had set up spotlights, showing the way to a green tent
where the graveside service would take place. The casket
was covered with a spray of white and red roses.

"Ashes to ashes, dust to dust, the Lord bless her and
keep her," Knupp said as Laurie's body was committed
to its final resting place.

Hazel's cousins had set up a light dinner of cold cuts
and cakes in the basement of the church. They moved
in from the cold damp night and relished the hot coffee
and the chance to be together. The Haases were a close-
knit family, and the tragedy seemed to draw them even
closer.

The day had worn Hazel down. She stayed only a
short time at the church and then went back to her
brother's house. Hazel ended up spending the rest of
the year there.

On Christmas morning, usually a time of such joy with Laurie, Hazel visited a great uncle and the husband of her deceased sister and his children. Hazel's nephew Dean Haas, who was more like a son than a nephew, stayed by her side, keeping her busy. They had dinner Christmas night at George's.

The days spun out like a dreary dream of despair. She stayed at George's house, bunking in the room of her fourteen-year-old nephew, Tim. Friends and family came and went. Hazel remained somber, her emotions dulled by prescription drugs. She needed a therapist, someone to help her cope—not just to cope with a life without Laurie, but also to cope with the trials she knew would be coming soon enough. She knew she had six months to get herself together before she faced a courtroom full of spectators, a judge, reporters, and the people who killed her daughter. That first week, she went to counseling every other night.

I have to testify, she thought. *I can't afford to lose it. This is all I can do for my daughter now.*

At the end of the week, she decided she needed to say something to the people of Lancaster County who had opened their hearts to her. She knew it would be sometime before she would write all the thank-you notes for flowers and food. So she sent a letter to the newspaper, published on the last day of the year, coincidentally the day she decided to go home.

She thanked her friends and family and said she hoped the tragedy would keep them as close as they had been those past few days. She thanked her coworkers at Community Hospital and the staff at Conestoga Valley High School.

"I saw how devastated Laurie's friends were at the funeral, and my heart goes out to you," Hazel Show wrote. "Please remain as close to each other as you were that day—you've lost one friend but you're forming new lifelong friendships through her death.''

Finally she thanked the people of the county, the strangers who showed concern.

"Your prayers are making life a little easier for me," she wrote.

In closing, Hazel said, "If there's one thing Laurie should be remembered for, it's her big heart. I'm sure she would have been touched by the way people have been drawn closer to each other and shown love for one another due to her senseless death."

Some thought Hazel should not go back into the condominium. But, to her, there was no choice to make. The Oaks was not only the place Laurie was murdered, it was also the place that had been their home together. The house they lived in for most of Laurie's life on Willow Road had been John's, too. The condominium was theirs alone. She and her daughter had shared such good memories there.

Shortly after Laurie's death, three of Hazel's friends had entered the apartment, carried out all of Laurie's things, washed them, and put them on the sunporch. A restoration company had stripped up the bloodied carpet and washed the blood off the closet doors. Blood had soaked through onto the plywood underneath and the workmen could not get it out. They had applied sealer to the floor and ordered new carpet. When Hazel returned home, after the New Year, the carpet was still not installed. She couldn't bear to see the bloodstain encased in sealant.

"I don't care what you put down, but put something on that floor," she demanded to a company employee. The company readily complied.

For her first week back in the condominium, Hazel was joined by her sister-in-law and Dean's mother, Alletah Haas. Then Dean moved in. Thirteen years younger than Hazel, he had been her companion from the time he was a toddler. When Laurie was born, he had been her baby-sitter. They played and roughhoused, teased and taunted. They were more like brother and sister than cousins. Dean and Hazel needed each other to get through the days and weeks and the rest of their lives without Laurie.

Sifting through the mail that had piled up while she was gone, Hazel found a postcard amid the cards and bills. She turned it over and saw it was from Lawrence Yunkin, written on the day of Laurie's funeral.

"When Michelle saw her somewhere, I would try to keep her from Laurie and that's the truth," he wrote. He told her how sorry he felt for her loss.

Show tossed the card down in disgust. Later she turned it over to Renee Schuler. Hazel felt numb.

Sperry New Holland, where John Show had worked since 1972, was on Christmas break for the last days of December. John tried hard to fill his days, but the pain of losing his daughter never dulled. Sometimes he'd find himself talking to her as he drove in his truck. They had shared many wonderful talks as they traveled the roads of Lancaster County while he taught her to drive. She was to take driver's education the next semester with the idea of getting her license in the summertime. She would never have a license now. She would not see her seventeenth birthday, less than a month away. So many dreams and plans dashed.

Guilt swept through him, too, worsening the grief. He had always wanted to make it up to her for leaving, for divorcing her mother. John believed Laurie understood more as she aged, but still, he knew it would take a grown woman to fully comprehend what had happened. He wouldn't have that opportunity now.

Part 2: The Families

Five

They were more alike than different: the Shows, the Lamberts, the Yunkins, the Bucks. All but the Bucks were Pennsylvania natives. They lived quiet, workaday lives in Lancaster County, the heart of what's known sweepingly as Amish country, a collection of rocky-soiled farms with neat corn rows and grazing holsteins. What most describe collectively as the Amish actually comprises about two dozen religious groups, with varying levels of conservatism. Old Order Amish, numbering eight thousand in Lancaster County and 65,000 worldwide, shun electricity and travel by horse and buggy. Mennonites drive cars and trucks, and tend to have more worldly ways. All the groups have a profound impact on the region. Most notably, the countryside, unaltered by stark steel towers and strings of power lines, unfolds serenely up hill and dale as far as one can see, pocked only by white farmhouses, red weathered wooden barns, and lots of cows.

Tourism changed the quietness of the place. On the major highways that lead to the simple farms, the tourist industry sprang up, fueled in part by the 1985 movie *Witness*, starring Harrison Ford. The movie was filmed in a hamlet called Intercourse and on the surrounding farms outside of Lancaster, the county seat. With elegant cinematography, the movie uses the rolling verdant farmland of Pennsylvania Dutch country as background for a story of forbidden love between an Amish woman and a Philadelphia detective. It was a huge hit and brought much exposure to a group of people who wouldn't even consider going to see their community or their lives portrayed on the big screen.

Today gawkers choke Highway 30 year-round, anxious for a glimpse of the simple life, of another time. While they gape at the simple life on the back roads, they spend lots of money on the main ones. Buicks and BMWs ease alongside black and gray Amish carriages pulled by husky horses, sidling up to clots of shopping malls and factory outlet centers. National chain restaurants bump against local eateries like Lapp's, a meat-and-vegetable place owned by an Amish family. In summer especially, the dozens of large hotels brim with guests. Camera-toting tourists seek the perfect shot: horse-drawn carriages, farms, Amish men in black pants and women in black skirts, their shirts and blouses of lavender, red, lime-green, royal blue, color-coordinated by family.

The Amish tend to keep to themselves, but there is a continual interaction between them and the people they call the "English." Their values and simplicity can't help but rub off on their neighbors. For much of her life, Laurie Show lived across the street from a one-room Amish school. Until he was a teen, Lawrence Yunkin lived and worked on an Amish farm, where his parents rented a house. Lisa Michelle Lambert lived across the street from an Amish family during her early teens.

Yet, the lives of the three as they grew proved to be anything but simple. Divorce, abandonment, death of siblings, at least one of the hard lessons of a modern-day, tumultuous world, touched the life of each one of those young people. Their lives intersected and diverged, as did their memories and the story they told of the day Laurie Show died.

The public image of Lisa Michelle Lambert could not have contrasted more starkly. She was either a troubled young woman who had been abused by the man she thought she loved, as her defense attorney tried to portray, or she was a vicious, sadistic killer who saw nothing wrong in taking out a romantic rival, as the district attorney believed.

Yunkin, too, had his own schizophrenic persona. He was either a blundering, less-than-bright day laborer who loved a bad woman, or he was an abusive, hard-drinking aggressor obsessed with controlling his woman.

The people of Lancaster County were hard pressed to know just who they believed. A girl was dead, three people were implicated. Beyond that, it just depended upon which one you knew as to whom you believed.

Lancaster is a place of routine, as predictable as the farmers' market through summer. Hazel Show's life followed a routine, too, as did the lives of the Lamberts, the Bucks, the Yunkins.

As a girl, Hazel Show lived in the hilly eastern part of Lancaster County, ten miles or so from the Amish farms. Her father and his father before him worked at New Holland Machinery, a farm equipment manufacturer that ultimately became Sperry New Holland and then through the years was bought and sold, changing names with every sale. Hazel worked there for a time, too, and there met the man who would become her husband, John Show.

Hazel's family included eight children, one of whom—a girl—died at three months of age. Times were tough in those hills. They lived in a small house of shared rooms and relied on a garden and a yearly steer for food. Slaughtering the cow was a family event and the meat was shared with an extended family of aunts, uncles, and cousins. They used an outhouse until Hazel was well into her teens and drew water for baths and drinking from a porch pump. Hazel didn't know her family was poor, though, until high school. For some reason, she suddenly realized how bad her clothes looked. Her school days spread out like a bland diet of nothing special, but there was strength in family.

"I never was anybody in school," Hazel Show said flatly some years later. Her speech bore no sign of self-pity, just simple truth. "I was not the smart kid, the sports player, just a nice person who smiled and was nice to everybody."

All the various groups—the nerds, hoods, aggies, home ecs, and athletes—seemed to like her just fine.

She had an awkwardness, a certain shyness about her in the way she cocked her head, the way she rarely wanted to be the center of attention. She carried the trait into adulthood. As a child, her life centered around her family, her brothers and sisters and parents and the extended group beyond, most especially her maternal grandfather, whom she called "Pappy." From him she learned the lessons of life: to tell the truth, to be kind to people. He was one of the people whom Hazel Show would look back on from middle age and thank for giving her the strength and the faith to make it through the horror that was to come.

Pappy lived just up the road from her childhood home. Hazel walked up there most nights to visit. Her cousins and aunts and uncles would be there as well. The grown-ups played Chinese checkers and cards as they laughed into the night. The young ones went for spirited contests of kick the can, tag, and goose. When she was nine, her grandmother died, and Hazel's life became even more centered around Pappy.

At thirteen, she switched from her family's Presbyterian Church to Cedar Lane Christian Chapel so she could go to church with him. Sunday afternoons meant visits with her father's parents in Churchtown, a few miles away.

"We always visited relatives," Show said many years later with the nostalgia folks feel for losing something special.

Her first job was at sixteen, in a local family-owned hardware store, where she sold everything from paint to antiques to pots and pans. That was followed by a stint in a drugstore, and then the job at Sperry New Holland, where she was a timekeeper. John Show was in training there when she met him, learning various departments to best see where he fit. He was the son of a local doctor who was also the county coroner. "Old Doc Show," they called him. Johnny, as the boy was known, traveled with his father to home visits. Doc Show delivered hundreds and hundreds of babies in the homes of area residents, especially the Amish. The Shows lived in a stately house in Bird-In-Hand, a crossroads community close to Lancaster that sports a few small shops specializing in Amish products like quilts and simple furniture. Doc Show's office was there, as was a drugstore of sorts. He rarely liked to leave home for long periods, fearing someone would break in to get drugs.

Hazel remembers John as someone with whom she instantly felt at ease, though their backgrounds differed so. Something about him made her feel they had known each other all their lives, a comfort she had not known before. She was twenty-one. He was twenty-two. He had rugged good looks and an easy smile. He had been a basketball player at Phelps School, a preparatory school in Philadelphia. His father sent him there because he feared he would not get a proper education in Bird-In-Hand.

John Show knew he did not want to be a doctor. The profession was around-the-clock. Many times, they would be eating dinner and someone cut and bloody would show up at the door. This was a farm community and accidents happened with some regularity. Doc Show would get up from the table and mend the man. John looked proudly on his father and saw the respect accorded him by the people he helped. But it was not a job for John. In fact, he really didn't want to go to college, even though he could have gone to his father's alma maters, Kent State or Temple. He spent two semesters at Brandywine Junior College, studying business administration, then came home to become a plumber's helper.

When John took the job at Sperry, he noticed Hazel. She seemed nice. They dated and soon were living together. They had talked on and off about having a baby. Hazel believes she got pregnant the day she went off the pill. She realized she was pregnant a short time later when she felt sick while cooking meat loaf. Four months later, August 23, 1974, Hazel and John were married by a justice of the peace.

"I just can't see spending all that money on a big wedding," she told him. He had already had a big wedding when he married the first time. She didn't want to replicate anything about that union. The newlyweds spent their honeymoon—a few days—in Atlantic City.

Hazel believed the Shows felt she had trapped their son with the pregnancy. Decades later, Hazel still reeled at the thought. The father was the one who wanted them to be married, she said. Their living together made him look bad to his Amish patients. A cold unease remained between Hazel and her in-laws for all the years of their lives.

But John remembers events differently. He did not think his parents felt distant or displeasure toward his wife. Life seemed uncomplicated to him.

Hazel and John bought a cozy one-story two-bedroom bungalow in Smoketown, yet another crossroads near John's parents in Bird-In-Hand. Two months before the baby was born, Hazel quit her job at Sperry New Holland. John continued working there.

Six

Laurie Michelle Show was born January 27, 1975. Laurie was Hazel's middle name. They chose Michelle because they liked it. Hazel counted every day of Laurie's life a blessing because of the way she came into the world: with the umbilical cord wrapped around her neck three times, knotted twice. The delivery had been difficult; Hazel had been given a spinal for pain, but she had the flu and threw up over and over. Because of the illness, she couldn't hold Laurie on the first day of her life. The nurses kept her in the nursery.

The woman in the bed next to Hazel had a perfect delivery. She had used Lamaze breathing exercises for a natural childbirth. Hazel thought it seemed so easy for her. Six months later, John and Hazel took Laurie along to the Fireman's Hall to register to vote and a couple standing behind them struck up a conversation. They were the grandparents of the baby whose mother was in the room with Hazel. The baby had been born with a hole in his heart and had to be airlifted to a more sophisticated hospital in Hershey, Pennsylvania. The baby had died. Hazel thought of that through the years as Laurie grew. Laurie could have died, too.

"Every day with Laurie is a gift from God," Hazel would say. A friend had lost a baby whose umbilical cord was only wrapped once around the neck.

When Laurie was two, the Shows moved into a two-story yellow house on Willow Road, a rural thoroughfare not far away in East Lampeter Township. It had a backyard big enough for animals and childhood adventure. Hazel and John's marriage had become less than happy. Hazel felt John blamed her for everything that went wrong. She had gained weight from her pregnancy. He thought Hazel's personality had changed. They had grown apart and he wanted out.

The day after they moved into the house, John Show left. That would be the pattern for eight years, splitting up and reuniting, splitting up and reuniting. They would agree to try to make it work, for them, for Laurie. It was the way Hazel was brought up. Marriages didn't end. John's parents had a long-term marriage as well.

Laurie was a happy-go-lucky kind of child, who started baton lessons when she was three, the youngest in the group. She loved to wear the glittering green uniform and prance proudly around the field, her curly blond hair flowing to her shoulders. Laurie's best friend, Shannon Miller, was on the squad, too. Shannon was a daughter of Hazel's high school friend. The mothers would watch the troupe march through its routine and as sure as the sunrise, the leader would stop and call to Shannon and Laurie to catch up. They had stopped midfield to chat. John and Hazel often decorated his pickup truck so the girls could ride in the various parades the surrounding farm communities staged every year.

Hazel did not return to work until Laurie was two, shortly after John Show left for the first time. She took odd jobs such as secretary for a water conditioning company, until 1981, when she went to work as a secretary at a flower shop. Laurie stayed at Little People Day Care in Greenfield Industrial Park, not far from their home.

Laurie liked it so much staying there and playing with all the children that Hazel took an extra job to afford the tuition.

She loved to swim and Hazel and John liked to take her to Atlantic City or Rehobus, anyplace with water. Her father's parents had a backyard pool that Laurie especially enjoyed. She also seemed to catch poison ivy by simply looking at it. Once Laurie touched a vine with a stick. Hazel spotted her and made her wash up immediately and well. She got it anyway. Swollen and puffy, Laurie looked like a blowfish, an image Hazel dutifully caught on film.

She was simply precocious. Laurie also broke bones so often Hazel Show asked the doctor whether there was something wrong with her.

"No, she's just a klutz," the doctor said, laughing.

When she was about four, Laurie was watching television downstairs while her mother cleaned her room upstairs. Hazel checked on her every so often. When she called down to her later, Laurie did not respond. Hazel ran down the steps, checked all over the house. No Laurie. She raced next door to the Hersheys, a retired Mennonite couple. Laurie liked to go over there for crackers. For some reason, their saltines were better than the ones her mother bought. They hadn't seen her. Hazel ran over to the Laymans, the other neighbor. Their daughter, Lynette, and Laurie often played together. She was not there, either. Hazel was beside herself. The woods behind her house looked ever more ominous.

Walking back toward her house, Hazel saw some buggies outside the Amish school across the street. Desperate, she walked in, knowing Laurie had not gone there. A group of bearded Amish men were gathered at the front of the room. It was the school board. There in a desk in the first row sat Laurie, coloring. She had stopped in to see what was going on and the men had simply offered her something to do.

Relieved, yet angry, Hazel went to yank Laurie back home when one of the elders looked kindly at her and said Laurie was welcome to stay to finish her picture.

"Let her stay," he said in the lilting accent of the Amish, a mix of American-style English and German.

Hazel complied, but as soon as Laurie got home, she scolded her daughter. "Don't you ever go out again without telling me."

Another time the Shows were visiting John's aunt in Delaware. She had a pond at the back of her property and they all decided to go fishing. It was a sunny Sunday afternoon. Laurie caught a catfish. She didn't want to let it go, though, and didn't want to cook it, either. She was about seven years old. John's aunt got a gallon bucket and filled it with pond water, and Laurie slipped the fish in. When it was time to go, Laurie decided she needed to take the fish home with her, a two-hour drive.

Reluctantly her parents agreed, and Laurie spent the whole ride home, petting and talking to the fish. When they got home, she said she wanted to take it to the Criders' pond nearby and release it. For years afterward, Laurie talked about that catfish and wondered how it was doing. She regularly asked the Criders if anyone had caught it or seen it.

They always had a garden and one year Laurie grew pumpkins in July. It made the newspapers. Pumpkins in July! Eight of them.

In the second grade at Fritz Elementary School in Leola, Laurie struggled with schoolwork and failed. Her mother became her staunchest defender, battling the school to figure out what was happening with her child. Ultimately tests showed Laurie had dyslexia and she spent years in resource classes and special education. She could read, but didn't always understand what she was reading. School became an obstacle, an object of hate. Hazel had trouble even getting her to school.

Matters only became worse when Hazel's mother died. Laurie loved her "Grammy." When Hazel would pick her up after spending the night with Grammy, Laurie would cry all the way home, wailing, "I want my Grammy." She and Hazel were at her home the day she died of a heart attack, April 6, 1985, the night before Easter. Hazel hadn't planned to be with her family for Easter—they were going to John's aunt's—but she wanted to help her mother prepare for the big meal nonetheless. Hazel, John, and Laurie had not been there long. Hazel had gone to the basement to get the big roasting pan for the ham. Mellie, Laurie's puppy, had wet the floor and Hazel cleaned it up. She looked at her mother.

"Mom, you look tired," she said.

"I am tired," her mother responded. Hazel asked her whether she had taken her high blood-pressure medicine. She hadn't, but went to get the pill bottle. She came back into the kitchen and was standing beside Hazel as Hazel handed her a glass of water. Her mother didn't reach for it, so Hazel absently put it on the counter.

Hazel tapped her mother on the shoulder and her mother fell over. She had suffered a massive heart attack and died standing.

Laurie was devastated. Her Grammy was gone.

That summer John and Hazel decided to take Laurie to Disney World, to cheer her up. Hazel remembers it as a mistake. She and John fought. He wanted to stay in the room; she wanted to see everything. Laurie was torn between her parents.

It was the Shows' last reconciliation. He left at the end of July.

Laurie was devastated. Problems between Hazel and her daughter grew.

"She saw it as me making her dad leave and she had lost her Grammy," Hazel remembered. "She really hated me."

The anger seethed. Hazel took Laurie to a counselor, but she wouldn't open up. She didn't want to let the hurt out. Laurie learned how to play her parents against each other. She could easily get her father to overrule her mother.

Ten turned to eleven, and there was no sign that Laurie's anger was tempering. Everything seemed a constant battle. One day Hazel had had enough. She had grown especially weary of Laurie telling her how bad things were at her house and how great they would be if she lived with her dad. Hazel put Laurie in the car, drove to John's apartment, and said, "She's yours." Laurie stayed three days.

Many years later, Hazel read Laurie's diary from that time. Laurie wrote, "Mom kicked me out," then three days later, "Mom and Joanne and I went out to dinner." The entry the next day was "went to movies with Mom." There was no mention of the blowup.

Seven

Laurie's relationship with her mother steadily improved over time. Laurie worked with her mother in The Bear Shop when she was twelve. A few years later, Hazel Show took the job as an aide at Community Hospital, where she was working when Laurie died.

They especially liked to go to Hershey Park, an amusement park owned by the candy company. It was about an hour away. The sweet smell of chocolate from the factory lingered over the town. They usually went with others, friends of her mother's or hers. The first time it was just the two of them, Laurie said, "This isn't going to be any fun, just us."

Hazel responded, "We'll just stay in the car."

She didn't, of course, and it turned out, Hazel said later, to be the best time they had ever had there. They rode every ride—except the "spinny ones"—over and over. They stayed until the park closed. Laurie often went places with her mother and her mother's friends. She was quite often the only child. She fit in no matter whether she was eating a hamburger at McDonald's or lobster in a fine restaurant, her mother said. Yet, Laurie could be silly and goofy, especially if there was a camera around.

Laurie and her mother were friends. The dark days faded. School became less of a problem as well. By high school, Laurie was taking regular courses, even though she was assigned to the counselor for "exceptional students" at Conestoga Valley High, Mrs. Cooper. It was a source of embarrassment. Everyone knew the kids had been labeled "slow." In eleventh grade, Laurie wanted to go to the vocational technical program to study cosmetology, but her true dream was to be a model.

Laurie spent a lot of time with her dad. He had bought a piece of property next door to his parents with a little house that Doc Show had built for John's grandmother. Laurie enjoyed spending time there, especially swimming in her grandparents' pool. John coached her slow-pitch softball team, which won the league championship one year.

Laurie and Hazel stayed in the roomy yellow house on Willow Road until Laurie was sixteen. They wanted a smaller place with no grass to cut. They found it in The Oaks, a condominium complex, just down the street from busy Highway 30 and the shopping malls.

That summer Laurie began to look for friends closer to her new home. She took up with a crowd of friends Hazel Show at first thought was the most polite group she'd ever met. Soon, though, Hazel realized they were trouble. She suspected they had taken $2,000 worth of jewelry from her. She knew they had taken the small bills she kept in the cookie jar for Laurie to buy pizza or snacks after school. Laurie seemed unaware, Hazel thought. Laurie was outside on the deck cooking hot dogs for her friends and they were stealing her thirty books of green stamps. She had a shy way about her, almost naive about people. That same way Hazel had. That same cock of the head.

One night in February 1991, Hazel asked two friends who were policemen to come to the condominium to talk to Laurie about the kids she was running around with. They explained to her the consequences of hanging around people who get in trouble. She could end up in trouble with the law, they told her. After that, the friends were not at the Show condo again.

Laurie stayed busy with school and work. She worked at the Deb Shop, a women's clothing store, to help her mother afford the condominium. That was part of the deal they made when they bought it. They would be a team. It was their own place. Just for them. Laurie took the front bedroom and filled two tall bookcases with her stuffed animals, mostly bears she had collected when she worked with her mother at the teddy bear shop. A passel more sat on her white iron daybed, which she meticulously made every morning. The one mess she usually left was the pile of clothes she considered wearing to school but rejected.

In May, Laurie met a girl on the bus, Rachel Winesickle. She seemed nice, Laurie thought, and then she discovered the girl lived in the apartment complex across the street. She seemed to have lots of friends, people Laurie might befriend as well. One spring afternoon at Rachel's, Laurie was introduced to a couple, Michelle Lambert and Lawrence Yunkin.

Eight

Where Laurie Show's life was relatively stable in its sameness, Tabitha Faith Buck's life was like a bird of passage. By the time she was seventeen, she had lived in eighteen houses in five states, literally spanning the nation from Alaska to Florida. She was born in Anchorage on May 26, 1974, the second child of Alvin and Joanne Buck. Her father had five children by a previous marriage; her mother two. Alvin and Joanne had daughter Kitty together, who was two years older than Tabbi.

Family dynamics are not easy anymore. They rarely fit a common mold, and the Bucks were no different. Children moved in and out, living with their mother for a time, and then on their own; but by and large, Joanne Buck raised the entire brood of nine children. The family divided, not by parentage, but by age: the ones known as the "older kids"—Kellie, Wendy, Archie, Kyria, Shannon, and Dan—and the younger kids—Dawn, Kitty, and Tabbi. They were all living together in a house in Anchorage when Tabbi was born. Her father worked on the commercial fishing boats and as a part-time preacher.

He had been wounded during his year as a squad leader in the infantry in Vietnam in 1968, shrapnel to the lung. It earned him a Purple Heart. The experience dragged him into the lifelong spiral of post-traumatic stress syndrome. He didn't settle well. He liked to keep moving, looking for the next job, the next opportunity. The U.S. Army paid him a monthly pension for his service.

Tabbi Buck has few memories of this time. She and her sister played in a run-down Volkswagen "Bug" without tires in a parking lot somewhere, pretending to drive to town.

They moved to the Yoncalla/Drain region of Oregon midway down the state about fifty miles from the coast, when she was four. Both her parents were originally from Oregon. Buck remembered they lived in a two-story house in Drain, located in the heart of the lush Willamette Valley. A pig and a Doberman served as pets. They had a swing in the backyard, which to a preschooler seemed huge. Once she darted into a road and was almost hit by two cars coming from opposite directions. Tabbi Buck remembers the older kids roughhousing. Once, Kyria was thrown through a wall.

"There was always something to do and someone to do it with," she remembered. "My aunts, uncles came over."

A year later, the Bucks moved to Wyoming, near a military base. Alvin Buck was working in an oil field. They lived in a trailer with a long driveway. When the field closed, not too many months later, Buck sent his family to Florida, near Satellite Beach, to be near friends while he headed for the fishing boats of Alaska. It was seasonal work and he had heard the fishing would be good that year. It wasn't. He was destitute. Meanwhile, in Florida, Joanne had three of her four biological children, Kitty, Dan, and Tabbi.

"We were very poor," Tabbi said. Her mother was the breadwinner, working various jobs, usually in a kitchen of some sort.

"My husband was always chasing rainbows. I worshiped the ground he walked on and I followed him literally to the ends of the earth. We were like gypsies," Tabbi's mother, Joanne, recalled.

Tabbi remembered her mother preparing dinner once from all that was in the cabinets: flour, baking soda, and salt. She cooked it on the grill outside and poured ketchup over it. The power was off. They had virtually nothing. The next day, Tabbi and the other children came home from school and found their mother crying. She led them into the kitchen, opening the cabinets, now full of canned goods. She opened the refrigerator, full as well, and the freezer, too.

"She was crying and laughing, she was so happy," Tabbi said. "She didn't know where it came from. Mom came home and found it."

It was the day before Christmas and they also found a decorated Christmas tree with presents underneath. Tabbi Buck clearly remembers her presents that year: three Barbies, a Skipper, a red Barbie Corvette, a yellow Barbie recreational vehicle, and a stocking brimming with candy and trinkets.

Tabbi especially liked being close to the ocean. She swam fearlessly in the salt-water currents. Her brother often carried her way out into deep water, while her older sister stood crying at the shore afraid to go in. Yet, Kitty was fearless on a bicycle.

After about a year, the Bucks returned to Oregon, living in the McKenzie River area in the small mountain community of McKenzie Bridge. It was a beautiful area near the volcanic mountains known as Three Sisters. For three months, the Bucks lived in tents. All of the Buck children except Wendy, her father's oldest daughter, were there then. They slept in sleeping bags and built dams in the creek, hiked and swam.

"It was all fun to me," Tabbi Buck recalled, "but I'm not sure it was to the older kids."

Or to her mother.

Her father built a kitchen area from some scrap wood. The children laughed at their mother for sweeping the dirt floor of the "kitchen." Her father also created some semblance of civilization in the outhouse, with a holder for toilet paper and a padded seat.

She remembers driving up the mountain one day in an aged pea-green car they nicknamed the Buckmobile. A tire went flat and they were stranded. Before long a man came along, stopped, talked to Alvin Buck, and then sped off. The children were tired and thirsty and not taking the situation well. Soon the man returned with a cooler full of Gatorade and a new tire.

The generosity of strangers fills a big part of a grown Tabbi Buck's childhood memories.

Joanne Buck took a job in the school cafeteria, while her husband worked for a convenience store called Phil's. They moved into a red two-story house with three bedrooms. The children packed in two-to-three to a room. Tabbi Buck was in the second grade. Before the year ended, they moved "downriver" to Bear Creek and then Leesburg. Tabbi enrolled in McKenzie Elementary, where she finished fifth grade. She remembers it as her favorite school, where she learned to play the flute and the piccolo. Her parents separated, and she moved with her mother, Kitty, and Dan to Arizona. Her mother had friends there.

Dan was a rebellious teen in those years, listening to heavy metal music, wearing his hair spiked. A few months before graduation, he dropped out of high school. A few months later, he got involved in a church and turned his life around. He elected to stay in Arizona when his stepfather came and took Joanne, Kitty, and Tabbi back to Oregon.

The household seemed even more turbulent when they got back. A friend of Tabbi's sister moved in after being kicked out by her own parents. She was pregnant, eventually had the baby, and kept it. The Bucks soon saw she was not properly caring for the baby and called protective services. Another friend of a sister moved in sometime later.

Her parents' reunion didn't last, however. Alvin Buck was accused of having sexual relations with a member of Joanne's family. Tabbi remembers being taken to a large office building and separated from her sisters and mother. She was asked whether she had ever seen her father do anything "mean" to anyone. She hadn't, nor had he ever hurt her, she said. She was twelve.

After that, she remembers her father coming into her room crying. She was crying, too.

"Why do you have to leave?" she pleaded. She felt confused and upset.

The Bucks divorced. Joanne and the girls moved to the Cottage Grove area in Oregon's central coast section to be near her family. Their house looked just like the one on *Little House on the Prairie*, a television show Buck watched faithfully in reruns well into her adult years. She wasn't happy in school there, though; it was too big. She gleefully returned to the high school in Drain, where she spent her happiest elementary school years. Kitty went to live with their father; Dan (who had returned to Oregon), Tabbi, and her mother lived in a trailer. She played softball and volleyball and enjoyed the small church they attended. She also played in the high school band.

Tabbi Buck became reacquainted with her cousins Carla and Carol, whom she had previously considered

"Goody Two-shoes." They, in turn, considered her and her brothers and sisters heathens. Carla and Carol's father—Joanne's brother—was a minister, and their home was full of rules; at the Bucks', it was often more of a free-for-all.

Carla remembers Tabbi as a fun-loving, sensitive child, who became upset if someone killed a snake or even a bug. Carla, Carol, Tabbi, and Kitty went to week-long church camp together and packed all the clothes they owned so they could share. When their mothers came to pick them up, they had a bigger mess than the Salvation Army on receiving day.

Dan worked in a mill; Joanne in a nursing home. Life spun happily around school, where Tabbi was first chair in the band and an honor roll student, and church, where her uncle was the associate minister.

When Joanne's oldest biological child, Kellie, got married, Joanne wanted to invite her daughter's father to the wedding. Kellie did not know her father well, and Joanne wanted her and her children to know him. During the festivities, Joanne and her first husband, Leland Guier, spent a good deal of time together. They rekindled their feelings for one another. He went back to Lancaster, Pennsylvania, where he had lived for some time. They talked for long hours on the telephone and wrote letters. Soon Joanne was making plans to remarry her first husband, the man she had married at sixteen to make things easier for her father. Lancaster, Pennsylvania—out east as they called it—would be their new home.

Nine

Tabbi Buck was fourteen when she moved to Lancaster. It wasn't a move she made willingly or easily. She didn't especially like this guy Lee, even though he was the father of her brother and sister. He seemed way too rigid for a girl whose family didn't follow too many rules. He ate dinner at the same time every day, had a certain routine with the newspaper and television every day. Tabbi thought he was like a robot. Moreover, she thought he was cold and unresponsive to her mother, whom she had always seen as a caregiver. But what really upset Tabbi was she thought he tried to buy her affection. Once she told her mother she'd like to give a friendship ring to her best friend back home. He bought it for her.

That was between Mom and me, the angry teenager had thought. Tabbi and her stepfather would go for long periods without speaking.

They lived on Hazel Street, a not-so-nice section of Lancaster near the abundantly run-down Seventh Ward. Their house was a row house, tucked so close the teen would sometimes feel smothered. She was used to the wide open spaces. She had once lived in a tent under the stars. It all seemed so foreign. To make matters worse, she attended Hand Junior High, one of the toughest in the city.

Looking back on the period, she considers it the worst time of her childhood. One cold winter day, she came home from school to realize she had forgotten her key. Lee and her mother were both at work, so she sat on the porch. One neighbor, whom she had only known from the arguing she heard through the wall, asked her to come inside and wait. She declined. The neighbor on the other side, who had ten children who seemed to cry all day, asked her in as well. No thanks, she said. She remembers feeling she would rather wait in the cold. The people scared her.

One night she pleaded with her mother, "Please let me go back and live with Daddy."

He was in Alaska with a new wife. At first Joanne agreed, but then she changed her mind. She agreed to let Tabbi live with Dan, her older brother, who was still in the Cottage Grove section of Oregon. He was a youth leader at his church and worked in a mill. She was in the tenth grade and acted like the happy homemaker. She remembers the time as the best year of her life.

She was reunited with her cousins Carol and Carla. She played in the band and went to church. They were so steadfast in their attendance, a car accident couldn't keep them away. Dan ran the car into a ditch, spitting out the window. They flagged down an eighteen-wheeler, went to church, and dealt with the car problems later.

Dan was there for emotional support when a girl from school was killed in a car accident around Thanksgiving. Four others were hurt. The school planted a tree in the girl's memory and held a memorial service in the gym. The entire town mourned.

On Father's Day, Tabbi was upset when all the other kids stood in church and talked about the good things about their fathers. Dan was there for that, too, comforting her as she once again felt like the odd man out.

Tabbi knew it was all coming to an end, however, when Dan met Sherry, who would soon become his wife. The two women could not live in the same house. They liked each other, but Tabbi had for too long been in charge, and she felt jealous.

Her mother and Lee separated and Joanne returned to Oregon. They rented a cabin on the McKenzie River. Kitty, whose husband, John, was in the service, came to live with them with her daughter. Tabbi returned once again to McKenzie High School, where she was first chair flute and piccolo. Then a call came from Lee in Pennsylvania. He was ill with cancer. Could Joanne come? Of course. Kitty was going to return to North Carolina, but Tabbi was torn. She could stay with a friend and finish school in Oregon, or she could go with her mother.

It seemed odd to her not to be around family, so she returned to Pennsylvania to be with her mother in 1990. They lived in an apartment in the Bridgeport section of East Lampeter Township and Tabbi enrolled in Conestoga Valley High School. Michelle Lambert had been a student there, but dropped out before Tabbi arrived. Laurie Show was in the grade behind her, and Tabbi knew her only from riding the bus. Tabbi got her first job, at Weis Market in Bridgeport as a cashier. A woman named Jackie Yunkin worked there, too, but Tabbi did not know her. Tabbi Buck made some friends at school, including Stacy Cassione, who had a car. They would cruise the loop, a several-block-long section of Lancaster. Fridays, though, were usually reserved for Tabbi and her mother to do something together. They'd go to the movies or to Friendly's restaurant, or else they'd shop.

One evening, as Stacy and Tabbi cruised, they saw a bunch of teenagers sitting on the porch of one of the houses. Each time they passed, a boy jumped out into the road toward their car, teasing them. Stacy decided to stop. They met a group of kids, including Keith Painter. Something about the young man intrigued Tabbi. They started seeing one another. On one of their dates, he introduced her to some friends, Lawrence Yunkin and Michelle Lambert. Tabbi had seen them before, when she was working at Weis. She noticed them, out of the dozens of people who came through her checkout every day, because they seemed so attractive. Michelle was so pretty, Lawrence so handsome, and they seemed so devoted to each other.

Ten

Lawrence Yunkin's biological father saw him on the day he was born in Coatsville, Pennsylvania—March 12, 1971—and a few times after. The twenty-five-year-old steelworker wasn't ready for a family, not even the blue-eyed boy with hair so blond it hardly looked like it was there. He had married the boy's mother, Johnie Mae Haines, when he was twenty-two and she was eighteen. She just wanted to get out of the house, out on her own, out of the dismal surroundings and a home she considered cold. Her mother didn't show her love for her five children. Sometimes Johnie Mae even wondered if she felt it. For a time, Johnie Mae aspired to be a model. She enrolled in modeling school in Philadelphia, but lasted only a month. Her funds ran out, so she got married instead. She was a street-smart girl who was never into drugs, but she did like a stiff drink. Shortly after her marriage, she took the name "Jackie." She never officially changed it, but she liked it, and everyone knew her as Jackie.

The couple moved to Christiana, Pennsylvania, in Chester County, the eastern neighbor of Lancaster County, after Jackie graduated from high school. They separated after two years there. Jackie didn't know it at the time, but she was two months pregnant with Lawrence. She didn't tell her husband about the baby, even though she suspected she was pregnant. She lived in a rooming house until the baby was born. Her husband came to the hospital the night Lawrence was born. She named him for a friend, a Vietnam veteran who had been like a big brother to her.

Jackie and her husband reconciled for about a month after the baby was born. It just didn't work, Jackie remembered many years later.

"He wouldn't buy milk for the baby," she said. "I was raised in poverty and I wasn't going to have that for my son."

They were divorced in June 1973.

She was on welfare and working at the counter at the Midway Restaurant, a hot dog shop, for $75 per week, and trying to make enough to pay for her apartment and support her young son.

At night Jackie liked to party. She and her friends would gather at a bar and drink Seven and Seven, glass after glass. Often Jackie couldn't remember what had happened. One night a man punched one of her friends. She hit him with a fist that seemed of iron, splitting his head open. She knew she had to stop drinking then. She had almost killed him. She would call the incident her "crude, rude awakening." Police didn't file charges, calling it self-defense.

Jackie had previously met a man she liked, Barry Yunkin, when he delivered the couch and chair she had long wanted and had finally saved enough to buy. She didn't think much about Barry at the time. He was three years younger, and she was the mother of a six-month-old son.

But Barry was smitten. He continued to ask her out until finally she consented. Barry immediately took to young Lawrence, who was called "Butch" by his family after his biological father. Barry coddled Lawrence more than Jackie did. She was the disciplinarian, telling Lawrence the things she had heard all her life: tell the truth, be loyal, don't make fun of others, don't give up. As a toddler, Lawrence almost drowned, but Barry took him right back to the same spot and made him swim until he got it. He wouldn't have a boy afraid of water, even if his mother still was afraid of the water.

Jackie and Barry married in June 1974 in Elktown, Maryland. They drove across the state line to avoid Pennsylvania's blood test and a sixteen-day waiting period. Family and friends gathered at the Little Wedding Chapel across the street from the courthouse, where they got their marriage license. They didn't take a honeymoon. Monday morning Barry was at work at Denlinger's, a roof truss manufacturer, and Jackie was at Carter's sewing children's clothing.

They just wanted to get married and have a simple life. They moved to Paradise, Pennsylvania, a township surrounded by Amish farms about seven miles south of Lancaster. They rented part of a house that belonged to an Amish couple, the Glicks. When the Yunkins worked, Lawrence stayed with Mrs. Glick, and he soon became much like one of her own seven children. The Glicks raised chickens and grew all sorts of vegetables for their own kitchen. They also grew tobacco. By the time Lawrence was thirteen, he was planting tobacco and spearing it, too, driving the team of horses. He learned a lot of the Amish existence, the simple ways on the farm, a life of sunshine and cool water and dirt beneath fingernails.

He seemed a bit shy around strangers and had something of an awkward smile, slightly crooked. But he had a good sense of humor. Work came easy, school did not. He struggled over math and English. His talents lay on the baseball diamond and the football field. He played both of those sports, plus soccer, hockey, and threw a javelin. He liked physical activity. He worked odd jobs for neighbors.

He had his first real job when he was sixteen, working for Merv King, an Amish man who built roofs. King had one firm rule for his business: no employees younger than twenty-one. But this Yunkin kid wouldn't go away. He gave him a shot and was stunned by how much he could accomplish in a day. King even took him deep-sea fishing off the New Jersey shore that summer.

Even though school was not his strength, he bided his time well enough. He didn't make too much trouble. Jackie Yunkin remembers being called to the principal's office one day because her son had had some trouble in the cafeteria. A boy had poured pepper into a handicapped girl's milk and Yunkin dumped the milk over the boy's head.

In the eleventh grade, he wanted to quit school. He'd rather work, he told his mother.

Jackie told him, "If you were walking ten miles and got to eight and were thirsty, would you go back and get water or keep going forward?"

"No," he said, a bit puzzled by the analogy.

"Same thing with school," she said. "Finish."

She added a threat to make her story stick. If he didn't go to school, she was going to drag him in there by the hair.

The next summer, he took a job as a lifeguard at Pioneer Woods Apartments, where the Yunkins had moved the year before. Within weeks he looked like a California beach boy with a golden tan across his broad shoulders. The girls noticed him, flocking around the lifeguard stand like adoring groupies. He reveled in the attention. Soon a young girl with big brown eyes started showing up at the pool with some friends who lived in the complex.

"Who's that?" he asked a friend.

"Lisa Michelle Lambert" came the response.

Eleven

Fall had taken hold of the New Jersey landscape with swirling, falling leaves and nippy mornings when Lisa Michelle Lambert was born September 9, 1972, amid the frenzy of Wilson Army Hospital at Fort Dix. Her father, Len, was in the air force and they lived at McGuire Air Force Base in central New Jersey.

It had been a tough delivery. Judy Lambert was in labor for almost twenty-nine hours and developed toxemia. Doctors worried she and the baby would not live. But once born, Lisa was fine. Judy needed some recuperation time and did not get to see the baby immediately.

Two years later, Judy Lambert gave birth to a son, Lenny junior.

A year after that, Len was discharged from the Air Force, and the family moved back to Lancaster County, where they were from originally. They moved to Bridgeport. Her mother remembers Lisa as a "sweet little girl, a perfect little girl." She had always wanted a daughter and she doted on her.

When Lisa was about four, she began to have trouble with the neighborhood children. Her mother believed they were picking on her. One boy—Judy considered him nothing more than a bully—hurt Lisa's arm so badly she was treated in the emergency room and the doctor made her wear a sling on her arm. Another time a dog tore her arm up, exposing the bone.

"She was always picked on, always tormented," Judy recalled.

The problem grew so great that the family moved to a rental house in Strasburg. They were building a two-story house in the Stumptown community in East Lampeter Township. Settled on a small hill, the house was sided in blue vinyl.

Judy Lambert ran a day care from the home for about five years, caring for six other children besides her own. Her husband worked for the United Parcel Service and obtained his bachelor's and master's degrees during that time.

Seven-year-old Lisa was especially excited about the prospect of a new baby in the family when Judy announced she was pregnant in 1979. They prepared a nursery for the child, carefully setting out the crib that hadn't been used for several years. Lisa, whose artistic ability was beginning to show, drew elaborate cards for her mother, especially after Judy was put to bed for the duration of the pregnancy. She told her mother she was praying for the baby. Lisa also easily stepped in to care for her little brother, Lenny, who was five years old. When Judy miscarried, Lisa was devastated. She went to the funeral home with her father to pick out a casket for the baby her parents named Justin.

It seemed Judy had no more lost one baby than she discovered she was pregnant again. She spent much of this pregnancy in bed, too, and Lisa again cared for her brother. Lisa remembered her mother just sitting in the bed, not moving, not talking. Lisa made her brother sandwiches and watched out for him. The baby, Jeremy, was born in 1980, a healthy boy.

The family attended Oregon Pike Presbyterian church

every Sunday morning, Sunday night, and Wednesday night, and Lisa attended Lancaster Christian School until she was in the fifth grade. It was a strict household: no smoking, no drinking, no rock-and-roll music, and certainly no sex before marriage. They taught Lisa that the only man she was to ever have sex with was the man she married. And only after she married him.

Len Lambert went to work as an accountant after he earned his master's, and the family's financial situation continued to improve. He worked for Custom Kitchens for many years.

Lisa was twelve in 1984, when her mother became pregnant again.

"Lisa took over like she was a mother," Judy recalled. She cared for Lenny and Jeremy. Doted on them. She moved furniture around. She ran the household as her mother slipped into depression. Judy stayed in bed for days on end, playing the same records over and over. Her emotional state grew worse when she lost that baby.

The next year, Judy Lambert was pregnant again. That summer Christopher was born with complications. Judy spent much of the next two years caring for him. Shortly after his birth, Lisa went with Judy's eighty-eight-year-old aunt to Everett, Pennsylvania, 150 miles west of Lancaster, to care for her after a stroke. The aunt had been used to living alone, but after the stroke, she lived with relatives in the Lancaster area. She wanted desperately to go home. It was an isolated area and the aunt had no phone or television. Lisa agreed to go to be sure she ate and to bathe her. Lisa stayed about a week, her mother recalled.

Lisa was a good student, her mother said. Art was always her strongest subject, math her worst.

In junior high school, Lisa was picked on again. She

and her friend Beth Eldridge were considered nerds, were decidedly unpopular, and were called names.

In high school, Lisa became disinterested in academics and her grades dropped. She wouldn't go to school and was hanging around kids Judy and Len believed to be bad influences. Lisa bristled at the strictness of her parents' rules. They seemed arbitrary and unnecessary to someone who could easily take care of herself. Len simply couldn't understand his daughter. A military man, an accountant, he liked things to add up, stay ordered. Lisa just wasn't that. Sometimes she would sneak out of the house at night and be gone for hours. He worried, fearing she might be hurt or involved in things she should not be. But she told her parents she was not sneaking out to meet people. She simply needed time alone to think.

Toward the end of tenth grade, Lisa left home. The incident seemed so inconsequential. Looking back on that time, it was still hard for Judy Lambert to figure out why it had happened. Three times a week, Judy drove Christopher to the hospital to get therapy. On that day, Lisa wanted her mother to drive her to work. When Judy told her she couldn't, Lisa told her she was leaving. But, Judy recalled, her relationship with her daughter continued with lunches and swimming together. She came for birthdays, Father's Day. After spending about six weeks with friends of her parents' in Virginia, Lisa returned home. She had been gone nine months in all. The Lamberts' friends called Lisa a "diamond in the rough."

"She was not a bad, bad kid," her mother said. "Family was important, even if we weren't seeing each other very much."

Twelve

Years after Lisa Michelle Lambert met Lawrence Yunkin, Lambert could remember the date they met without hesitation: July 26, 1989, the day she met the man who became her whole world. On a beautiful Pennsylvania summer day, she was at the swimming pool at Pioneer Woods with her brother Jeremy. As she recalls it, her parents and brothers had been telling her for some time she needed a boyfriend. She was sixteen. Jeremy introduced her to the lifeguard: Lawrence Yunkin; he lived with his parents in the complex. When she told him her name was "Lisa," he asked her middle name.

"I don't like Lisa, so you are going to be Michelle," he said.

He asked her out. That night they saw the movie *Batman*. Years later he would say he fell in love with her that very night. On the next date, they saw *Dead Poets Society* and he took her to meet his parents.

"I liked her," recalled Jackie Yunkin. "She was a polite young lady, a lot of help."

On their third date, they saw another movie. On their fourth date, Yunkin picked Lambert up from work at the Dutch Wonderland Castle gift shop. At an apartment of a friend of Yunkin's at Pioneer Woods, a group played Dungeons and Dragons, donning period costumes to fulfill their roles. Lambert felt spooked.

"I had never seen anything like that," she said later.

The men left the apartment to complete their "missions" and Lambert stayed behind with the friend's wife. After what seemed like a long time, Yunkin returned and drove Lambert home in his parents' van. They were sitting in the back, feet swinging, talking. In court testimony years later, Lambert would accuse Yunkin of raping her that night. She said he suddenly pushed her over on the van floor and raped her in the driveway of her parents' home.

"Why did you do that to me?" Lambert said she cried. He beat her neck, back, and legs.

"I curled into a ball and he was just beating me," she testified.

Finally he stopped and started crying, she said. He apologized and said he didn't know why he would do such a thing. He carried her into her parents' house. It was about 2:00 A.M. She went to sleep and did not tell her parents about the incident. She said she did not think they would believe her. After all, she reasoned, they liked him. His uncle Bumpy Yunkin, a truck driver for a convenience market chain, was a leader in their church, Oregon Pike Presbyterian. It was a good family.

The next morning, Yunkin showed up with roses and told Lambert he would marry her. They had had sex. It was the right thing to do. He drove her to work; her life just seemed to float along like that.

Yunkin denies raping her. In fact, Yunkin and Lambert tell far different accounts of how their relationship progressed through the next two years. He says he was madly in love with her. She says he abused her unmercifully. Friends say they never saw Yunkin hit her, although she has pictures of an angry gash on her face where she says he punched her. Jackie Yunkin says she saw her son hit Michelle, but it was clearly an accident.

Several friends say it often appeared that Yunkin was actually henpecked, putting up with Lambert verbally abusing and sometimes punching him. Many people who knew Lambert before she met Yunkin were shocked by the change in her appearance. She says she did it to please Yunkin.

It started a few days after the alleged rape. He wanted her to look more like a Barbie doll, she claims. He asked her to bleach her brown hair and get blue contacts to make her brown eyes blue. He also told her she didn't look "sexy" enough. She wasn't showing enough skin. And he wanted her to wear more makeup. She changed her clothes, sometimes three or four times a day, she said, because Lawrence tired of the outfit.

Lawrence brought Michelle around the Yunkin house a lot and she'd set the table and help Jackie wash dishes. She started calling Barry "Pappy Barry." Jackie noticed Lambert's new look. She thought Lambert wore too much makeup, and looked like a clown or worse.

Soon Lawrence asked Jackie if Michelle could move in with them. Her parents had thrown her out, he said. Reluctantly Jackie agreed.

The next September, Lambert enrolled in classes to earn her GED. She had planned to go back to high school—she would have been in the eleventh grade—but changed her mind, she says, when Yunkin balked at the idea. He told her he didn't want her around high school guys. He preferred for her to work at the gift shop because all the employees were women.

They went to a play one night at Lampeter Strasburg High School, where Yunkin was a senior. Lambert testified many years later that he beat her that night when he became enraged at locking his keys in his truck.

The evening had started off so well, Lambert recalled. Yunkin was pleased with the way she had changed her looks. He wanted to show her off to his high school friends. But he lost control when he found out he had locked the keys in the truck and called her a bitch.

"Shut up. Don't tell me what to do," he screamed after she had told him to call his father for another set of keys. She testified in court years later that he grabbed her hair and slammed her face into the truck.

The next month, they went to a cabin in Dushore with his parents. Jackie and Barry Yunkin went hiking for the day, leaving their son and his girlfriend alone in the cabin. They were talking about the future and Yunkin mentioned he was going to join the army after he graduated.

Lambert remembered the exchange in court testimony:

"Oh, well, you didn't tell me that before," she said. "How long will you be in boot camp?"

"Three months."

"OK, I'll just work while you are gone."

He looked at her and said, "What are you going to do, mess around on me? What are you going to do, sleep around?"

He started screaming at her, she testified, and kicking her. He knocked her to the floor and beat her until she ran into the bedroom. He kicked the locked door and beat on it. She stayed inside. When his parents came back, they took her to a clinic, she said. Yunkin's parents have steadfastly denied it happened, however.

Lambert said she thought it was her fault he was hitting her. If she had been nicer or prettier, he would not do such things.

Another time, she said, he hit her with a lamp and a Crock-Pot. One summer he became jealous of the attention she got from other men when she wore a bikini. After he closed the pool, he dragged her into the water, scraping her leg. He held her underwater, time and time again. Finally he let her go, saying, "Next time, don't flirt."

In June 1990, Yunkin graduated from Lampeter-Strasberg High School. By then, he was a stocky six-footer, with bleached blond hair cropped short on the sides, longer on top, and grown past his shoulders in back. Jackie Yunkin remembers their fights growing worse, but from her perspective, it was Lambert who caused them. She became jealous of everything Lawrence did. Suspicious, questioning his every move. She'd get mad if he wanted to go somewhere without her. She'd ask Jackie if she saw lipstick on his collar. She was jealous of his relationship with his mother. One night Lawrence turned to say good night to his mother and kissed her on the cheek. She heard Michelle in the bedroom saying in a cold tone, "That's your mother. You're not supposed to kiss your mother."

Lambert said to Jackie, "Why do you hug him like that? He's a man!"

Jackie was astounded. She had made of point of hugging her son since he was a baby, because her own mother rarely hugged her, never told her she loved her. Jackie Yunkin would not make that same choice with her son. Never a day or night passed when she didn't tell Lawrence she loved him. And it didn't matter to her what Michelle Lambert thought, either. Soon Jackie Yunkin began to seethe. This Michelle was really getting on her nerves. And the fighting was growing worse by the day.

Michelle seemed to want to be the center of the universe or she wasn't happy. It was almost as if she were a television star and she heard her theme song every time she walked into a room. The queen has arrived. Notice me.

Once Jackie Yunkin saw her son hit Michelle. She thinks it was an accident, but years later Yunkin would admit he had indeed hit her. Sometimes, he told his mother, he wanted to "put her through a wall," but he said he remembered mild-mannered Barry, who never hit his mother, never raised his voice, never cussed.

At the end of 1990, the management at Pioneer Woods asked the Yunkins to move out. No explanation, Jackie says, but she believes it was because of her son's fights with Lambert, which were growing in intensity all the time. The Yunkins moved to another apartment complex in East Lampeter. Jackie asked her son to take his girlfriend and move out.

Lambert tells it differently. She says the beatings became so frequent, she could not differentiate between them. Yet, in October 1990, Lambert moved into an apartment with Yunkin on Old Pennsylvania Pike. It was the upstairs of a two-story mustard-yellow house in a commercial section of Bridgeport, the same community where Tabbi Buck lived, the same community where Lambert was taunted as a child.

Not long afterward, Yunkin became enraged that she had talked to a sixteen-year-old boy at the Good N Plenty Restaurant, where they all worked together. He beat her so badly that night, she ended up in the emergency room at Lancaster General Hospital, Lambert testified years later. He told the nurses she had been in a car accident and then never left her side so she couldn't tell something different. He stayed even when the technician came in for X rays.

Lambert said Yunkin would not let her go out with her girlfriends, except one, and when she did that, he followed her.

"He was always there," Lambert said. He got her paychecks and cashed them, controlling all the money. And he always seemed to need to hurt her in order to become sexually aroused.

He got drunk drinking Jack Daniel's on Christmas that year and smashed a ceramic bear collection her parents had given her. He threw weights at her. She begged him to leave her alone.

"He sodomized me," she would testify in court years later when she was trying to overturn her conviction for killing Laurie Show. The next day, she was bleeding and throwing up. The room was spinning. Lawrence's mother told her she should get used to it, Lambert testified. She called her parents, who came over and pleaded with her to leave.

"Mom, you don't understand. He follows me everywhere. He's going to kill me."

Jackie Yunkin remembers the incident much differently. She said Lambert was menstruating heavily.

"She asked me about it and I said I was like that, too, before I had gotten pregnant," Jackie said.

A few months later, Lambert and her mother were talking. Judy Lambert told her daughter of her deep religious conviction that women should marry a man if they had sex with him. He was the man for the rest of your life, she told her daughter. But her situation was different.

"Lisa, Lawrence is not the right man, he's not the right man," Judy Lambert said. "You can't let church and the Bible, you can't let that make you stay there. I know you have had sex with him, but you can't marry him. He's horrible. If you ever have babies, he'll kill them. He's a monster."

A few days later, Lambert had another confrontation with Yunkin. She said she threw the engagement and wedding ring he had bought her at him as he beat her. Once she had thought she was a pretty girl. Now she felt ugly and hopeless.

"Just kill me," Lambert said. "Just please kill me, because I can't take this. Get it over with."

He looked at her and started laughing hysterically.

"I hate you and I don't love you and I don't want to be with you and just kill me. I'm not with you anymore, we're not together and I am leaving."

He stopped laughing then and said, "If you leave, I'll kill you."

He agreed they were not together anymore but forbade her to move out. One night they had a party and Yunkin got drunk, Lambert said. He started beating her, but Allen Rudolph interceded and threw Yunkin to the floor. Yunkin passed out. It was the first time Lambert had seen anyone hold his own against Yunkin. She started sneaking out at night after Yunkin was asleep to meet Rudolph. He would pull her into his bedroom window and they'd sit up listening to music and talking. They'd play basketball in the dark and go swimming in the creek.

On Easter Sunday, Len and Judy Lambert saw for themselves how troubling their daughter's relationship with Yunkin truly was. The two came for Sunday dinner at the Lamberts'. Michelle's brothers, aged sixteen, eleven, and six, were there as well.

Yunkin began calling Michelle names, Judy remembered. He accused her of sleeping with other men and used foul language. In court testimony years later, Lambert admitted she had crept out at night to meet Allen Rudolph and their relationship became more than platonic. They slept together regularly until June.

That Easter Sunday, the Lamberts asked Yunkin and their daughter to leave.

Two times earlier, Lawrence hit Michelle's brothers. Judy saw her rush between Lawrence and her brother Christopher, saying, "You can't hurt him! Get away from him. Leave him alone." Judy asked her son what happened and he said Lawrence got mad because he accidentally spit on his shoe.

In June, Lawrence called and asked to borrow Barry's van. His car was broken, he said. When he brought the van back, he asked his mother if he could move back in at home. He was sick of Michelle's crazy jealousy.

"I just want to forget about her," he told his mother.

Jackie was relieved; the Lamberts, who were receiving calls from their daughter accusing Yunkin of beating her, did not know of the breakup.

"We honestly thought she was going to end up dead," Judy said.

Her parents had talked with her about Lawrence; they encouraged her to leave him. On June 24, 1991, Michelle called, crying deeply. Her father was off from work. They picked her up and she spent most of the day with them at their house. Her parents tried to reason with her. They wanted her to take control of her own life. She could live in the basement of the house. It had its own entrance, so she could have some measure of privacy.

"She was crying through the whole day," her mother said. "We just couldn't get through to her."

She talked about a "friend" who was pregnant. Judy believed Michelle was talking about herself, but she also knew a doctor had told her when Michelle was fourteen she would probably need drugs to stimulate ovulation to get pregnant. She didn't take it seriously.

After they took her home, the boys told their mother that Michelle had taken "pregnant things," pamphlets and other information.

Meanwhile, at the Yunkins', Lawrence Yunkin was getting frantic phone calls from Lambert. She called over and over.

"If you don't come back, I'm going to kill myself," Michelle wailed into the telephone to Yunkin.

The phone seemed to ring incessantly, and when Jackie answered, the caller would hang up. Once Jackie punched in *69 and heard Michelle's number. She redialed.

"I'll have you arrested for harassment," she said bitterly, all the months of frustration welling up and flowing out with each word.

Soon Lawrence brought home a new girl, Laurie Show. She seemed like a sweet girl, Jackie thought. A bit young, perhaps, but nice. They had been swimming at the girl's grandfather's house, a doctor in Bird-In-Hand, and to the fair.

A few days later, Lambert called again. This time when she asked for Lawrence, she was calm.

Jackie watched her son as he spoke into the phone. His face seemed to go white. He recradled the receiver and started crying.

"Mom, she's pregnant," Lawrence said. He'd have to go back to her.

He told his mother, "Didn't you always tell me if I make a child, I'm responsible?"

It was like some out-of-world experience. For years Michelle Lambert had thought she would never be able to have babies. Even her parents had said so. Everyone thought she was lying. Yunkin went with her for an ultrasound. It was a baby all right. This time the girl whom everyone considered a pathological liar was telling the truth.

At about the same time, Lambert called Hazel Show. She told her she was pregnant with Yunkin's child. Hazel wasted no time in telling Laurie she had no choice in the matter. Laurie would have to break it off with Yunkin. No debate. Laurie agreed.

Yunkin moved back into the second-floor apartment in Lancaster. Michelle Lambert had won back the man she considered the love of her life, but for some reason, she could not forget about the girl she believed had almost stolen Lawrence away from her. Even though Laurie and Yunkin dated for a week only, Michelle was convinced that Laurie still wanted him. She never called her by name. Laurie was merely "The Bitch."

Two weeks later, the Lamberts realized their daughter had taken something far more valuable than information on pregnancy: her mother's coin collection and $150 in cash. On September 11, 1991, the Lamberts took a letter to the East Lampeter Police Department, dated August 20, 1991. The letter warned Lambert to stay away from her family or face prosecution because of the theft.

"You are not permitted on our property at any time, you are not to call our home for any reason, and you are not to bother or disturb any of us in any way whether it be at home or in a public place." It spelled out that she was not to contact her father at work or her brothers at school. The letter also accused her of "ransacking" her parents' bedroom.

It was one of those times parents of troubled children know so well. Loves flows inside them like a wide river as they feel empathy and sorrow for a child's bad choices, yet just as quickly come anger and resentment when they become aware of the child's betrayal. It is the one constant in the lives of parents of children who have veered off course. The children of those families experience a path of twists and turns—drugs, bad relationships, alcohol, violence, no school—yet the circumstances for the parents remain immutable; they live their lives on an emotional roller coaster. Most certainly, the Lamberts felt they had no choice. Their sons had been hurt by Yunkin; their daughter had been abused and would not leave him. Now she had stolen something valuable. Not just their coin collection. Not just their money. She had stolen their trust. They had to shear off one child, no matter how much they loved her, to protect the others.

The police delivered the letter to Lambert personally at the apartment she shared with Yunkin. It was two days after Lambert's nineteenth birthday.

They did not see her for six months, not until the day she was arrested for murder.

Thirteen

One trait of Lisa Michelle Lambert's on which everyone agrees is that she is a smart woman. Hazel Show says it; her lawyers say it; Jackie Yunkin, Lambert's friends, her codefendants in the case that made her famous. Her foes call her calculating; her friends cunning. Evil. Sweet. Manipulative. Considerate. Polar opposites.

Laurie Show considered Lambert overbearing and self-centered. They met at Rachel Winesickle's house one afternoon after school. Laurie had been in a fuss with Rachel and with another friend, Laura Thomas. Both girls accused her of spreading rumors about them around Conestoga Valley High School, where Laurie Show was a tenth grader.

Laurie Show had a way about her that some found snobby. In many circles of teenage girls, it's not well received to seem confident and self-assured. Tall and thin, she could seem much older than her sixteen years. She was no angel, either. She'd had boyfriends, and she'd given her mother some trouble. But as she moved toward her seventeenth birthday in January, Laurie Show was figuring things out. She thought she'd like to be a model one day. If that failed, then cosmetology. She had a nice boyfriend, Brad Heisler, who went to her school. He was a good-looking boy—about her height. They spent most of their free time together, often hanging out at Laurie's condominium.

Laurie Show mentioned to Lambert one day that she'd like to be a model.

"You can't be a model," Lambert scoffed. "Look at your hair, and you're not pretty enough."

Laurie went home and told her mother about it. Hazel said, "Who's she to tell you what you can and cannot be?"

A few weeks later, Laurie was dating Lambert's ex-boyfriend. Hazel Show believes Laurie took up with Lawrence Yunkin because she felt sorry for him. He seemed dejected about his breakup with Lambert. To Hazel, it seemed they were merely friends. They went to Park City Mall, the petting zoo. Laurie got another hole pierced in her ear. They swam at her grandfather's pool. John Show let Yunkin come over and watch television. He seemed like a nice enough guy, even though John thought Yunkin at twenty was a bit too old for his sixteen-year-old daughter. He also didn't like the fact that Yunkin drove a van. But he always had her home on time.

One Saturday Laurie and Yunkin were supposed to go to the fair with her father and his girlfriend. But when they got to John Show's house, her father had gone on ahead. Laurie came home and told Hazel she was angry her dad had done that. Hazel wondered what had made Laurie so mad about that.

When Hazel discovered Yunkin had gotten Lambert pregnant, the friendship—in her mind—was over. He was standing outside the Shows' condominium with Laurie after Lambert called Hazel and told her about the baby. Hazel went outside and said to Yunkin, "Michelle just called. She was very abusive and told me she was pregnant. You have a problem you need to take care of, Lawrence. You need to talk to Michelle, to her parents, your parents, maybe even get guidance from a counselor. But you need not involve Laurie in this."

She looked at the young man and said, "You're not to see Laurie anymore."

They all agreed it was for the best.

Life went on. Laurie was working at the Deb Shop, a clothing store in East Towne Mall, which could almost be seen from the Shows' condominium. She had gotten her permit to drive but had not taken driver's education yet, so she did not get her license when the six-month waiting period ended in the summer.

Hazel told John about the baby and he backed her up on the decision to make Laurie stop seeing Yunkin.

On July 5, Laurie was working when Lambert came into the store.

"You fucked my boyfriend," she screamed at Laurie, and then called her a slut and a whore and left. That night, Laurie called Lambert and told her not to do that again. Hazel was listening on an extension. Lambert cussed and called Laurie names. Finally Hazel said, "Michelle, this is Laurie's mother. You've got Lawrence. She doesn't want him. You must leave her alone."

Hazel Show felt sure that would end it. But a few days later, as she was waiting for Laurie to leave work, she saw a carload of teens in a car. When Laurie walked down the hallway, a blond girl stepped toward her and shoved Laurie against a wall. Hazel had never seen Michelle Lambert until that day. She wanted to confront her, but as Laurie got into the car, crying, she told her mother to please go on. It would make matters worse.

Hazel called East Lampeter Township Police to report the incident, but the duty officer told her nothing could be done. They had left the scene. The Shows created an elaborate schedule so Laurie would not be in public alone. John or Hazel picked her up from work, Brad took her to and from school.

But a couple of days later, Lambert confronted John Show, telling him Laurie had had sex with Yunkin. She called her a slut and a whore.

John remembers his daughter was so scared of Lambert she would cry and shake whenever she saw her. That day at the mall, when Lambert confronted him, Laurie had wanted to stay inside the mall so they wouldn't have to walk past Yunkin and Lambert.

"Hey, you're with me," the father said. "They're not going to hurt you. We're going."

Lambert marched right up into his face. John felt like he wanted to smack her. He could not get over the nerve she exhibited in screaming at him—an adult—in such a way. Yunkin stood in the background.

Show said, "You better get her out of here. I have really lost respect for you to let your girlfriend do this."

It seemed to the Shows that no one was immune from the wrath of the woman. The Shows did not understand it. That night Laurie told her mother why she had been so mad at her father on the night of the fair. Yunkin had taken her to a secluded road, somewhere she did not know, and raped her in his parents' van.

"It's up to you, whatever you want to do about it," Hazel told her daughter. They would let it be for now. Laurie did not want to make them madder.

On August 1, Laurie called Hazel at work, frightened.

"Lawrence and Michelle are outside," she said.

Hazel called the police. Officer Robin Weaver was dispatched to East Towne Mall. He took Lambert and Yunkin aside and questioned them. Hazel brushed past and went into the store. Laurie was in the back room with her boss. Weaver came into the room and asked Laurie what was going on. She told him about the rape.

"Do you want to bring charges?" he asked.

"No," Laurie said. He told her if she changed her mind to let him know.

On his way out, he said to Lambert and Yunkin, "Stay away from her."

In the later part of August, Hazel and Laurie were at Root's Market, an outdoor farmers' market in East Petersburg, with Hazel's friend Rose and Rose's four-year-old son, Zach.

Hazel spotted the six-foot-tall Yunkin towering over the crowd. Lambert was by his side.

"Don't panic," Hazel told her daughter.

"Let's go," her daughter said quickly.

Hazel told her they wouldn't live in fear. They weren't changing their plans. They stopped at a booth. People were packed around them.

"Your daughter fucked my boyfriend," Lambert screamed, moving toward them.

Laurie, holding Zach's hand, got behind her mother.

"Michelle, will you just stop this," Hazel demanded, peering down at the girl. Rose said something to Lambert, who in turn called her a bitch.

Hazel blurted, "Michelle, if you want the truth, Lawrence raped Laurie, and if you don't stop this, you're going to force us to bring charges against him."

She turned to Yunkin and said, "Lawrence, you better get her out of here or I'm going to call the police."

Rose yelled, "Where's a phone? Where's a constable?"

The couple quickly left. Hazel was struck by the look on Yunkin's face as the encounter transpired. She thought he looked like he enjoyed it, having women fight over him.

Lambert left Laurie Show alone for a few weeks, until October when they all were at the New Holland Fair. Standing in line to get food, Laurie spotted Lambert.

She told her mother they were leaving. Laurie looked over her shoulder all the way to their car, four blocks.

At some point in November, Hazel dropped Laurie off at East Towne Mall for work. At shortly after 8:00 P.M., Laurie was standing with Jackie Weakland and some other friends in the parking lot. Lambert and Yunkin drove up. Lambert jumped out of the car and pushed Laurie to the ground. At five feet nine inches, Laurie could have easily knocked Lambert down, but Lambert was six months pregnant at the time and Laurie did not want to hurt her. Lambert screamed, "You ruined my life. You ruined my baby's life."

Lambert struck her several times. Yunkin sat in the car and watched.

Laurie replied, "I'm sorry. Let me make it up to you. I'm sorry I ever did anything to hurt you."

Lambert raced to the car when she saw a security guard come out of a nearby Burlington Coat Factory store.

Hazel Show had had enough. She had Laurie take out a warrant for simple assault that night against Lambert. She was tired of her daughter looking over her shoulder everywhere she went. She did not want her to be afraid any longer.

Fourteen

Tabbi Buck met Michelle Lambert and Lawrence Yunkin in September through Keith Painter, a boy she had met on the loop. They were all just young people hanging around and cruising the loop. They didn't drink or use drugs, just rode around, talked or listened to music. Often they'd end up at Longs Park, near Park City Mall. Buck was still in high school. Lambert, who had just turned nineteen, had dropped out many years before. Yunkin, twenty, had graduated and had not gone to college.

Buck thought Lambert and Yunkin were obsessed with each other. Sometimes they were so affectionate with one another that it made her sick. Other times Lambert would get mad at Yunkin, call him names, and hit him. It seemed to Buck that in Yunkin's eyes, Lambert could do no wrong.

After Buck and Painter broke up, she relied on Lambert and Yunkin for rides, something to do, someone to do it with. She never considered Lambert her confidante, nor did Buck her. They were simply her ride. In fact, Buck did not know a lot about Lambert. She didn't know until after they all were arrested that Michelle's real name was Lisa. She had never seen the cold side of Lambert until the morning in Laurie Show's bedroom.

She had just seemed nice. Some questioned Buck

about hanging around with an unmarried, pregnant high school dropout, but Buck thought nothing of that. Some of her sisters, after all, had done the same. It didn't seem like such a bad thing. Buck also didn't see anything particularly unusual about Lambert's dark eye makeup or the light, thick foundation and deep red lipstick she wore. It was a lot of makeup, but what is too much to a teenager? Lambert told her she wanted to be as white as she could, a comment that annoyed Buck because she was then dating a boy of mixed race. Lambert never told her she changed her looks to satisfy Yunkin.

Buck did not know of Lambert's plots to lure Laurie Show from her house and embarrass or hurt her. She did know Lambert did not like Laurie, a girl Buck knew from riding the school bus.

Joanne Guier saw traits in Lambert, though, that her daughter did not see. Lambert seemed to make up stories, but there was also something about her that made Guier feel sorry for her. Lambert told her she didn't really have a mother. Her mother was a prostitute on K Street, Lambert told her. Years later, when Guier learned the Lamberts were pillars of the community, she was stunned.

Guier took her to a prenatal visit and drove her home a time or two. She tried to be a role model to Lambert. Nevertheless, there was something about the girl that Guier simply did not like, did not trust. She told her daughter to beware.

"I don't like that girl, Tab," Guier said.

Buck casually responded, "Oh, Mom, she's OK."

Part 3: The Trials

Fifteen

Lawrence F. Stengel came late to the law. His father, Lawrence E., was a lawyer in Lancaster. But Lawrence F.—known as Larry to distinguish him from his father—wanted to be a teacher. Drama was his passion, one he discovered and nurtured as a high school student at Lancaster Catholic High School. In his senior year, he won the coveted part of the diabolical Fagan in the musical *Oliver*. He also was involved in forensics, or debating, and won some state tournaments.

The Stengel family was one of the more prominent in Lancaster. They lived on Buchanan Street, across the street from Buchanan Park, a refuge at the edge of downtown. Stately well-preserved homes line the street. Larry was the oldest. Three brothers and two sisters followed. Sacred Heart of Jesus Church centered their lives. Although not especially tall, Larry played on the Catholic Youth Organization basketball team. His friends remember him as a leader when he was as young as elementary school age at Sacred Heart School. After high school graduation in 1970, he studied English at St. Joseph University in Philadelphia and returned to Lancaster Catholic to teach English. He also was in charge of the school's drama program.

After his first year teaching, he married Barbara Senkowski, whom he had known since the eighth grade. Two years later, Stengel decided he did want to follow in his father's footsteps after all, and he enrolled in the University of Pittsburgh Law School, graduating in 1980. A decade later, he was appointed to a circuit court judgeship to fill out the term of a Lancaster judge who had been appointed to the federal court. The next year, he won the spot for himself in a general election.

So when he mounted the bench on July 9, 1992, to preside over the Lancaster area's most horrific murder ever—the slashing death of sixteen-year-old Laurie Show—Stengel had been a judge only a matter of months. He was thirty-nine years old, Lancaster County's youngest judge, but he was a popular one, having won the majority of the votes of both Republicans and Democrats. He had told them he wanted to make a difference in the community. They considered him intelligent and fair. It didn't hurt that his father was still practicing law, as was his brother John, and that his brother Robert was a doctor. The Stengels were connected and well respected in the community of sixty thousand.

John A. Kenneff, known as Jack, would present the case for the commonwealth; Roy D. Shirk would represent Lisa Michelle Lambert. The lawyers gathered first in the judge's chambers, reviewing evidence such as hair samples from the accused, the black leather gloves she supposedly wore. Shirk handed the evidence back to the commonwealth for inclusion in the trial.

Lambert had made the unusual decision of asking the judge to decide the case, waiving her right to a trial by a jury of her peers. Shirk believed the egregious nature of the crime and the resulting publicity would make it more difficult to find an impartial jury. The judge could render a fairer verdict, he thought.

Stengel told the lawyers in chambers he would normally instruct a jury to refrain from watching television news or reading articles about the case while the trial was under way.

"I decided yesterday that was probably a good instruction to give myself," he said. He had stopped reading newspaper coverage and watching television reports on the case the day before. He would have someone keep his papers until the trial was over.

"Then I'll read what we supposedly did," he said. He had already slapped a gag order on lawyers in the case. He was tired of seeing the case tried in the *New Era* and the *Intelligencer Journal.*

This would go by the book. Fairness would be preeminent in his mind. He did not want a reversal on appeal if the girl was convicted.

Hazel Show was nervous that morning as she dressed to go to the courthouse. She had bought a new wardrobe for the trial, because she wanted to look presentable for Laurie. She didn't want Laurie to be ashamed of her mother. As a nurse's aide, she wore scrubs to work and rarely went anywhere that required anything dressier than jeans. A friend who owned a dress shop had given her quite a price cut—seventy-five percent in some cases—and let her pay as she could. Hazel Show was not a woman of means; she scratched by on limited education in jobs that paid modestly. Every day she sat in the courthouse was a day she was not paid anything.

Her niece Deb picked her up for the ride into Lancaster. Deb told her she was in the bathroom that morning getting ready, when as clear as she was hearing Hazel, she heard Laurie's voice.

"Take care of my mom," Laurie had said.

Without thinking, Deb, a thirty-three-year-old mother, responded, "I will. I'm going to go get her now."

Hazel did not find that odd or unsettling. She often

felt Laurie's presence. She felt it in the courtroom that morning and on every day, every minute of the trial.

John and Hazel Show sat in the back row. They wanted to be as far away as possible from Judy and Len Lambert, who sat on the opposite side of the room, near the front. Spectators—lawyers and the just plain curious—filled every other seat. Hazel remembers feelings squished in like sardines. Newspapers from Philadelphia sent correspondents. Also well represented were the local media—the afternoon *Lancaster New Era,* the morning *Intelligencer Journal,* the *Sunday News,* all owned by the same company. Everyone, it seemed, wanted a look at the made-up blonde accused of the crime, the woman known as a stalker and insanely jealous.

Instead, in walked a carefully coiffed woman with doe eyes, wearing a youthful-looking pink flowered dress. Like many criminal defendants before her, she had been remade. And now she preferred to be called Lisa. Michelle was dead, she told her family. That was some other more sinister person, an artificial wonder created to hold on to a man, Lawrence Yunkin. She wanted only to raise her daughter, Kirsten, who had been born the previous March. Lambert had delivered the baby in the hospital and then was carried back to Lancaster County Prison, where the baby's father, Lawrence Yunkin, was housed as well. Yunkin had asked to be there for the baby's birth, but the warden had not agreed.

Lambert's parents were caring for Kirsten. Lambert did not do this crime, she told her lawyer. Yunkin was the mastermind, and he and Tabbi Buck carried it out. She was not even in the room when Laurie Show was murdered.

"This is the time scheduled for trial in the matter of the *Commonwealth of Pennsylvania* versus *Lisa Michelle Lambert,"* Stengel said, opening what would become a

ten-day trial. He told the courtroom he had intended
to start precisely at 9:00 A.M., but was sidetracked by
some procedural matters in his chambers.

"Mr. Kenneff, is the commonwealth ready to proceed?" the judge asked.

"Yes, Your Honor," Kenneff responded as he stood
to begin a recitation of his side's story. Laurie Show was
living with her mother, he said beginning the tale.
Through friends Laurie met Yunkin, who was living with
Lambert. Laurie and Yunkin dated for ten days, which
"started a course of events that led to the demise of
Laurie Show."

Kenneff said testimony would show that Lambert devised a plot to kidnap Laurie Show, drive her into Lancaster, tie her up, and embarrass her in a most public
way. She had tried to get other girls to help her, Kenneff
charged. It was retaliation, nothing less. But the girls
Lambert had tried to bring into her plan went to Laurie
instead and told her about it. Lambert was undaunted.
She followed Laurie. She tormented her. She hurt her.
She knew, however, she needed help to lure Laurie into
the open. She found Tabbi Buck, someone "who lacked
the moral fiber to say 'I'm not participating in this,' "
Kenneff said.

He laid out the prosecution's case. Step by step. When
Yunkin woke up. Where he went. Who drove. Times.
Specifics. Details. Hazel Show sat weeping in the court.
She held a handkerchief in her hand all day, every day,
for what seemed like days on end. She had to get
through it, she thought. It was all that was left for her
to do for her daughter. Her ex-husband was there, too,
by her side, through it all.

"The lung of Laurie Show was punctured by one of
the wounds to the back, and the girls heard a hissing
sound," Kenneff said. "As a result of what they heard,

they decided that they would slit Laurie's throat in order to put her out of her misery."

Laurie asked them to take her with them, he said.

"But they turned their backs and left the apartment."

They ran. They cleaned up. They went about their day as if nothing had happened. They washed clothes. They disposed of evidence. Witnesses would show it all, he said.

Shirk decided to defer his opening statement until he began his case.

Kenneff called Robin Weaver as his first witness. Weaver, an East Lampeter Township Police officer since 1984, was the second officer on the scene that morning. Corporal Jan Fassnacht had arrived moments earlier. Already there were three medics from the East Lampeter Township Ambulance Association and three from Medic 3 unit, dispatched from Community Hospital.

"When I first walked in the apartment, I observed Hazel Show," Weaver said as he sent a shy glance at the mother in the courtroom, "seated at the dining room table directly in front of me. She was in a hysterical state, crying. She was yelling, 'Michelle did it. It was a setup. Brad seen it. He was here.' "

Weaver told the judge he saw Hazel's neighbor Marie Chapman in the apartment. He noticed a bloodstain or splatter on the wall in the hallway, to his left, about chest high. Fassnacht pointed toward the bedroom and Weaver said he knew the corporal was telling him where the body was. He walked in, he said.

Kenneff picked up some photographs and showed them to the officer. He asked if they showed the outside of the condominium. Weaver said they did and showed how there was only one entrance to the home, up a staircase. He also identified the sketches he made that day.

The sketches showed where he picked up certain

pieces of evidence. He had painstakingly drawn a detailed floor plan of the home, from the balcony into the front door. A narrow hallway led into a combination living and dining room. Immediately to the right was a small kitchen with dark-stained cabinets. To the left was Laurie's room and bath. A laundry room separated her room from her mother's, which was entered from the living room. A sunroom stretched across the outside wall and overlooked a grassy area. It was not a big place, but for Hazel and Laurie it had been their one true home, theirs alone.

Weaver recounted his movements. Laurie was lying faceup on the floor. Large bloodstains and pools of blood encircled her upper body. The closet doors were smeared with blood, three patches in all. Small clumps of hair, saturated with blood, dotted the white carpet. A length of rope—twenty-three feet long—lay under Laurie's body. Weaver also described Laurie's neck wound, four inches across her neck, a smaller gash on her leg, tiny cuts on her fingers.

"Now I would like to direct your attention, then, to later that day," Kenneff said, changing subjects. "Did you respond to a bowling alley in the Strasburg area?"

"Yes, I did," Weaver answered, and recounted scouring the parking lot with Officer John Bowman to locate Lawrence Yunkin's brown Mercury Zephyr. It was 10:40 P.M. Once they found the car, the officers entered the Garden Spot Bowling Center and saw Lambert. He took her into custody and he and Bowman drove her in an unmarked police car to the station in East Lampeter, Weaver testified. He took her into Chief Jacob Glick's office, removed the handcuffs, and asked her to sit down. Glick and Sergeant Carl Harnish of the Pennsylvania State Police came into the room to question Lambert, he said.

"I have no further questions," Kenneff said.

Shirk stood and walked Weaver through his day once again. He drilled Weaver on footprints seen on the floor. Were there footprints on the carpet in her room? he asked. No, Weaver said, the footprints were in the hallway on the white linoleum. They were not there when he arrived, but were there when he left. They were made by paramedics, Weaver said.

After a brief recess, Kenneff called Officer Randolph Sensenig, who witnessed Laurie's autopsy the day after her death. He was the one who obtained the clothing she had worn when she was murdered. Step by step, Kenneff was building his case, showing the trail of evidence, putting pieces out that he could eventually stitch back together.

Kenneff next called Enrique Penades. At the sound of his name, the Shows quickly left the courtroom. The judge had instructed the bailiff to let the Shows come and go as they needed during the trial. But no one else could disrupt the proceedings.

Penades was the pathologist who performed most of the autopsies in Lancaster County. In the previous twenty-one years, he had performed thousands of autopsies, 250 or so each year. He toiled in a basement room, beneath the "old folks' home." Originally from Spain, he had been in the United States since 1953, when he arrived to train in pathology at Pennsylvania Hospital of Philadelphia. He went to Richmond's Johnston Willards Hospital for his internship. He went to work for the Medical College of Virginia and then moved to Lancaster in 1960 as associate pathologist at Lancaster General Hospital. He was not board certified in forensic pathology, a specialty that provides extra training in homicide investigations. But Penades had studied under Dr. Russell Fisher in Baltimore, a world-renowned pathologist who was a consultant in the autopsy of President Kennedy.

Kenneff put drawings Penades had made of Laurie's wounds on a board for display. More than one in the courtroom was relieved Hazel Show had left the room. Penades described Laurie's wounds in exacting detail: six bruises to the head, three cuts on the back, a cut on the thigh, one on her lower leg, fourteen cuts on her left hand, seven on the right, many more on her palms. Then Kenneff asked about the neck wound.

"The neck had a big slashing wound, which is actually the result of more than one stroke," the pathologist said. "The one in the center of the neck measured five inches from side to side and up to two inches from the upper to the lower end. If you tilt the head back, it gapes; if you put it back, it closes."

The cut went from the skin of her throat to her spinal column, he said. The knife sliced through Show's Adam's apple, the cartilage between the larynx and the hyoid bone, the windpipe, and the epiglottis.

Could Laurie Show talk with all that trauma to her neck? Kenneff asked.

Penades answered with an extensive lesson on how a person talks. The vocal cords close and vibrate as air is propelled into the body. The tongue and lips form the words. Laurie's injury was higher than the vocal cords and her tongue and lips were not harmed, he said.

Finally Kenneff asked, "Are you able to form an opinion with a reasonable degree of medical certainty as to whether or not Laurie Show could have spoken approximately ten to fifteen minutes after the cutting of the neck?"

"Yes."

"What is your opinion."

"Yes."

"That she could have done it?"

"Yes. Of course, as I said before, not in a regular tone but a whispering, mumbling, intelligently enough for someone who is close to this person to understand."

Penades also said Laurie suffered two fatal wounds, the neck and a wound to the back that entered her chest. She bled to death, he testified.

Stengel adjourned for lunch, and Shirk began his cross-examination of the pathologist at 1:45 P.M. He asked immediately about the back of an earring Penades found during the autopsy. Where was it now? the lawyer wanted to know.

"Anything I had I gave to the police," he said.

"The police indicated they don't have it," Shirk responded, hoping to make it look like the police were incompetent or hiding something. He pressed the doctor for details on the cuts and bruises.

Could one wound be caused by one person, another by another person? Could be, Penades said, but probably not in this case.

Aren't bruises on the head sometimes caused by simply falling? Yes, but not in this case. The bruises were on the top of the head.

Point after point, the well-seasoned doctor held forth. Asphyxiation, couldn't Laurie Show have died of that? Possible, the doctor said, but he didn't believe that was the case. Blood could have gotten into her windpipe and suffocated her, but he believed she bled to death.

How long does it take to lose consciousness from asphyxiation? Shirk pressed.

"I do not think she died of asphyxiation, that's what I said," Penades said flatly.

"But you said it was a possibility." Reasonable doubt. That's all it takes to win. Create doubts.

"Case like this could die of asphyxiation, but in this case, I do not think she died of asphyxiation."

"If you had a case of asphyxiation, how long would it be?" Shirk would not let it drop. He knew he could get the doctor to say what he wanted to hear.

Finally the doctor replied, "If you had asphyxiation, they have a lot of blood in the tracheal bronchial tree, they can die in ten or fifteen minutes; lose consciousness. You are talking about several minutes."

Several minutes. Not the fifteen it took Hazel Show to get home and find her dying daughter proclaiming Michelle did it. Now it was out there, on the record.

Then he got Penades to admit he did not do any specific tests to see if she died of asphyxiation. Shirk had done his research. He started asking about the nerve system in the neck. The vagus nerve, did he see it? Shirk asked.

"I did not," the doctor answered.

Recurrent laryngeal nerve, did he see that?

No.

Esophagus, pharynx, trachea bronchi, larynx—the defense lawyer went over and over the parts of the neck and throat. Penades held firm to his central theory, however. Laurie Show could talk.

Shirk moved on. What about the knife? he asked. He noted Penades did some experiments with the knife believed to be the murder weapon once he realized it had a serrated edge. He wanted to know whether the jagged edge could make a clean cut like those on Laurie's body.

"I was doing an autopsy and I got the new knife and stabbed someone's leg and made a thin, straight clean cut and I wanted to make sure that that serrated edge would not produce a jagged edge," Penades said.

"What concerned you was the knife that was thought

to be the murder weapon had a serrated edge?" Shirk asked.

"It has a serrated edge."

"The cuts you had seen did not seem to be made with a serrated edge?"

"No, it didn't," the doctor said.

"Weren't they clean cuts?"

"The one I seen was clean cuts, but I had never seen a knife or had an autopsy on a knife with the thinly serrated edges as this one."

"I understand."

"I got one leg and stabbed that leg and it came out with clean cuts."

"You stabbed someone's leg with the new knife?"

"That's right."

"To compare it with the cuts you had seen in the victim's body?"

"That's right."

"You were in the middle of an autopsy and you cut the cadaver's leg?"

"I guess you could say that."

In true television-lawyer fashion, Shirk said crisply, "I have no further questions."

Sixteen

As the trial moved on through the first day, Ronald Barley, a Lancaster County detective, testified to finding the clothing Lawrence Yunkin had said Lambert wore when she killed Laurie Show. He and two other officers searched a garbage truck at a local incinerator and quickly found a pink trash bag containing two black knit caps, black gloves, white gloves, white socks, yellow socks, Levi's jeans, black sweatpants, and a flannel shirt coat. They were the clothes Yunkin had said Lambert and Buck had on when he took them to Laurie Show's home that morning. Barley also went to the Susquehanna River at Pequea. Yunkin had said he would find the murder weapon there.

A group of police officers, as well as Smokey Roberts's diving team, trudged to the water's edge underneath the railroad bridge and found the knife—its tip broken off—in shallow water near the river's edge. The power company lowered the water in the river with its dam to help with the search. It was Sunday, he said, two days after the murder. On Monday morning, he went back out and found the rope that had been tied around Laurie's neck. It was a foot or two downstream from the spot they had found the knife.

Next Kenneff called on Ronald Savage, a detective with the East Lampeter Township Police, to set the

scene. Using aerial photographs, Savage showed the
judge the lay of the land around the Shows' condominium: where the McDonald's is located a short distance
away on Route 30; East Towne Mall, where Laurie had
worked in a clothing store; the state police barracks,
oddly right at the front door to the condominium complex.

He also showed where Lambert and Yunkin lived in
Pequea in a mobile home beside the river. They rented
from a man who lived on the property, too. At 4:30 that
afternoon, Stengel adjourned for the day. Lambert
swapped her pink floral print for prison blue and went
back to the Lancaster County Prison, where the man
she loved so feverishly was imprisoned as well, the man
who was waiting to testify against her.

Yunkin appeared in court the next morning, striding
somewhat shyly into the courtroom at the sound of his
name.

"Mr. Yunkin, please," the district attorney stated.

The Shows, sitting as usual in the back row, eyed him
coldly. Hazel Show had not seen him for months, not
since he and Lambert had confronted Laurie at the New
Holland Fair. He had changed his appearance. Gone
were the long, stringy strands of bleached blond hair.
It was pulled back in a ponytail. He wore white jeans,
a white shirt, and a tie. His parents had picked up the
wrong tennis shoes that morning, so he still had on his
prison boots.

Lambert glared. She knew Yunkin, the father of her
daughter, had cut a deal with the state. In return for
testimony against her and later against Buck, he would
get a three-year sentence on a charge of hindering apprehension. More betrayal.

She and Yunkin had written a series of letters to each
other as the months passed in prison. In January he

had written, "If I would just think with the head on my shoulders and not with the one between my legs, everything would have been alright. I blame myself for bringing Laurie into the picture of our feud."

On January 11, he wrote that he had never meant to hurt her. He guessed he was just a heartless soul.

She wrote back to him that he shouldn't worry, he wouldn't do any time in prison, because he had nothing to do with that horrible morning. She reminded him that she hadn't, either, but had seen part of what happened. She guessed they could put her in jail for that. Lambert wished it had never happened.

Another time she wrote him that she didn't understand how Tabbi could drag him into the case, because he'd been at the McDonald's.

In a January 11 letter, Lambert tried to get Yunkin to understand that either Tabbi or she would be going to jail for life. An outside source had told her he would say whatever he had to say to get out of jail. She told him she expected he would cut some kind of deal, but couldn't understand why he told the police that she had said she helped Tabbi do what she did.

"State your name, please," Kenneff said.

"Lawrence Stewart Yunkin," came the response as the young man looked at the district attorney and then back at his mother in the back of the courtroom.

Responding to a series of questions from Kenneff, Yunkin told the judge he and Lambert had been engaged since the summer of 1991 and had lived together about six months before the murder. He said he met Tabitha Buck that summer, in the loop in Lancaster, a route young people cruise and where they hang out. He met Laurie Show through a friend of hers, Rachel Winesickle, in front of the Oaks Condominiums, where Laurie had lived. They dated for eight days in June

1991. Lambert was jealous of the relationship, he said, and the jealousy continued until the day they were arrested.

Kenneff took him back to the day before the murder.

"Do you recall what time you got off work that day?" he asked.

"Four o'clock."

"After you got off work, what did you do?"

"I drove home to where Michelle and I lived."

"In Conestoga?"

"Yes."

Michelle wanted him to take her to Buck's house to see if she could spend the night there. They left about 7:00 P.M. and stopped at Kmart at Kendig Square. Lambert went in; Yunkin stayed in the car, parked in the fire lane. She came out with a plastic bag. They drove to Buck's apartment on Columbia Avenue in Lancaster County, but Buck was not home. She arrived a few minutes later, however, with her mother. Buck said she wasn't sure whether Lambert could spend the night, because she and her mother were going grocery shopping. He and Lambert left and went on the loop for a bit, before returning to Buck's apartment. Michelle went inside to see if she could spend the night. Yunkin stayed in the car.

"Did you look in the bag?" Kenneff asked, referring to the bag Lambert brought out of Kmart.

"Yes, I did."

"What did you see?"

"A rope and a ski hat," Yunkin answered.

Yunkin identified the hat and the rope, which had already been entered into evidence.

Lambert came back to the car about thirty minutes later and told Yunkin she wasn't going to spend the night, but instead they were going to come back first thing in the morning to pick Buck up. Lambert woke up at about 5:30 A.M., told him to go back to bed, and then woke him at six o'clock. He hurriedly threw on blue jeans, a black T-shirt with the rock band AC/DC insignia on it, and Nike shoes. Yunkin also wore an army jacket that had belonged to Lambert's father.

They picked up Buck at about 6:40 A.M. and then went to The Oaks. He dropped the women off in a wooded area near the condominium complex. Lambert had on a red flannel shirt, a gray, green, and blue hooded sweatshirt and sweatpants; Buck wore a Miami Dolphins jacket and black jeans. The hood was pulled up over a black ski hat. She wore white knit gloves. Lambert had on black gloves, he said. He identified the clothing already in evidence as those worn by the women. He said the sweatpants were his. Lambert often wore his clothing, he said, because she was pregnant.

"Michelle told me to go to McDonald's and come back in a half hour. Tabbi said not to lock the door, because they might have to make a fast getaway," Yunkin said.

Lambert carried a white bag, but he didn't know what was inside. He drove off. It was about 6:50 A.M. when he arrived at the McDonald's just around the corner from the complex. The restaurant was closed. When it opened at seven o'clock, he went inside and ordered hash browns and orange juice. He saw the brother of a friend, spent about fifteen minutes inside, and then drove back to The Oaks. He drove by and didn't see the women, drove around and returned. Still not there. Again. Not there. Fourth time, still no sign of them. Fifth. On his sixth pass, he spotted Lambert and Buck in the wooded area where he had dropped them off. Lambert had the white bag. Buck bolted into the backseat, Lambert dropped into the front.

"I asked Michelle what happened and she wouldn't tell me," Yunkin said. "Then I noted a scratch on

Tabbi's face, because Michelle pointed it out. Tabbi said, 'The bitch scratched me.' Michelle lifted up her upper lip and said, 'Yeah, she kicked me in the face.' "

They rode the rest of the way—twenty-two miles—to the trailer he shared with Lambert in silence. He noticed Lambert had a bruised ring finger and blood on top of her hands.

At the trailer, Yunkin lay down on the couch and began to fall asleep, when he felt someone staring at him. He opened his eyes to see Lambert standing over him, shaking. Buck was in the shower.

"I asked her what was wrong and she didn't say anything. And then I asked her what happened at the house and she said, ah, she didn't know, so I asked her what happened. I said did you do anything to her or did you kill her? I don't know why I asked that, but I did. She said she did not know. I asked her what was that supposed to mean? She said that she and Tabbi and Laurie were wrestling around and Laurie accidentally got stabbed in the back and they heard a hissing sound like they had punctured a lung, and Michelle asked Tabbi what they should do and Tabbi said she didn't know. She said she should slit her throat to put her out of her misery so she would die, that they both agreed to do that, but she didn't tell me whether they did or not."

They left about 8:30 A.M. to take Buck to school, Yunkin testified. They dropped her off at Penn Manor High School about 9:00 A.M., with the understanding she would explain the scratch by saying she had gotten into a fight at McDonald's with two Puerto Rican girls. Yunkin and Lambert drove to Farmers First to cash his Denlinger's paycheck and they went to Green's to do some wash, two basketfuls and a plastic bag. Yunkin washed the clothes in the baskets, Lambert the items from the bag, including the jeans, flannel shirt, and other items she and Buck had had on earlier that morning. On the way back to their home, Lambert said she wanted to dispose of the clothing in the plastic bag. They threw it into a Dumpster behind Kmart.

Lambert and Yunkin went back to their home, ate, and watched television. She wanted to pick up her paycheck at Miller's Smorgasbord and then go to his grandparents at Parkesburg to get an artificial Christmas tree. On the way to Miller's, she told him she had another bag to throw out. He drove down a back road toward the Susquehanna and she threw the bag into the river.

They picked up the check, cashed it, and went to his grandparents'. They left there about 5:00 P.M., returned home, ate dinner, and watched television. Michelle went to the landlord's house to make two calls, one to a friend, the other to Buck. When she returned, she told Yunkin they needed to go to Buck's house, but before they did that they went back to the river to throw Lambert's hooded sweatshirt away.

They arrived at Buck's at about 7:00 P.M. They devised an alibi, a convoluted tale, rich with detail.

"Tabbi heard out at Park City that Kmart at East Towne Mall opened up at seven A.M. We picked up Tabbi to take her and Michelle, and we went down to the Kmart at East Towne Mall. I dropped them two off in front of Kmart and went back up to get something to eat at McDonald's. I would've been at McDonald's fifteen or twenty minutes, came back to pick Michelle and Tabbi up, and Kmart wasn't open, so we headed back toward Old Philadelphia Pike."

Michelle forgot her purse. They went back and got it. The tire on his car was low. They stopped at McDonald's to get something to eat and two Spanish girls approached. One of the girls said something about him or her. Lambert cursed them and the girl punched her. Buck said that's no way to treat a pregnant lady and shoved the other girl, who in turn scratched Buck in the face. He separated the women, got them in the car, which they took to the car wash; then they took Buck to school.

They agreed that would be their story.

They drove over to the Weis Market, where Buck worked, and picked up her paycheck. They went to Park City to get a leather jacket Lambert was giving Yunkin for Christmas and then went to the bowling alley. Yunkin's mother worked there, but was not working that night. It was about 10:00 P.M. Shortly afterward, he was arrested.

At the East Lampeter Police Department, Yunkin recounted the alibi. He stuck with the story for three hours or more. But when told Lambert was talking, he caved. He told police what he knew and told them where to find the clothes and the knife.

Shirk began his cross-examination. He wanted to show that the clothing—all of it—that Yunkin said Lambert was wearing on the day of the murder actually belonged to him. And that the sweatpants in particular were among his favorite clothing for lying around the house. He pressed him for details of that morning.

"She got you up at six o'clock and you went to Tabbi's."

"Yes."

"Never asked why."

"No."

"Just drove her over to Tabbi's at six o'clock in the morning."

"I did ask why, but she wouldn't tell me."

Shirk recounted Yunkin's tale of going to Buck's and the woman coming outside and getting in the car.

"You had no idea where you were going."

"No."

"They just said drive through town and you did it."

"Yes."

"Told you to go down Route Thirty."

"Yes."

"You got to the light and they told you to turn left."

"Yes."

"Didn't ask where you were going." Shirk's voice was tinged with incredulity.

"No."

"They told you to stop, so you stopped."

"Yes."

"It's your testimony they got out of the car, dressed as you say they were, and Michelle had a bag in her hand."

"Yes."

"Same bag as the night before?"

"I'm not positive about that, no."

"Didn't that seem kind of strange to you?"

"A little, yes."

"But you just went along with it?"

"Yes."

"With no knowledge whatsoever of what was going on."

"No."

Shirk asked him to tell once more where he was after he dropped off Buck and Lambert. He asked who Yunkin knew that lived in the area. Laurie, police officers Jere and Renee Schuler, and Rachel Winesickle, he responded.

"Did you think they were going to visit Mr. and Mrs. Schuler?" Shirk asked sarcastically as spectators chuckled.

"No."

"Where did you think they were going?"

"To see Laurie."

"But you didn't ask any questions about it."

"No, I did not."

Shirk asked when he figured out he was taking the women to Laurie Show's house. He said he knew it when he got to East Towne Mall, just around the corner from the Shows' home. He didn't say it might not be such a great idea going to Laurie's? No, Yunkin responded.

"You just silently did what you were told?"

"Yes."

And, Shirk pointed out, Yunkin didn't ask whether Laurie had been killed.

"You didn't say maybe we ought to go to the authorities."

"No."

"You just went about your business . . ."

"Yes."

". . . like it would be a normal thing somebody would say to you."

"It's not normal, no."

"What did you do next?"

"I went back to bed."

"You went back to bed?"

"Yes."

Shirk's disbelief at the blasé way Yunkin went about his day was barely hidden. At one point, he asked, "Like everything that happened in the morning was just a blank, we're going to make plans as to how we're going to enjoy the rest of the day."

"Yes," Yunkin responded.

He participated in making up the alibi, Shirk said, drilling the young man.

"Yes."

"Why would you do that if you didn't know what was going on?"

"Because I loved Michelle and I would do anything for her, just about."

Finally Shirk said, "Mr. Yunkin, yesterday in court, Mr. Kenneff said you were either the most naive person in the world or you are stupid. I can't believe you are that dumb. These two girls planned this, had you drive them there, and you didn't know anything about it?"

"No, I did not."

He asked Yunkin about the deal he worked out with prosecutors the February before. In return for testimony, no further charges would be brought against him. Shirk asked about his relationship with Lambert.

"We were constantly at each other's throats," he said. "We had our good times and bad times."

"Did you beat her?"

"No."

"Never have?"

"I hit her once, yes, actually, three times but once intentionally."

He said he hit her the first time when she tried to jump out of his dad's van. He reached for the door and hit her accidentally on the lip. The next time was after he told her he had slept with Laurie Show, she grabbed his hair. He spun around and hit her with his elbow. Another accident, he said. The time he meant to hit her, he said, occurred the previous September. It was about three o'clock in the morning. He was trying to sleep, but she was mad and sitting on top of him.

"I backhanded her," he said.

"So that was self-preservation."

Yunkin did not respond.

Shirk continued. "What about November 1990, when she was admitted to the hospital?"

"That's when we were living in Pequea. We didn't really have any fights there. I don't know about that one."

"You don't remember taking her to the hospital?"

"No, I don't. I can't recall."

What about August 8, 1991, Shirk asked. East Lampeter Township Police had been called.

"That was when I backhanded her."

But, Shirk reminded him, that was in the middle of the night. The August incident occurred at 10:30 P.M.

"I don't know," Yunkin said, obviously confused. "I'm not sure on times. I don't look at a time when I hit her, so I wouldn't know the time."

"I'll bet you don't," Shirk responded disgustedly.

He asked Yunkin about cutting his own face.

"I did it a lot," Yunkin said. "I used to break things in the house and I didn't want to take it out on Michelle or anything, and I felt it was my fault that we were fighting, so I would do something to myself."

Shirk asked about a day when Yunkin cut a large gash across his face. In June 1991?

Yunkin said he and Lambert were fighting because she was seeing a lifeguard at Town & Country Apartments. He kicked the bathroom door down. As he held her down, he cut his face and let the blood drip onto her. Isn't that how it happened? Shirk pressed.

Yunkin said he had already cut his face when he was on top of Lambert, and he couldn't remember whether the blood dripped on her or not.

"You just said a minute ago it happened," Shirk fired.

"Could have. Couldn't have. I don't recall back then."

Shirk changed course, asking how many piercings Yunkin had in his ears.

"I had four at the time."

Through a series of questions, Shirk gleaned that Yunkin liked to wear earrings with cubic zirconia and diamond stones, loops, dangling earrings, all kinds, and that on occasion, he wore pearl earrings that Lambert's parents had given her, pearl earrings like the one found in Laurie Show's bedroom on the morning of her murder.

"You were wearing it that morning, weren't you?"

"No, I was not."

"Was Michelle?"

"I don't believe that she had any earrings on."

"Nobody was wearing that earring."

"I can't recall."

"I bet you can't."

Shirk continued pressing the point. Didn't he wear those earrings? Didn't the men at Denlinger's call him Goldilocks because he wore earrings, especially pearl ones? No, he only wore them a few times. Lambert didn't like them. She said they made him look like a gypsy.

He pressed Yunkin on the details of what was thrown out and when. The hooded sweatshirt? Was it his or hers? It was his. And what about the companion knives to the murder weapon? Didn't he encourage Lambert to throw them out, too? The two remaining Tristar knives could tie them to the crime. How many sneakers did he own? Were his the ones thrown out? Why didn't he tell the prosecution about any of this? No, no, no, Yunkin said. He didn't know anything about any of it. Shirk forged on, steamrolling through the cross-examination, changing courses, darting and weaving like a coyote in pursuit.

"Why were you and your family giving Michelle money while she was in prison?"

"Because she was pregnant, and her mom and dad didn't seem to be supporting her."

"So every week a deposit was made to her account?"

"I believe so, yes."

"Your money?"

"I wouldn't know that."

"You wouldn't know?"

"No."

"Was it your money or wasn't it?"

"I had an income tax check that came in for seven hundred dollars. I don't know if my parents used some of that or not."

Finally Shirk drove home his point: Was the money intended to keep Lambert happy?

"I still cared about her," Yunkin said. "I cared what happened to her."

Shirk then dropped a bombshell that would reverberate through the case against Michelle Lambert for years and years, one that would be used to cast doubt on her guilt. The document came to be known as the twenty-nine questions. Lambert had used the law library to pass a list of questions to Yunkin. Shirk handed him two pages.

"Did you indicate sometime in the last—since May 26, 1992, to Detective Barley, did he question you at some time and ask you if there had been a document sent to you by Michelle consisting of approximately thirty questions and you answered those thirty questions?"

"Correct."

"But you are saying this isn't the document."

"Well, it looks like it's been tampered with."

"Well, we have an expert to come talk about that. I'm asking if this is the document."

"Questions like that, no."

"Is this the document you saw in the library?"

"No, it was not."

Yunkin maintained the questions and answers had been changed. That words were added, crossed out. He looked down at the pages, a childlike handwriting covering both sides of each sheet.

It read:

Listen to me. I guess I won't tell on you. But please answer these questions honestly. There are some things I need to know if I'm supposed to take the blame for WHAT YOU DID! MAIL THESE BACK TO ME.

1) Do you still love me? Yes

2) I'm still scared of Tabbi. Were you ever afraid of her? No.

3) Tabbi looks crazy. She scary like you when you beat me and kill me. Do you ever think of killing me when you have evil eyes? Yes

4) Do you remember where the jergo (hooded sweatshirt) is? We had your jergo to hide (me & you)? like yesterday

5) I think about Tressa and Laurie. I think you guys are sick. I think about her life you took! All those people at her funeral! And I know very well that you don't feel sad. You were happy. You weren't sad Friday. Do you remember seeing Laurie dead? Yes I remember seeing dead.

6) I don't understand. WHY NOT tell about Laurie? Are you afraid you couldn't? Did she look scary DEAD, like Tressa? I want to go home and have MY BABY twins. What if one of them dies because they need mommy? I don't want to cover up for you. I never

should've agreed, and I'm MAD and still sad. Yes and yes.

7) It's not my fault that things went wrong (our prank) Friday morning! Do you even care? Still blame YOU and TABBI! Just wish it didn't happen

8) The TRUTH - WHEN did YOU stop CARING about me? Never, always will

9) TELL TRUTH - You ONLY stayed happy Friday so I wouldn't be terrified of you. You did because you were sorry. I know you didn't mean to kill and you were sorry and guilty and feel SORRY for Hazel, right? wrong

10) I KNOW I'M not an angel, but Lawrence, I never got MAD enough to kill! Your temper blew and you hurt her, THIS time So BAD that she can't get better. To me it's a surprise it was on her, And she will NEVER LIVE AGAIN, I wanted to get goddam Tabbi away from her. You got in the bedroom and BLEW UP and went decided to do things your way - VIOLENT. That should've been me you killed. I hate you. I don't hate anyone. God said it is wrong to hate.

11) Were your sweatpants and flannels that you got blood on, did we dumpster them? Yes

12) Will you promise to love me if I lie for you? Always and forever

13) You won't forget? No, never

14) Will you always stick WITH me as long as I still don't tell that you held Laurie down for Tabbi? will always

15) Weren't you scared of Tabbi after she killed her? I think you ARE STILL evil. AFTER

you guys killed HER, didn't you think SHE'D kill you? No

16) Do you remember when we used to make pee-bee in the back of your van? Oh, yes

17) Do you PROMISE not to beat my face up anymore if I lie 4 you. That's why I said I hated you. Will you be nice like our first date? Yes

18) Do you REMEMBER after 4th date at my Mom and Dad's, AND we had been talking and then at 2 a.m. you forced sex on me, beat me up when I cried - that was MEAN. Yes, your mom and dad's house

19) Do you promise not to beat me? I am scared of YOU! I never slept with Allen. Yes

20) Why weren't you sad at all on Friday after you and Tabbi killed her? You were happy at grandma's. Are you glad she's dead? Yes, we had fun at grandma's house

21) Do you remember in the mountains when you choked me? That was mean. Yes, the mountains are pretty

22) And also remember when your mom and dad left us alone in the cabin and you beat me a lot. Yes, the cabin was nice

23) Tabbi scares me. Gives me evil looks! Do you still think about Laurie's scary dead-eye stare. No not anymore

24) Do you honestly promise to STICK by me (if I lie for you)? Yes, I love you

25) Do you love God? Yes

26) Do you promise? Yes, I love God

27) Do you play with John? No

28) Do you know that Rachel and Josh and Allen lied to you? Yes, I know they lied Are you

sure that if I take the blame for you that I'll
get less time? Absolutely sure? yes
29) Are you sure you never cheated on me (except for all the little girls)? Never cheated on
you with anyone else Should I still cover up
that you helped Tabbi kill Laurie? Are you absolutely sure? Yes, I'm positive

The rest of the document included a note Yunkin
wrote saying he couldn't write to her anymore and that
his parents would not be sending her any more money.
He also said he had heard that someone outside of
prison had $2,000 available to anyone who would rape
him or castrate him.

"So, bye for now, Might drop a line once in a while
and let you know how I'm doing. Love you always
Butch."

Shirk took him through all the questions and Yunkin
said most had been altered. Words were squeezed in,
crossed out, all to change the meaning, to implicate
him. The answers were his and in his handwriting. The
questions had been changed, he contended.

"Isn't it a fact, Mr. Yunkin, that upon returning to
your house on the morning of the twentieth of December 1991, after taking Tabbi to school, you broke down
and started crying?"

"No, it's not."

"Isn't it a fact, Mr. Yunkin, that you told Michelle that
you are a man and you would get life, they would put
you in prison forever?"

"No, I did not."

"Isn't it a fact that you convinced her that if she took
the blame for whatever you did—she was pregnant, she
was a woman—she would get a lot less time?"

"No, I did not."

"None of that is true?"

"None of it is true."

Then Shirk asked whether Yunkin had seen Lambert the morning before and said, "You are dead, bitch." He denied that, too.

Shirk cut to the heart of the matter:

"Isn't it a fact, Mr. Yunkin, that on the morning of December 20, 1991, you were in that apartment and were involved in the murder of Laurie Show?"

"No, I was not."

Seventeen

After lunch Alan Goldberg, Shirk's cocounsel, began questioning Isidore Mihalakis, a forensic pathologist hired by the defense to testify about the nature of Laurie Show's wounds. Stengel allowed him to testify out of order, because he would not be available later. Mihalakis worked as the director of postmortem services at Lehigh Valley Hospital, one hundred miles north in Allentown. He had studied the photographs of Laurie's autopsy, the crime scene, and the knife, as well as Hazel Show's statement. Mihalakis said he believed Laurie died from the stab wound to the chest and the throat cut, and that suffocation from blood in the windpipe was indeed possible. If that had in fact happened, Mihalakis said, Laurie would have passed out within minutes. If she had bled to death, the doctor testified, she could have lived thirty minutes. A combination of both would have brought unconsciousness in a shorter time span.

Under Goldberg's questioning, Mihalakis talked on about the workings of the tongue and the voice box. He talked about the hyoid bone and how the larynx was "compromised," causing the tongue to lose "dexterity." He made sounds based on Laurie's injuries, slurring his words like a drunk man. The testimony centered on technical, medical terms, but the basic thrust left no doubt as to his meaning: Laurie Show probably could not have talked.

The lawyers asked that Hazel Show be asked to leave the courtroom, because the doctor's testimony could directly affect her own. She went into a room nearby.

Mihalakis was asked about the knife believed to be the murder weapon with a broken tip. Laurie's wounds were made with a knife with a sharp edge. The only place the knife could have been broken was when she was stabbed in the thigh, but the tip was not found during the autopsy. The doctor said he had taken a similar knife and broken it by holding it with a vise. The blade snapped and the end was bent, he said. Plus, it took "substantial force" to break it.

"While it is not beyond the realm of a woman [to stab someone with such force that a knife lodges into a hip bone and then breaks], it would be extremely unlikely, very unlikely," the doctor said.

On cross-examination Kenneff pinned the defense's technical expert down on the length of time Laurie probably lived.

"Multiple minutes," the doctor said.

"What does multiple minutes mean?"

"Up to twenty minutes."

"No further questions."

Kenneff resumed his case, calling Sergeant Carl Harnish, the investigator with the Pennsylvania State Police, who interviewed Lambert the night she was arrested. He recounted his interview with her, from the moment he started talking to her at the police station around 11:15 the night of Laurie's murder until Solt took over the questioning. At the time, Solt had been with the Pennsylvania State Police for twenty-four years and a criminal investigator for nineteen. He first saw Lambert just before 2:00 A.M. on the day after Laurie's murder.

He took the stand next, but his testimony was not finished before Stengel called a recess for the weekend.

Solt again took the stand first thing Monday morning. He testified that after he had Lambert write out the statement she had given to Harnish, he told her he believed she was lying. Within minutes she admitted she had been. She and Buck went to Laurie's as Yunkin was going to McDonald's. Buck pushed inside when Laurie answered the door. The door slammed. Lambert said she followed Buck inside and told Laurie to be quiet.

"I told her I was going to leave her alone," she said. "She was fighting and yelling. Tabbi pushed her into the wall. She yelled the lady's name downstairs; Jackie, I think. I got scared and I ran out."

She didn't know what Buck was doing to Laurie, Lambert told the investigator.

"I don't know what Tabitha did. I don't want to know. Tabbi's my best friend. I don't want her to go to jail."

"Where did the knife come from?" Solt said he asked Lambert.

She did not know. Solt left the room and got Renee Schuler, a corporal with the East Lampeter Township Police, to come inside to witness Lambert's statement. It was 4:45 in the morning.

He told her he didn't believe she was not in Laurie's bedroom when Laurie was killed.

"I stayed in the hallway," the investigator's notes say. She was in the apartment for five, perhaps ten minutes and ran out through the buildings and into someone's backyard at a cream-colored house with blue shutters. Buck ran a different way, but they met in the bushes near the woods. She said she asked her what she did inside and Buck replied, "It's better if you don't know."

Later, at McDonald's, she asked Buck if she had

beaten Laurie up "real bad." "Don't worry about it," Lambert said her friend responded.

"As far as I know, Lawrence did not know we went there," Lambert told Solt.

After talking to the district attorney, Solt went back into the police chief's office and told Lambert, "Lawrence is telling us what you told him about what happened to Laurie while you were in the apartment. Will you please tell me what you did and saw happen to Laurie?"

"I know one thing: the scratches on her, Tabbi's face, was when Laurie tried to get the knife from Tabbi. I lied about that before. I got elbowed in the mouth by Tabbi. Lawrence doesn't know anything because I didn't want him to. I wanted him kept out of it."

Lambert began to tell the third version of her story. She wanted to talk to Laurie that day and suggested she and Buck go to her house. Yunkin dropped them off at Kmart, and she and Buck walked over to The Oaks. Lambert wasn't sure which condominium was Laurie's, so they walked around as she tried to remember. Buck had her hood up, while Lambert did not. Lambert didn't like to wear the hood up, she said.

"It looks stupid."

Lambert pointed out the unit she believed to be Laurie's and Buck started up the stairs.

"I don't know if I want to go up, because her mom knows me," Lambert recalled saying. "Going up to the door with her mom there wouldn't be real cool."

So Buck went up alone. Lambert told Solt she heard Laurie ask, "Who are you?" She walked up the stairs to find Buck and Laurie struggling. Laurie was kicking, so Lambert grabbed her ankles and told her to calm down. Laurie was yelling, and kicked Lambert in the mouth, busting her lip. She asked Laurie why she was crying.

Laurie ran into the bedroom and Buck ran after her. Laurie tried to reach the telephone, but Buck grabbed it and threw it across the room.

"I saw she had a knife, and I saw her bring it down," Lambert told Solt, referring to Buck. "It looked like it bounced off. It didn't look real."

Laurie fell to the floor. Lambert said she heard a sound like "whoosh." Coughing, Laurie said she was sorry and asked them not to leave her there. Her body jerked. Lambert told the investigator she felt like she was going to throw up and she ran out of the condominium. She ran into a field and by a creek, tripping over a barbed-wire fence. She fell into a briar patch, she said.

Solt asked who called Laurie's house the night before. Lambert said she didn't know Laurie's number, that she had tried to call her several months earlier on the wrong exchange, but it was a law office now.

"Who cut her throat?" Solt asked.

Lambert responded, "Oh my God! Are you serious? Are you serious?" She cried briefly, and then said, "I didn't see anything like that."

At about eight o'clock the next morning—twenty-four hours after Laurie Show's life ended—Lisa Michelle Lambert signed her name in red ink across a seven-page statement. It was Tabitha Faith Buck who did the killing, she said. She brought the knife. She did the attacking. Lambert and her beloved boyfriend, Lawrence Yunkin, were innocent victims.

Shirk had several points to make on cross-examination, clearing up the timetable some, but he especially wanted Solt to acknowledge that Lambert held Laurie's feet down when Laurie kicked her, before Buck raised the knife. It was an important distinction. He did not want it to appear that Lambert had been holding Laurie down as Buck wielded a butcher knife at her. In addition, he asked about the clothes Lambert was wearing that night and showed him a black leather jacket, pants, pink sweater, and a pair of white sneakers. Solt said the items appeared similar to what Lambert wore that evening.

Building his case block by block, Kenneff ran through the testimony of several law enforcement officers who worked the Show murder. Renee Schuler, the East Lampeter corporal who watched Solt interview Lambert, testified that she searched Lambert's body for bruises or cuts but found nothing but a small bruise that looked old. In addition, Schuler said Hazel Show gave her a pearl earring that her nephew found in the foyer. It was not one of Laurie's, Hazel said.

Kenneff wanted to lay the groundwork for what would prove to be one of the most emotion-filled parts of the trial: the testimony of Hazel Show. Everyone who had followed the case knew Hazel contended that Laurie said, in her dying breaths, "Michelle did it." The contention had already been called into doubt by earlier testimony from a forensic pathologist that Laurie's wounds might have left her unable to speak. The local pathologist who performed the autopsy said she could, but he was not a forensic pathologist and Kenneff was unsure just how much difference that distinction might make to the judge. He called to the stand Joseph Annese, an ear, nose, and throat doctor in Lancaster for fifteen years. It was his first time testifying in court. He watched the autopsy performed on Laurie.

"She was able to speak," he said firmly.

On cross-examination, Shirk asked him about his report where he said she would have been able to produce "some kind of speech."

He responded that her speech would have probably

been weaker, but not altered in any other appreciable
way. The mouth needs air passing through to make loud
sounds. When Hazel Show propped her daughter
against her, Laurie's neck wound closed enough to allow
air to pass through the mouth, enabling her to speak,
he said.

Kenneff brought in Officers Barley and Jere Schuler
to testify to their interrogation of Yunkin, before calling
Joanne Guier, Buck's mother, to the stand. Guier, a dietary supervisor at Moravian Manor in Lititz, said Lambert had come to her home the night before the
murder. The next morning, Guier awoke to the closing
of the front door. It was 6:40 A.M. She wondered what
her daughter was doing leaving for school so early. The
bus didn't come until 7:00. She always waited until the
last second, especially in the cold. She looked into her
daughter's room, confirmed she wasn't there, and
headed for the bathroom. A note was lying on the
counter. It said she had gone to school early.

Guier showered, dressed, and went to work. She
talked to her daughter on the phone once during the
day, but when she returned home at a few minutes before 9:00 P.M., Tabbi was not there.

As the Monday afternoon wore on, Richard Kleinhans
was called to the stand. He was Hazel Show's downstairs
neighbor. The morning of Laurie Show's murder, he
was sitting reading the newspaper at about 6:45. He had
been up about an hour and was sitting beside the front
window of his condominium. He watched as Hazel got
into her car and drove off. Odd, he thought then, she
didn't usually leave for another thirty minutes.

Shortly afterward, Kleinhans heard the Shows' door
slam. A woman screamed. Seconds later there was a
thump. The door slammed again about five minutes
later. Kleinhans said he rose from his chair and looked

out the window in time to see two people of about the same height running across the patio and around the corner of the building.

He ran into his bedroom.

"Jackie, did you hear that noise upstairs?" he asked his wife.

"Yes, I heard a thump," she answered.

He stood in the kitchen for a few minutes before his wife joined him. She looked at the clock on the microwave oven as she entered: 7:17. It was strangely quiet upstairs, Kleinhans thought. Usually they would hear Laurie getting ready for school. They decided to go up and see if she was all right. Jackie opened the door as Hazel pulled in.

"Is anything wrong?" Jackie inquired as Hazel bolted from her car.

"No," she said, and scurried up the steps.

Shortly they heard Hazel scream. Jackie, who had a bad back, lumbered up the steps and then came back down again, ran to the phone, and dialed 911. Laurie'd been hurt, she exclaimed.

Another neighbor, Frederick Fry, took the stand next. Kenneff stitched the day together, person by person. A habitual clock-watcher, Fry recalled glancing at the digital clock in his car as he turned on the ignition and seeing 7:13 displayed. He backed out and saw two people walking from a part of the development where people generally do not walk. His impression was from the way they walked and their mannerisms that they were both women, although he did not see their faces. They had on dark clothing, he said. One had a jacket on with some sort of insignia.

His wife, Patricia, followed him to the stand. She said after he left for work she went back into the kitchen. She looked out the window and saw two people coming down the steep hill behind the condominium. She thought it odd and went to the den window to see where the girls had headed.

"They went down between the garages and the condos and down along the woods," she testified. "Well, that was another thing that was entirely different, because that happens to be a drainage ditch and people just do not jog in the drainage ditch."

Upon questioning from Shirk, the Frys said they could not identify the clothing the police recovered from the river as the clothing worn by the two women they saw the day of the murder.

Darrell Welk, a neighbor of Yunkin and Lambert's, testified he saw them and a woman with "long frizzy brown hair" leaving their house at about 8:30 the morning of the Show murder, as did Ray Warfel, who owned the trailer they rented. Warfel said he saw Lambert and Yunkin again at 3:30 that afternoon. Lambert used his telephone at about that time. At about 5:00 P.M., Warfel received a call from a man who said he was Yunkin's father. He said it was a matter of life and death; he needed the exact address of the trailer Yunkin lived in. Warfel refused to give him the address, but he did go down to the trailer and give Yunkin the message.

"They seemed indifferent," Warfel said.

Kenneff established that Yunkin had been in the McDonald's that morning by calling as a witness Ivette Rodriguez, a cashier there. She said the night of the murder she was watching the television news and saw a photograph of a man she had waited on that morning. He was one of her first customers and she remembered him ordering an orange juice and hash browns. He sat down, got up and paced a bit, and left after about twenty minutes.

Kmart, at the request of the East Lampeter Township

Police, produced a register receipt from December 19, 1991, showing that at 8:47 P.M. someone bought a rope and two knit hats. Shirk, however, asked Kmart employee Timothy Puchalski whether he knew specifically who made that purchase. He said he could not tell.

Donald Bloser Jr., a chemist in the Pennsylvania State Police crime lab, testified the phenolphthalein test performed on the clothing recovered from the incinerator showed it all had been "washed in blood." He couldn't tell if the blood was animal or human, probably because it had been washed. Detergent destroys the characteristics of blood that show whether it comes from a person. Everything in the wash becomes contaminated as the blood swirls around the washing machine.

Shirk wanted to know the answer to one key question: "Did you find any [blood] sample that matched the blood of my client, Lisa Michelle Lambert?"

"No, sir, I did not."

In addition, none of Lambert's hair was found at the scene of the crime.

Eighteen

On Tuesday the defense and prosecution shuffled back in for the fourth day of Lisa Michelle Lambert's trial. The district attorney planned to continue with a litany of the cleanup witnesses, those brief appearances by people who played bit parts in the human drama of Laurie Show's death, but whose presentations were essential in putting people where they said they were, in establishing the integrity and credibility of each witness. But the Lancaster County Courthouse bristled that morning because most in the legal community knew the day would bring the testimony of Hazel Show, Laurie's mother, the prosecution's key witness because she would say her daughter identified her killer.

Kenneff began by calling the man who drove the garbage truck that picked up the small pink trash bag that contained the clothes Yunkin and Lambert said were worn that day. Next came Kelly Gladfelter, who was twenty years old, and then her husband, David, who lived near Yunkin and Lambert. Kelly remembered that soon after Lambert moved in, she told her that she wanted to "beat up" and "kill" Laurie Show. She didn't take Lambert seriously, but she said it more than once, probably six times.

"One minute she'd be fine and the next minute it was like a split-personality-type thing," Kelly testified.

Victim Laurie Show, 16. (*Photo courtesy Hazel Show*)

Laurie Show at 6.
(*Photo courtesy Hazel Show*)

Teenager Laurie Show with her dog.
(*Photo courtesy Hazel Show*)

Laurie Show poses for camera, a few months before she was murdered. (*Photo courtesy Hazel Show*)

Apartment where Laurie Show lived with her mother Hazel. (*Photo courtesy East Lampeter Township, PA Police*)

Like many teenage girls, Laurie Show filled the shelves in her bedroom with stuffed animals. (*Photo courtesy East Lampeter Township, PA Police*)

Laurie Show's throat had been cut several times.
(*Photo courtesy East Lampeter Township, PA Police*)

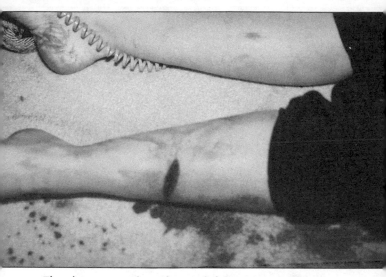

The deep wound in Show's left leg was made
during the struggle with her attackers.
(*Photo courtesy East Lampeter Township, PA Police*)

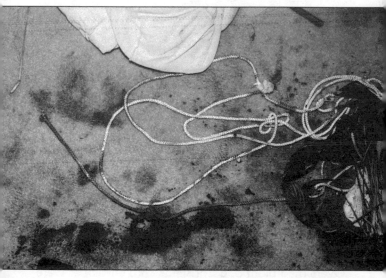

A white cord had been wrapped around Laurie Show's
neck. (*Photo courtesy East Lampeter Township, PA Police*)

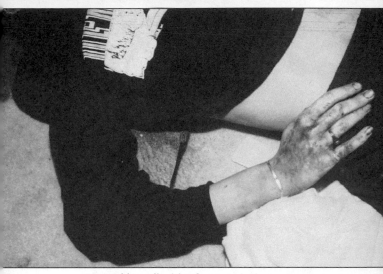

Wood-handled knife Hazel Show used
to cut cord from Laurie's neck.
(*Photo courtesy East Lampeter Township, PA Police*)

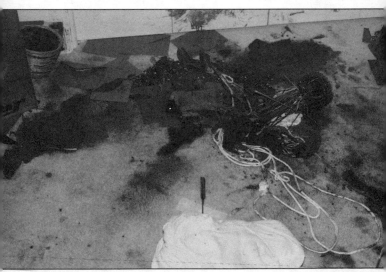

Overturned plant and Christmas card envelopes were
among the items strewn on the blood-soaked bedroom
carpet. (*Photo courtesy East Lampeter Township, PA Police*)

Lisa Michell Lambert at 18, two years before her
trial for the murder of Laurie Show.
(*Photo courtesy Jackie Yunkin*)

Lawrence Yunkin dated Laurie Show briefly making
her the object of Lambert's jealousy.
(*Photo courtesy Jackie Yunkin*)

Tabitha Buck, 17, charged as a juvenile in the murder, but tried as an adult, had only known Lambert for a few months. (*Photo courtesy Alvin Buck*)

Yunkin, 18, and Lambert, 17, at a Christmas party in 1989. (*Photo courtesy Jackie Yunkin*)

Yunkin and a pregnant Lambert had lived together in the upstairs of this house prior to the murder.

Michelle Lambert's sentence of life in
prison was upheld on appeal.
(*Photo courtesy East Lampeter Township, PA Police*)

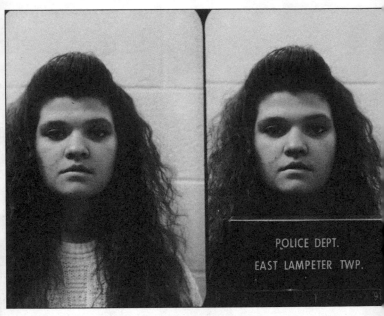

Tabitha Buck was sentenced to life in prison with no parole. (*Photo courtesy East Lampeter Township, PA Police*)

Lawrence Yunkin pleaded no contest to third degree murder and was sentenced to 10–20 years in prison. (*Photo courtesy East Lampeter Township, PA Police*)

Tabitha Buck's father, Alvin, and stepmother, Sharon. (*Photo courtesy Alvin Buck*)

Lt. Renee L. Schuler, who served as chief spokeswoman for the East Lampeter Township Police, lived across the street from the Shows.

A tree was planted in Laurie Show's memory
at her high school.

Hazel Show at the gravesite of her daughter
Laurie in 1999.

Shirk objected to the comment, saying it was opinion, and the judge sustained his objections and struck the comment. But it was out there. The judge had heard it. Such inappropriate comments probably made less of an impression on a judge deciding a case than on a jury, but nonetheless, it had been said.

When she talked about Laurie, Lambert would "get angry and say that she wanted to beat her up, and most of the time she just said she wanted to kill her." About half the time, Yunkin was with her when she made such comments and he'd tell her to let it go, Kelly said. Hearsay, Shirk charged. Strike it, Stengel said.

Shirk, on cross-examination, reminded Kelly she had not taken Lambert's threats seriously.

"I'm sure you heard on more than one occasion from people other than Miss Lambert a comment like 'I'm going to kill them. I'm going to get them.' "

"Yes."

"From a lot of different people."

"Yes."

"Is that correct?"

"Yes."

"Maybe you even said it sometimes yourself."

"If I can recall, yeah."

There were no further questions.

David Gladfelter told the court that virtually every time he and his wife were around Lambert and Yunkin, Laurie Show's name came up.

"Basically the same thing would be brought up where they would be fighting over her and the fact Lawrence had slept with her," he said. They fought physically, not with words only. Lambert was usually the instigator. They'd hurl words at each other, then stomp out and head for home, he said.

Kenneff continued to set the groundwork to prove

Laurie Show's murder was premeditated. He called Laura Thomas, a sixteen-year-old who met Laurie when Thomas's brother Benjamin worked at the Fudge Shoppe in East Towne Mall. Laurie was working at the Deb Shop, also in the mall. Lambert was bitterly jealous of Laurie when she started dating Yunkin on June 22, 1991. Laurie had spent the night with Thomas, and Yunkin was there until about 3:30 A.M. Lambert phoned at five o'clock and told Laurie if she slept with Yunkin she would kill her. But later Thomas got mad at Laurie, because Laurie was spreading rumors about her at school. She told people Thomas was a lesbian, just because she didn't like to date, because school and good grades were important to her.

Thomas took up with Lambert as Lambert plotted revenge. The week of the Fourth of July, she asked a number of people to meet her at the mall, where they agreed to lure Laurie from her house, take her to Green Street downtown, and tie her to a telephone pole. Lambert was going to cut her hair, slit her throat, beat her up, and paint the words "free black pussy" on her.

Thomas and a friend, Kimona Warner, were designated as the ones to get Laurie out of her house. They started driving over to the Shows' condominium and Warner said she thought the whole plan was ridiculous. Instead, she said, they ought to warn Laurie about what Lambert wanted to do. But when they got to the door, they just told her to stay home with her mom and Jackie Weakland, a friend.

"Lock your doors and don't answer the phone, and don't ask me any questions," the girls told Show. Thomas and Warner went back to East Towne Mall and told Lambert they couldn't get Laurie out of her house.

The next day, Thomas saw Laurie at work and told her to call at 11:00 P.M. and she would tell her what was going on. They talked for about two hours, Thomas testified.

Some time later, Lambert resurrected a plan to get rid of Laurie.

"I swear to God I'm going to kill her," she told Thomas. "I'm going to slit her throat."

Yunkin said, "Well, why don't you just beat her up?"

Another time Lambert wanted Thomas to lure Laurie from her house and once on a lonely road pretend her car had broken down. When they got out to check the engine, Lambert and Rachel Winesickle were going to come out of the bushes wearing black ski masks and beat Laurie.

Other friends of Lambert's stepped up to the witness stand to verify the threats, the plans Lambert had to take care of Laurie Show. Lambert sat quietly at the defense table as her attorney tried to pluck away at the stories. None of them had told him in interviews in his office before the trial that Lambert had said she wanted to slit Laurie's throat. They felt like she was a blowhard and a braggart, didn't they? None of the plans were ever executed. Piercing the guilt bubble raises reasonable doubt.

Laurie lived in constant fear of Lambert, Jackie Weakland testified. Weakland had known Laurie for about two years, since the beginning of her own sophomore year. She had known Yunkin and Lambert for about a year.

"She was afraid something was going to happen, you know. She hated living in fear," the seventeen-year-old told the court. Jackie had been there the day Lambert hit Laurie in the parking lot of East Towne Mall. She had seen the look on her face.

Nineteen

The courtroom was packed when Hazel Show, wearing a blazer and skirt, took the stand. She had been waiting for this moment for six months. She felt tremendous pressure. She had been in counseling for some time, telling herself she was doing it to prepare for this day. It was, after all, all that was left to do for her daughter.

Kenneff began: "Would you state your name, please."

"Hazel Laurie Show." Her daughter had been named for her. Her only child. Stay strong, she told herself. She looked straight into the face of Michelle Lambert. She wanted the girl to see her, to see the pain and devastation she had caused. Hazel suspected Lambert did not care, did not grasp the depth of her sorrow, but she stared nonetheless, throughout her entire testimony. Lambert did not look up often. But when she did, Hazel was looking at her.

Hazel said she lived on Black Oak Drive still, in the condominium she shared with her daughter, the place her daughter died. She worked as a nurse's aide in the operating room at Community Hospital of Lancaster.

Kenneff asked her to recall the summer of 1991.

"Was your daughter, Laurie Show, living with you at that time?"

"Yes, she was."

"And did you become aware in the summer of 1991 that she started to date Lawrence Yunkin?"

"Yes."

"What is your recollection of the first time that you were aware of that relationship?"

"I would say probably around, just a guess, around the middle of June she started dating him. At first it was more or less just being friends, going out shopping, swimming, that type of thing, but I would say approximately the middle."

She stopped dating him a little more than a week later.

"Did Laurie Show know Mr. Yunkin prior to meeting him around that period of time?"

"Yes. I think it probably would've been a couple of weeks. She met them through a mutual friend, Rachel Winesickle."

"Would that be both Mr. Yunkin and Miss Lambert?"

"Right."

Kenneff asked when Hazel realized the relationship with Yunkin was going to be a problem for her daughter.

"The day that Laurie and Lawrence discontinued this relationship, I received a phone call from Michelle Lambert."

"And in general, what was said in the phone call?"

"Did I know that she was pregnant? I said no, I did not. And did I know that Laurie and Lawrence had had sex in my house and I said no, I didn't. Continued on a lot of screaming and yelling and I said, well at this point there was really nothing that I could do for her and I ended up hanging up the phone because of the obscenities that she was using."

"Did you confront Mr. Yunkin with the occurrence of this phone call?"

"Yes. He was outside talking to Laurie; he was inside his van. She was standing at the side of the van. I immediately went out, told him I had received a call from Michelle stating that she was pregnant, and I told him that he had a problem he needed to take care of. Whether he needed to go see Michelle, talk to his parents, her parents, get counseling, whatever, but this would end the relationship with Laurie."

"To the best of your knowledge, did that in fact end the relationship between Laurie and Mr. Yunkin?"

"Yes."

"Now did you become aware of problems that Laurie was encountering as a result of the termination of the relationship with Mr. Yunkin?"

"There were phone calls made to Laurie and a lot of times we just hung up. Then starting July fifth, Michelle and Lawrence went into the Deb Shop, where Laurie was employed, and Michelle was calling [Laurie] names in front of customers; and when I picked Laurie up that night, this was stated to me."

Shirk rose to object. Hearsay. Sustained. Strike the comment.

On July 5, Laurie called Lambert and told her not to come into the store harassing her. It was a new job. She liked it and wanted to keep it. Hazel was listening on the extension.

"So was that the general tenor of the conversation? Did you identify yourself during it?"

"At that point when she said that she was there, she said she could do or go wherever she wanted to and started using obscenities to Laurie, and then I broke in and said, Michelle, this is Laurie's mother. I am on the other extension and you have to stop this; you cannot jeopardize Laurie's job."

Later in that month, about July 22, Hazel saw an incident herself. She went to pick Laurie up and pulled in, directly facing the mall entrance so she could watch.

"Michelle and Lawrence and two other people were waiting. There is like an island inside the door that has beverages around. They were waiting there and kept turning their head to look around to see if anyone was coming up the hallway. Laurie came out of the Deb Shop. Michelle got up and went toward Laurie. At that point, Laurie crossed the hallway to the other side. Michelle grabbed hold of her and pushed her into the wall. At that point, I pulled right up in front of the door and was ready to get out to go in to get Laurie and to confront Michelle when Laurie came out holding her head and crying."

About a week later, her ex-husband told her of another incident involving Lambert.

"It was time to talk to the police. I had called the police after the incident where I saw Michelle push Laurie, but I called them from home and they said really there was nothing that they could do at that point, we needed to stay at the crime scene and report it from there. So after further harassment, on the thirty-first, I believe it was, we called the police to discuss this problem."

Police were called again after another incident at the Deb Shop.

"Did you actually observe another incident in August that involved harassment of Laurie by Michelle?"

"Yes."

"When did that incident take place?"

"That was August twentieth."

"Where were you when that incident took place?"

"We were at the Root's Market in East Petersburg."

"Who was with you?"

"Laurie, a friend, Rose Metzger, and her son, Zach."

"What did that incident consist of?"

"We were in a building and I looked out and I saw Lawrence and Michelle walking through a crowd of people and I told Laurie, I said Lawrence and Michelle are here, and immediately she wanted to leave. She just panicked and I said no, this is our fun thing that we do. We're not going to run away from here, but we will avoid them. We'll keep looking and go to other areas of Root's to avoid them."

"Were you successful in avoiding them?"

"No."

"What happened when you came in contact with them?"

"We were at a stand looking at some things and Michelle came up and started screaming and yelling all kinds of obscenities and just being very vicious."

"What did you say or do?"

"Well, first of all, I got Laurie behind me and I said, Michelle, please stop this. Laurie does not want Lawrence and just leave us alone. Then she started screaming that Laurie had had sex with Lawrence in our house so many times. I said, Michelle, Lawrence raped Laurie and, I said, if you continue to harass her, there is a possibility that we could press charges. Then I looked at Lawrence and I said, Lawrence, get her out of here, because we are calling the police."

"Did you on that date attempt to find a police officer inside of Root's?"

"We did. We tried to find a phone and we couldn't, and then we found the constable that surveys the area."

"By the time you found the constable, were Mr. Yunkin and Miss Lambert gone?"

"Yes."

In early October, they saw Yunkin and Lambert at the New Holland Fair. They were waiting in line to get something to eat when they saw Yunkin and Lambert walking down the street. She told her daughter to stay calm. Hopefully, they wouldn't see them. Laurie panicked and they got out of line, got over onto a sidewalk, and she begged to leave.

After the November incident, Hazel said, they went to the police. Laurie came running to the car, crying.

"I said that's it, we're going to the police."

Each time during the confrontations, Yunkin stood in the background, arms folded, and after several abusive minutes, he would say in a patronizing way, "Michelle, don't—" or "Michelle, don't hit Laurie; she really didn't do anything."

"He would stand there with a smile on his face like he was enjoying it so much, having someone fight over him."

Her daughter was scared to death, Hazel said. She was always on the lookout for them.

"If we went anywhere and saw their van or their car or something, we didn't go in."

Hazel recounted her conversation with the woman who called herself Mrs. Cooper. She didn't recognize the controlled female voice.

On December 20, 1991, Hazel woke before 5:00 A.M. She left at 6:45 and arrived at the junior high school at about 6:58. She went inside and waited in the office. She looked at the clock and decided she had waited long enough. She left Conestoga Valley Junior High School at about 7:11. She drove home in nine minutes.

"I pulled into my parking space, got out of the car, and Jackie, our downstairs neighbor, came out and said is there a problem. And I said no, I have a day's vacation. I was over to school to see a teacher and now I'm going to do the rest of Laurie's shopping and wrap presents. And then Jackie said no, I meant is there a problem upstairs. And she said they heard terrible noises and maybe something happened."

Hazel Show went upstairs. The door was closed. She put her key in the door and went inside.

"I opened the door and I went in and I looked in my kitchen. I have swinging doors at my kitchen. I looked in the kitchen to see if something had dropped that caused a commotion for Jackie. The lights were still on, so I glanced in Laurie's bathroom. Her hair dryer and curling iron were still out and her light was on. I turned to go into her bedroom and I saw spots on the floor, and at first it didn't dawn on me what it was. It was kind of a brownish color and I thought, oh, Laurie spilled mouthwash.

"Then I turned and I saw Laurie lying on the floor with her arms moving and making a noise and there was blood. So I quick turned, ran to my front door, opened it, and screamed for Jackie to call nine-one-one. Laurie's hurt. I screamed again: Call nine-one-one! I ran back into the bedroom to Laurie's side, and then I saw that she had a rope around her neck, so I ran to the kitchen and got a sharp knife. I ran back in, slipped my fingers under the rope, and Laurie moaned, and I told her it would be okay, I would cut the rope.

"So I cut the rope and she breathed deeply; and I went to pick her up to cradle her, and that's when I saw that her throat was cut. So I cradled her head in my arms and I said, honey, I'm so sorry. I said this was a setup. Who did this?

"And she told me Michelle did it. And I said I'm so sorry, you were so good. You didn't do anything wrong; and again she said Michelle. And then she said Michelle again. And I told her that I loved her and that her father loved her and then she said I love, love you, approximately four times, and I told her God was going to take care of her and I just held her."

Hazel was sobbing, twisting the handkerchief someone had given her at Laurie's funeral. The courtroom could see her deep, deep anguish, the kind unknown to anyone who has not lost a child. Yet, through her tears, she kept her gaze on Lisa Michelle Lambert. In her head, Hazel Show was saying to Lambert, "Look at me. Look at what you did. Feel it. Know it."

"Now, a little bit of concern came up in the case regarding the tightness of this rope and you said you are a nurse. Could you explain to the judge how you handled that?"

"The rope was here and I slipped two fingers under and then cut between my two fingers."

"Now, at the request of Detective Savage, did you try to demonstrate on Corporal Schuler the manner in which you held Laurie on the morning when she was speaking to you?"

He handed her a photograph—Commonwealth Exhibit 42—showing Renee Schuler and Hazel Show reenacting the position in which she had held Laurie.

"She might've been a little different, but I did hold her so I could try to keep the wounds together."

"Mrs. Show, I don't want to belabor this, and I know I asked you this before in the other hearings. Can you do one of the phrases? You don't have to do all the phrases. Can you imitate as best you could the way Laurie sounded when she did this?"

"Miii—shhh—el did it."

"Cross-examine."

Shirk said, "Your Honor, perhaps this would be a good time for a break. I don't know if Mrs. Show would appreciate that or not."

Stengel asked, "Are you all right, Mrs. Show?"

"I'm fine."

"You may proceed."

Shirk began slowly. Defense attorneys know cross-examining a victim's mother is like walking through the proverbial minefield. Slow and steady. No attacks. Demonstrate empathy, but protect the client's case.

He asked her to review her testimony, when Laurie met Yunkin and Lambert, when she started dating him, when the incidents with Lambert began.

She patiently plodded through it, for Laurie.

He questioned her about changing dates and times in her testimony that day and in the earlier preliminary hearing. She had said Laurie and Yunkin dated in July, now June. That she went to lunch the day before the murder between 1:10 and 1:50. Now, 1:00 and 1:30. That was when the mysterious call from Mrs. Cooper came into the nurses' lounge on extension 161.

"If I were to call you at any given time and say to the hospital representative: 'Hello, I would like to speak to Mrs. Show.' Where would they route that call?"

"One-sixty-five."

"That is where?"

"The nurses' station in the OR."

"And they would never route my call through to the phone you got it on?"

"Unless you asked for that extension."

"Specifically for that extension?"

"Yes. No one is there usually."

"So I would have to have some type of knowledge of that extension to reach you at that extension."

"Yes."

He asked her whether she was familiar with Michelle Lambert's voice.

"Not her normal voice. All I've ever heard is screaming and swearing and abuse."

"But I think you indicated before at the preliminary hearing that you did not believe that was Michelle Lambert's voice that called you that afternoon on the nineteenth."

"I wouldn't know. It was [a] very controlled, medium type [of] voice. It could have easily have been, I don't know."

"After you got the calls, you contacted your daughter that day."

"She got home from school around four o'clock and I called to ask her if she knew anything that had happened."

"You testified here this morning that you arrived at six fifty-seven or six fifty-eight. Do you remember testifying at a preliminary hearing in this matter on February 11, 1992?"

"Yes."

"And you indicated at that time that you arrived approximately seven oh-three."

"No; I'm usually not a person that would be late."

"Excuse me?"

"I usually don't get anywhere late, I'm always early. I might've meant three minutes of seven."

"I think what I was referring to here when I was asking you questions was, you testified a week before at a preliminary hearing for Tabitha Buck before this hearing."

"Uh-huh."

"Am I correct?"

"Yes."

"And, question: I indicate now I was at the preliminary hearing last week, Mrs. Show. Some of the questions I might ask involve some of your testimony. I think you testified you arrived at the junior high at approximately seven oh-three. Your answer was: It was around approximately, yes."

He carefully grilled her on times: 7:07 A.M. at the school, 7:11 A.M. in her car. She told police on December 31 it was 7:17 A.M. when she left the school.

"I think I probably was confused, thinking that was probably about the time I was passing the high school."

"But that is what you told the police, seven-seventeen."

"Yeah, if that's what's there."

"And you indicated you left today at seven-eleven, and it took you, you figured, nine to eleven minutes to drive it."

"Yeah. I have driven it twice since and I've never gotten—I've always gotten red lights, so it's usually around eleven minutes, and that morning I didn't."

"Which would put you home somewhere around seven-twenty or seven twenty-one."

"Right."

"On the other hand, at the preliminary hearing, you testified that you arrived home approximately seven-thirty."

"No. Those were approximate times, at a very stressful time."

"I understand. I think I was looking at the police report. The police report from December thirty-first indicates you arrived home, you felt, at seven-thirty?"

"Yes. At that time I was a mess."

"I apologize. The preliminary hearing was seven-twenty to seven twenty-five. You told the police this on December thirty-first."

The point of tediously pursuing a timetable was setting the stage for the judge to believe Laurie simply could not have spoken. That her mother got there too

late and her daughter was unconscious and very near
death.

Hazel Show went in and saw the spot on the floor.

Shirk asked, "If I was in Laurie's bathroom and
looked through the bedroom door, I know—"

"I couldn't have."

"Excuse me?"

"You couldn't. If you were in Laurie's bathroom, you
couldn't."

"Okay. Again, I'm going to get to see your apartment,
but I haven't yet. But from my understanding, if I had
just entered Laurie's bathroom door, not up by the
counter—"

Hazel shook her head no.

"No way?" Shirk asked.

"If you were standing straight, you couldn't see."

"What I was going to indicate is, if I entered the bathroom door, had just entered the bathroom door and
turned left, I can see into her bedroom."

"No, you would've looked into the door to her bathroom."

"You walked into her bedroom."

"Yes."

"And you found your daughter."

"Yes."

"I think you testified that her arms were moving."

"Her hands were moving."

"And she was making noises?"

"Yes."

"What noises was she making?"

"Taa, taa, taa."

"Taa, taa, taa?"

"Yeah; something. Trying to breathe, get air in. I
don't know, just making some kind of noises."

"So she had—"

"I don't know if at that point she had seen me."

"You don't know if that means she saw you or not?"

"Yeah."

Hazel Show ran outside, leaned over the railing, and screamed for the neighbor downstairs, Jackie Kleinhans, to call paramedics. She rushed back inside, she said, to Laurie's side. Cradling her daughter, she asked who did it.

"And your daughter, you indicated, said three times, 'Michelle'."

"Right."

"Did she actually say just the word 'Michelle,' or 'Michelle did it'?"

"She said, 'Michelle did it,' and then she said 'Michelle' two other times."

"We've had a lot of discussion in this courtroom about the nature of your daughter's injuries. We had a lot of discussion in this courtroom about lip sounds and tongue sounds. And certain sounds are easier to make, depending on the type of injury.

"Did she say 'Michelle,' or did she say 'Maa'?"

"To the best of my knowledge, it was, 'Michelle did it.' "

"Did she perhaps indicate Maa and you filled in the rest, 'Michelle did it'?"

"No."

"And she communicated, it might be right, in some other way?"

"No, she said it. She whispered it, whatever you want to call it, she told me."

"My cross-examination is finished," Shirk said.

Hazel left the stand, and as she walked back to her seat, she looked at Lambert, who did not return her gaze.

Stengel asked, "Mr. Kenneff, do you have any additional witnesses?"

"No, Your Honor."

He asked that numerous charts, photos, and diagrams be entered into evidence and with that taken care of, Kenneff said simply, "The commonwealth then rests, Your Honor."

It was before 4:00 P.M., early to end a court day, but Shirk had asked for a little more time to prepare. Lambert's defense would begin the next morning at 9:30.

Twenty

Day five. July 15, 1992. The lawyers began in the judge's chambers. Shirk had three motions for the judge to decide: that the prosecution did not prove that Lambert committed first-degree murder, that Laurie Show was not dead and that there was no reason for Lambert to be facing the death penalty. Judge Stengel ruled against all three.

Moving into the courtroom, Shirk began Lambert's defense. In his opening argument, he focused on what he considered the district attorney's single-minded pursuit of Lambert as the killer. Decided early on by the commonwealth's lawyers was the idea that Lambert was the liar and Yunkin was the truth-teller. Shirk said he would show that was simply not the case.

"He's been lying since day one; he is lying now, all to protect himself. He lied about his involvement and he lied about the letter that was presented to him, or the questionnaire, in this courtroom."

Yunkin is not only a liar, Shirk said, he is also an abuser. He was not a meek guy standing by while his girlfriend told him what to do. He's a violent man, the attorney claimed.

Shirk also said Lambert has an aversion to blood, "can't stand the sight of it." Moreover, he has evidence that Buck did in fact commit the murder as Lisa Michelle Lambert said she did.

As his first witness, Shirk called to the stand once again Detective Ronald Savage. He asked about a hooded sweatshirt that Yunkin told police about three weeks earlier. It was one he had worn the day of Laurie's murder and was thrown into the river. Shirk asked why police did not look for it.

"We just felt that it would be in vain, it would not be worthwhile."

He asked Savage about the crime scene and whether there were any signs someone had broken into the condominium. None, he said.

Shirk also wanted to know about the injuries Tabitha Buck had on her body the day after the murder. Renee Schuler, the only woman on the East Lampeter Township police force, had conducted a physical search of both Lambert and Buck that day. Buck had various scratches on the side of her face, Savage responded. A small scratch at the corner of her mouth, one on her shoulder.

Savage got up from the witness stand, walked to the table where the assistant district attorney sat, and looked through some photographs. He pulled out the ones showing Buck's injuries and went back to the stand. Using the photographs to refresh his memory, he described Buck's facial scratches and said the shoulder injury wasn't exactly a scratch, more like a "disturbance of the skin," faint marks.

Shirk also raised a question about the timetable laid out by Richard Kleinhans, the Shows' downstairs neighbor. In one interview, Kleinhans said he saw the two people leaving at 7:08 A.M., in another he said 7:20 A.M. Savage had said Kleinhans's estimates differed only a few minutes each of the three times he interviewed him. But Shirk charged, "That's more than a few minutes."

He also asked why Savage did not write up each interview with the neighbor, so that the information could be provided to the defense.

"I don't know," the detective answered.

On cross-examination Kenneff pointedly asked if Kleinhans was guessing at times based on the only time anyone looked at the clock, at 7:17, when his wife noted the time on the kitchen clock.

"That's correct," Savage said.

"When you went to the crime scene, was Laurie Show dead?" Kenneff said, still bristling a bit from what he considered to be Shirk's inane motion in judge's chambers a few minutes earlier.

"Yes," Savage said emphatically.

The defense called John Gencavage next. A forensic document examiner now in private practice, Gencavage had spent twenty-four years in the field with the Pennsylvania State Police and a year with the U.S. Treasury Department's Alcohol, Tobacco, and Firearms division in Rockville, Maryland. Shirk's office had hired Gencavage to review the so-called twenty-nine questions, the document Lambert had sent to Yunkin at the Lancaster County Prison. He sent the examiner examples of Lambert's and Yunkin's handwriting.

Shirk handed Gencavage Defense Exhibit 5, the original questionnaire. He said he used a microscope to examine the document, as well as filters, longwave and shortwave ultraviolet, infrared. All helped to show what was used to write the document, different inks, pencil.

That particular document was written with two different types of pencil on "very, very cheap paper," he said. He could also tell that the answers were written with a defective ballpoint pen; the roller on the pen was damaged, leaving small skip marks in the ink. All of the answers were written by Yunkin, he said.

"There is a considerable amount of individuality," he said. "It is good line quality, no simulation, imitation. Good free-flowing movement."

The questions, he said, were written by Lambert.

Gencavage walked to a slide projector, which had been placed in the courtroom, switched it on, and showed two samples—side by side—of Yunkin's handwriting. He pointed to the word "yes" and showed how the known sample was precisely the same as the answers.

"It would be highly unlikely that any of this writing could've been interjected after the questions were answered, in my opinion, because why would someone end a piece of text here and answer clear over here after they had been going, following the question throughout the writing. I think not."

Throughout his testimony, Gencavage kept referring to Yunkin as "Mr. Lumpkin."

"The person that wrote these standards, Mr. Lumpkin, also wrote the answers to the questions," he said. He found no indication the document had been altered, he said.

Finally Shirk said, "I'm not sure how you're pronouncing it. It's Mr. Yunkin."

The judge announced a lunch break. Hazel Show knew the judge wanted to see her condominium, but she didn't know when. He sent word to her that they would go during the break.

The trial then moved to the Shows' residence. Hazel and her brother Butch were taken through a side entrance to the courthouse into a waiting car, driven by Pam Grosh, the victim's advocate from the district attorney's office. They wanted to avoid the press and the spectacle that came with them at the Show condominium. Judge Stengel was waiting for them when they arrived. Also present were the court nurse, bailiff, court reporter, lawyers for the commonwealth and the defense, four law enforcement officers, and Lambert.

Hazel Show was already inside when Lambert came in. Hazel stood in the living room and glared at Lambert, who stood uneasily in the hallway on the spot where investigators laid Laurie's body as they collected evidence on that cold December day, the last time Lambert had been there. Hazel stared and stared; the anger, the hatred, built up more and more with every minute the girl was in her home.

Lambert started to weep quietly. But Hazel's eyes locked onto her even more. She did not even blink. A deputy told Lambert to go stand in the kitchen. *Just ask me for a tissue*, Hazel thought. *Just ask.* The deputy, a woman, handed Lambert a tissue from her own pocket. The kitchen cabinets obstructed Hazel's glare then; all she could see was Lambert's midsection through the gap between cabinet and countertop.

Hazel knew she was making Lambert uncomfortable.

The judge spent seven minutes looking around the condominium. He left, followed by Lambert, who was guided into a police car by a deputy. Hazel stepped out on the porch and watched Lambert as she got into the car. Lambert looked up once. Hazel's gaze was glaring and cold.

After lunch Shirk called as a witness Forrest Adams, the assistant principal at Conestoga Valley High School. He brought to court the emergency information card filled out by Laurie Show at the beginning of the 1991–92 school year. Each student fills out an assortment of cards for the office, school nurse, guidance, district office. They include emergency contacts, parent work numbers, place of employment. One number listed for

Hazel Show had been crossed out and another number had been written above it.

Shirk continued to build his case. He had to disprove the perception of Lawrence Yunkin as an innocent bystander, as asserted by Hazel Show. He called Randolph Sensenig to the stand. An officer with East Lampeter Township, Sensenig responded to a call at the home of Lawrence Yunkin and Michelle Lambert on August 8, 1991. Lambert had a cut on her upper lip, he said, showing Shirk a photograph taken that day.

On the sixth day, Lisa Michelle Lambert came to court wearing a conservative dress. As usual her long blond hair was clean. She still wore too much makeup, but all in all she looked like a Sunday school girl. This was the day people were really going to be looking at her; the day she was to tell her side of the story. She was nervous. That gutsy confidence she had shown so often in her life had vanished, or at least was not evident to outsiders.

Shirk had a few more points to make before calling Lambert, including getting on record the news release issued by East Lampeter Police saying a man and a woman were wanted in connection with Laurie Show's murder. Chief Jacob Glick tried to explain the mix-up.

"When I arrived at the scene, we were—I was getting details from three or four different investigators, and at that time, we had information that there were two people seen leaving, coming down the steps or the immediate area of the steps of the victim's residence," Glick testified. "We were told by the investigators there that it was two people, and I believe they [were] described as being five foot four, five foot five, somewhere in that vicinity, short, and we also had determined that at that time we were told that Miss Lambert was one of the people that was in the apartment and we were attempting to get as much information as we could to put a release to county radio for other police departments to help us find Miss Lambert."

They found out she lived in the southern part of the county, had no car, and that she was usually seen with Yunkin.

"The report is a bit ambiguous in that it states a male and a female, but actually we were attempting to locate Miss Lambert," the chief said.

Richard Jeffries, a private investigator hired by the defense, showed a number of enlargements he made from original police photographs of the crime scene. He found what he considered to be footprints in Laurie Show's bedroom, including some that had blood on top of them.

But the bombshell from Jeffries's pictures came from the next witness for the defense, John Balshy, a former Pennsylvania policeman who had worked in the photo lab for seven years. He had printed Jeffries's pictures. Balshy said he was making a routine print of one of the footprints when he noticed something odd in the picture. On the bottom of the closet door, Balshy said, was a "B" written in blood.

"It's plainly made," Balshy said, pointing at the photograph now displayed on an easel, "and you can see as the finger just drops off onto the carpet area, all right?"

He also saw a "T."

"Now keeping in mind at this particular time I didn't know whose name was who," he said. "I didn't know any of the people who were involved in this case." He believed Laurie rolled onto her left side to print the letters on the door. As she did that, her head brushed up against the other door. It would explain why there was blood on top of the footprint Jeffries found.

Shirk was wrapping it up, tying the loose ends that

would add up to reasonable doubt, the hallmark of all criminal defense. Not just no doubt, but some doubt. He had shown Yunkin to be an abuser. He had shown Buck had prior problems with Laurie Show. He had shown Laurie had left a message of who had killed her.

He had one more witness: Lisa Michelle Lambert.

She walked stiffly, almost timidly to the stand.

"Lisa, I know you are scared. If there are any questions about what either Mr. Kenneff or I ask, just ask us to repeat them."

"Okay."

"Now you've been sitting here throughout this entire trial and we're talking about the events that took place on December 20, 1991. I'm going to ask you a few questions, however, first, about the months that led up to that. Now, there has been a lot of testimony here in this courtroom of different activities you were involved in and different things you've said. Have you ever said in those months between June and December that you wanted to kill Laurie Show?"

"Yes."

"Did you ever say you wanted to slit her throat?"

"No, I don't recall ever saying that."

"Is there a difference in the two to you?"

"Yes. If you say you are going to kill somebody, that's a figure of speech. If you say you are going to slit somebody's throat, that's a specific—sounds like a specific intent."

"Why would you say you want to kill someone if it's a figure of speech?"

"Something people say when they are angry or even joking around."

"Would you say it about other people other than Laurie Show?"

"Yes."

"So you are indicating it's something you might say when you are angry."

"Yes."

"Now, there was testimony that sometime in June you and about five other individuals were going to kidnap Laurie and take her downtown, cut her hair, and put a sign on her."

"Yes, that is true."

"What was the purpose of that?"

"To embarrass her."

Lambert said she never talked about slitting Laurie's throat. She was angry and just wanted to humiliate the girl who slept with her boyfriend, the father of her child. She was angry, too, because Laurie had told Yunkin that Michelle had slept with his best friend. Laurie wanted to break up her relationship with Yunkin.

"And subsequently you went after Laurie Show."

"Yes."

"There was testimony here that—I don't remember the exact document—but I think sometime in August that there was discussions, although nothing ever got off the ground again, luring Miss Show out of her home, something about taking her in her car to Manor Street and perhaps beating her up. Is that correct?"

"Yes."

"Were you involved in that?"

"Yes, I was."

"Again, what was the purpose of that?"

"Just to embarrass her."

"Embarrass her and hurt her?"

"Embarrass her and hurt her."

"Did you want to kill her?"

"No."

He asked when the planning began for the incident at Laurie's house on December 20, a Friday. Lambert said it was the Sunday before. She was with Buck and Yunkin at Park City. Yunkin said several times that day he was scared Laurie was going to press rape charges against him. Yunkin and Buck told Lambert they had a plan to "keep her mouth shut."

"But they wouldn't tell me what it was," Lambert testified. "They said they would tell me later on in the week."

They talked about it the next Thursday night, the same night she and Yunkin went to Kmart and bought a rope and knit hats.

"And what was the purpose of that purchase?" Shirk asked.

"Friday morning we were supposed to go down—Friday afternoon—around one o'clock we were supposed to go to Lawrence's grandmother, go back to their woods and cut down a Christmas tree."

"The hats, too?"

"They were to keep the wood chips out of our hair."

"You were going to cut your own tree?"

"Yes."

"At that point on Friday night, was there a knife in that bag?"

"There was a bag put in—a knife put in the bag Thursday night when we got home."

"Home from Kmart?"

"Yes."

"What was the purpose of putting the knife in the bag?"

"Because last year when we had gotten our Christmas trees, we forgot to cut the littler branches off of the bottom. When we tried to put it in the tree stand, it wouldn't go in. We had to drag it outside again, so we took it along to cut the branches off the bottom."

Lambert said she and Yunkin then went to Buck's,

and differing from his version of events, claimed both of them went inside.

"I went upstairs with Lawrence, and Tabbi said to be quiet, because her mother was sleeping. We sat down on the couch in the living room, and Lawrence started calling Laurie a bitch and he was saying that she was going to put him in jail and he was scared; and they both told me that they had planned—Tabbi said that that day she had called Conestoga Valley and said that she was Laurie Show's mother and wanted to change her phone number, and she asked them what phone number they had down there for her work. Then she told them it was something different and she told them to cross it off and change it. Then she wrote down on a piece of paper something for this guy Duane to read that she knows. I think it was like her boyfriend."

"Let me stop you there a second. Tabbi indicated that she had called Conestoga Valley High School."

"Yes, from a pay phone at Penn Manor High School."

"And indicated she was Hazel Show?"

"Yes."

"And asked them that her number, or said that her number had changed at work, and asked them what number they had."

"Yes."

"And that's the way she got Hazel Show's work number."

"Yes."

"That's what Tabbi told you."

"Yes."

"And that she had written something down for someone to read."

"Yes."

"What name did she give you?"

"She said Duane."

"She had written it for him. Do you know if he made the call?"

"She told me he did. She wrote it down on a piece of paper and told him it was part of a joke and asked him if he would do it for her, and she dialed the number and he read off the paper."

"Did she indicate that he made two calls?"

"Yes. She said that he made the first one and then she said she realized that she messed up because she said the high school was too close to Laurie's house and her mother wouldn't be gone long enough."

"When she told you this, had a decision already been made to do something Friday that you knew of?"

"They said they were going to do something, but Tabbi was telling me first what they had already done to see that it went through."

"What did they tell you they wanted to do?"

"Lawrence said that they wanted to make sure her mom wouldn't be there, and they were going to knock on the door and pull Laurie out onto the porch, and Lawrence and Tabbi were going to beat her up bad enough to put her in the hospital."

"Did you agree with all that?"

"First I just sat there and I said, Well, Lawrence, that's really stupid. You'll go to jail if you beat her up like that. I said that's dumb. That's even, you know, that's even dumber than you getting charged with rape. I said to him, I don't think anything is going to come out of those rape charges. It's your word against hers; and he said, well, he goes, I think they will. Then I said I heard Laurie is pregnant, I heard Brad got her pregnant."

"You heard rumors that Laurie was pregnant?"

"Yes."

"Go ahead."

"And I said I didn't think we should beat her up, because if she is pregnant, I don't want to do that."

"You were also pregnant at the time, were you not?"

"Yes."

"Go ahead."

"And then I said, Why don't we do what we were going to do this summer? Why don't we cut her hair off? Then he said, Well, I don't know. I said, Well, why don't we? You want to fight Brad anyway. Why do you have to beat up Laurie? If you want to fight Brad, why don't you cut her hair?"

"Is that the plan that was eventually developed?"

"Yes."

They picked up Tabbi, and on the way to Laurie's house, Buck realized the scissors Lambert had put in the bag with the rope and hats were no longer in there.

"She was digging in the bag. It was right when we got—I think it was close to the East Towne Mall, like right before East Towne Mall, and she said there is no scissors in here. I said, Yes, there is. She said, No, there are not. I said, Lawrence, you brought the bag out. Where are the scissors? He said you put them in."

"All of a sudden, the plan goes awry. You have no scissors. What did you all decide to do?"

"Tabbi reached in the bag and she pulled out the knife and she said we could use this. I said you can't cut hair with that. She took a piece of hair from the back of her hair. It was pretty thick and she took the knife and went like that. She cut the hair right off, like no problem, and she rolled down the window and threw it out and said see, we can do it. I said to Lawrence, What do you think? He said okay. I said all right; so we just agreed to use the knife then."

"I think Detective Savage indicated that the rope purchased was approximately fifty feet, and the rope they found at the scene was approximately half of that. How did that happen?"

"We were in the car and went over. We got to the intersection where you would go to turn onto the road that Laurie's house was on."

"You are talking about the intersection of East Towne Mall?"

"Yeah. She said she was going to cut a piece of the rope, and she, like, cut open the bag with the knife and then she took out the rope and she cut off a piece so we could tie her hands together so she wouldn't jump all around."

"That's an awful lot of rope for tying hands, twenty-four feet."

"She just cut a piece, and Lawrence said, too, that we should tie her hands and her feet together. He said, you know, tie them so she couldn't run away or jump around or anything."

"Okay. And you made your left turn at the stoplight."

"Yes."

"Did Lawrence drop you off? What happened?"

"Well, we got right in front of where the gazebos are, and he—"

"The what?"

"Right in front of where the gazebos are at the entrance to The Oaks. He drove about a hundred feet past the gazebos and then he started coughing. He was going to turn around and then he had stopped the car and then he drove up to where Rachel Winesickle lives, Town and Country, and he turned around and came back and he was still coughing and he said, I'm going over to McDonald's to get a drink. He said, I'll go through the drive-in if it's open, because I have something stuck in my throat."

"Why didn't you all go with him?"

"Because he said that, he just said you guys go ahead and start up; and he said her bus gets here around twenty-five after seven."

Buck, who used to ride the same bus as Laurie, and Lambert got out of the car and walked down a path toward the Shows' condominium. She said they threw leaves at each other and laughed. Buck had the rope and the knife in her pocket.

"Now, when you get up there, what was the plan?"

"We were going to wait until she came outside to go to the bus stop; then we were going to tell her we wanted to talk to her and we were going to ask her if we could walk down with her. When we got down to the gazebo—"

"Let me stop you there. You were going to stand by her house somewhere."

"Yes."

"And wait for her to come out and go to the bus."

"Yes."

"And ask if you could talk with her and, hopefully, walk down to . . . Did you use the word 'gazebo'?"

"Yes."

"Weren't you kind of wondering where Lawrence was?"

"Not yet."

"Okay. What was he supposed to do?"

"Originally, he was going to walk up to the house with us, but when he started choking, he said he would meet us down at the gazebo, he would wait down there."

"So you were going to walk down to the gazebo with her, I take it. Well, you tell me. What were you going to do when you walked down to the gazebo with her?"

"We were going to ask her if we could walk down with her and we were going to walk down there. Tabbi was going to, like, grab her from behind, and Lawrence and

I were going to tie her hands and feet together, and some-one was going to cut her hair, but we didn't figure out who. It was just that that's what we agreed on."

"Tabbi was going to grab her from behind, and Lawrence and you were going to tie her up?"

"Yes."

"Tabbi had the rope."

"She was going to give it to us."

"What happened instead?"

"Well, we were outside, and Tabbi was standing there stomping her feet and— Should I say exactly what she said?"

"Yeah, I want to know exactly what she said."

"She said, 'God, it's fuck'n cold out here'; and she said, 'I'm sick of waiting like this. I'm going up to the door.' "

"Do you have any idea what time that was?"

"No. I said to her okay. I said if you want to, go ahead up and ask her what's taking so long because it is cold out here. And then I went—"

"Where exactly were you standing when you said this?"

"Well, first we were standing like right at the en-tranceway, the brick arch where the stairs go up. And then when we were talking, I said I'll wait here. And we went up the first couple steps. It's shaped like an L. We went up the first couple steps, and I was standing on that landing and said go ahead, ask her what's taking so long. She went up the stairs and I heard her knock three times and then I heard the door open. And right then I heard—like there was a car that pulled in or pulled out or something, and I couldn't hear exactly what they were saying, but I could hear Tabbi's voice and Laurie's voice, but it was, like, muzzled. I couldn't hear what they were saying. I heard a scuffle sound and

I heard the front door slam. I said, Tabbi! And she didn't answer me. I said, Tabbi! Like that. She still didn't answer me. So I walked up the steps and I knocked on the door and I could still hear scuffling and nobody answered the door, so I turned the door-knob and went in and pushed the door open and it didn't shut the whole way; it went open and I could hear it, but it didn't close. And Tabbi, I saw Tabbi. Laurie was on the floor and Tabbi was hitting her."

"Laurie was on the floor?"

"Yes."

"Where?"

"It was by a table. It was like—right like two feet in front of the table."

"Inside the hallway?"

"Yes. It was—I think it was a little past the hallway."

"Near the entranceway to the bedroom?"

"It was past the entranceway to the bedroom, I know that."

"That's where Tabbi was on the—I'm sorry, Laurie was on the floor."

"Yes."

"Where was Tabbi?"

"She was hitting her. She was bent over hitting her."

Shirk showed her a diagram of the Shows' apartment and asked her to show where Laurie and Buck were when she walked in. She pointed to a spot in the hall; Laurie was on the floor, Buck was bent over hitting her with her hands.

"Tabbi was calling her a bitch and she was saying you are not pregnant. And I went over to Tabbi and I put my hand on her arm, right here, and I said, Tabbi, what are you doing? She brought her arm up like this and she brought it back and smashed me in the face with her elbow, and I, like, stumbled and fell back into the wall. I went over again, and Tabbi was still hitting Laurie, and I went over again and Laurie brought her feet, like, up. The way she was on the floor, she was going like this, trying to get Tabbi to stop it. The way she brought her feet up, they came real close to my stomach, so I put my hands like this, and her ankles came like this."

"So you grabbed her ankles?"

"Yes. I said calm down, nobody is going to do anything to you; we just want to talk to you."

"But you were. You were going to cut her hair."

"Yes. Tabbi took her fist and she hit Laurie really hard in the head and her head snapped over like that. She screamed and got up and ran into the bedroom. She ran into the doorway and she turned left and she ran into the bedroom and she tried to shut the door. She was terrified. I could see it on her face—she was really scared. And Tabbi, she just hit the bedroom door and just, like, barreled Laurie over. She flew and landed right beside the bed, ran right over her."

Laurie was on the floor and grabbed for the phone, but Tabbi picked it up and threw it across the room. Laurie tried to stand up.

"That's when I saw the knife," Lambert said. "It came out of nowhere and it was in her hand. Laurie tried to stand up and Tabbi grabbed the back of her sweatpants and tried to pull her back down. That's when I saw Laurie had on turquoise underwear, I saw that. I saw scissors laying on the floor. I said, Tabbi, there are scissors. Put the knife away! Put the knife away! Because of the way they were fighting and everything. And Laurie saw the scissors, because, I guess, I was saying it. She picked up the scissors and Tabbi lunged the scissors out of her hand. I thought she was going to cut her hair and everything would be okay. When she grabbed the scissors away from Laurie, she threw them—"

"Let me stop you," Shirk said. "To the best of my knowledge, there was never any scissors found at that scene."

"They were orange-handled scissors."

"Okay. Go ahead."

"And then when Tabbi threw them, she pulled Laurie down and she was taking, like, Laurie's hair and holding it and she was hacking at it with the knife. Laurie had her hands up here, going like this, pulling at her hair and trying to get the knife away or save her hair or something. And they were fighting and I kept telling Tabbi [to] stop it. I said [to] put the knife away! I kept telling her and telling her, and she wouldn't listen to me. The knife flicked up across Tabbi's face; I saw that.

"And I lunged into the bedroom and I tried to grab Laurie underneath the arms to pull her away from Tabbi, because I didn't know how else. I yelled at Tabbi. I tried to pull her off Laurie. I didn't know what else to do. Whenever I went to do that, the knife came down right in front of my face and it looked like it bounced off Laurie's back.

"I had picked her up and I was, like, dragging her away from Tabbi and I heard this *whoosh*, like it went *shoosh!* I felt something; it was, like, warm on my hand and I pulled my hand away and I looked down the back of her sweatshirt and it was black. There was a spot in her sweatshirt and it was black. I looked down at my hand and I saw blood on my hand and I just—like my knees went out from under me and I started shaking and I, like, fell on the floor with her and I fell, like, half over her, and I said to Tabbi, I said, Oh, shit! You cut her!

"And I was on the floor and I was shaking really bad

and Tabbi just—she looked at her glove and she had hair on her glove and she shook her glove and the hair, like, went all over the place. And then she crawled over to Laurie, and Laurie was crying and she was, like, really hysterical; and Tabbi had the knife and she looked at Laurie and she said, Shut up! Shut up! Like that. Laurie got louder and louder and Tabbi said, Shut up! Shut up! She took the knife and she acted like she was going to cut Laurie with it. Laurie put her hand up, grabbed the knife and Tabbi's gloves, they started getting red streaks on them."

Lambert continued, "Laurie's hands were bleeding. I started to get up. I started to crawl over to the bedroom door and Laurie looked at me and said don't leave me here, take me with you. She said it louder again: Please don't leave me here, take me with you. She put her hands out. She had blood on her hands. I didn't take her hand, I had her wrists. I pulled her up halfway. I said, Laurie, get up! Get up! I looked back and I saw Tabbi had her somehow by the back of her sweatpants. She had her somehow.

"And then I, like, kind of let her wrist go slack and jerked her really hard to get her away and I pulled her out into the hallway. Tabbi fell back, lost her balance. I pulled Laurie toward the front door and I opened up the door and right when I stepped out onto the porch I felt, like, Laurie was still in there but I felt this.

"I had my hand on her wrist and it felt like she pulled away like this. I thought she pulled her arm out or her wrist out of my hand and I got, like, down a couple steps and I heard: You are not going anywhere, bitch! Tabbi said that.

"And then I, like, turned around and a split second later there is, like, this person in the way. I smashed into him. I fell up against the brick wall and all of a sudden someone was shaking me really hard by the shoulders. It was Lawrence. He said, What happened to your hands? What happened to your hands? I said she's hurt. He said, Who? I said Laurie. He said, What are you talking about? He had me by the shoulder, shaking me really hard. And I said, She's hurt! She's hurt! I said Tabbi stabbed her. Do you want me to say what he said?"

"Yeah."

"He said, Oh, fuck! And then he took me down to the bottom of the steps and he told me to sit down where the landing is, down on the first part of the steps, and he jumped up the stairs; like he took three or four steps at a time. He ran up the steps in like three leaps. And then he went—I guess he went in, because I heard him go ugh! Really loud like that. Then I heard, you fuck'n bitch! That's what he said. And then I thought, Oh my God! Tabbi stabbed him, because I heard him yell that. He said your ass is done now, bitch.

"And then I heard Laurie. She said, I'm sorry! I'm sorry! I'm sorry! I heard this thump and the front door slammed and then I was waiting down there—I don't know how long I was down there—and Lawrence came. He came flying down the steps. He ran down three at a time again. He took the steps in three leaps. He said, I'm going to get the car.

"And then I looked up like a split second later. Tabbi was there and she had, like, red streaks all over her jeans and she had the knife in her hand and her face was all twisted up and her face was like twitching, and she was staring at me, staring right at me, but it was like she was looking through me. She had the knife in her hand and she started down the steps and moving the knife in her hand, back and forth.

"She was coming toward me and everything. I started

to back away . . . I was half like walking and running.
I kept backing away from her. I heard Lawrence yell,
Tabbi! Get her! I took off. I don't know which way I
went. I just took off and so I got to this one part where
it was, like, really steep and she almost caught up to
me. She was a couple inches behind me, because I was
afraid I was going to fall."

"When Lawrence yelled, 'Tabbi, get her,' do you think
he meant to get her with a knife?"

"I wasn't sure."

"Go ahead."

"I was running away from her. I ended up in somebody's backyard. It was a cream house with blue shutters, I think. I ran down along the road and Lawrence
came flying out of The Oaks. He came flying out of the
car and peeled out and everything. I heard it. And then
I saw the car, and Tabbi and I got to the car at the
same time; and I had to go around the front of the car,
so she got in a second before I did, and Lawrence, he
peeled out and turned around right in the middle of
the road and he started going out. He was saying, Oh,
shit! Oh, shit! I said, What's wrong? He said he was
coming out of The Oaks and he passed Hazel Show and
she looked right at him. We got right out to the intersection at East Towne Mall. He said, Duck your fuck'n
head. I said, What? He grabbed my head by the back
of my neck and he pushed my head down on my lap
like that," she said, pushing her head down from the
back.

"He held my head down. We were driving. He held
it down for about ten seconds. I said, What did you do
that for? He said it was Laurie's school bus that was
there. He said it was her school bus. We were driving
down the road and it was like ten seconds later I noticed

this smell. It was like this horrible smell. It was making me gag.

"Tabbi was in the backseat and she kept saying, If you tell, I'm going to kill you. If you tell, I'm going to kill you. We were driving home and Lawrence kept saying, Oh, shit! Oh, shit! The whole time. He took his jergo and his flannel shirt and pulled it up over his face, because I saw him go like this. I think he smelled that smell and Tabbi was telling us about this dream that she had. It was making me sicker. We drove the whole way home and she was telling us about this dream that she had the night before.

"She was sitting in the back and she was saying her stepfather, she said that he was impotent and she said in her dream her and her mom decided to cut off his genitals and that's what they did. This was this dream she was telling us on the way home. She said that after they did that, that they just decided to cut them up and put them down the garbage disposal. She went into detail and it was making me sick and I was gagging.

"When we got to the house, we pulled in the driveway and Tabbi went in. I followed her out to the kitchen and she started taking off all her clothes and put them in a trash can. I said, What are you doing? You can't put those clothes in my trash can. I went into the living room and said, Lawrence, do something. Tabbi is putting the clothes in the trash can. He started to walk out to the kitchen. I said, She doesn't have any clothes on, don't go out there.

"Then I came back in the living room. Lawrence was in there. He took off his sweatpants and all over his knees there was blood, like matted on his knees and into the hairs of his leg, and I started shaking and I said, How did you get that on you like that? And he wouldn't answer me. And then he—Tabbi was in the bathroom and he took off the rest of his clothes and went out to the kitchen and I heard the garbage bag rustle. He came back in. I said, What happened in there? He said, Tabbi killed her. I said, Huh-uh! He said, Yes, she did. I said, How come you didn't stop her? He said, I couldn't do anything about it. I said, You mean you couldn't stop her? He said no. I said, Oh!

"And then he was just telling me Tabbi was hitting her all over the place and stabbing her and everything and he couldn't do anything about it. And Tabbi came out of the bathroom and she was all dripping wet. She had her hair, like, all down in her face and she had on Lawrence's bathrobe and she came out and said I'm sorry. And she like tried to hug me and I pushed her away. I said, Don't touch me! And then Lawrence said to Tabbi, You are so goddamn stupid. He said, I didn't tell you to kill her, like that. She said, You were choking her.

"And then they started arguing, fighting really bad, and she said, You were choking her. He said, What the hell would you do if someone kicked you in the nuts? That hurt. They were arguing and fighting, blaming each other, saying it was each other's fault and everything. Then Lawrence just finally—he, like, yelled really loud and grabbed Tabbi up by the arm and me by the arm and he said, Get the hell back to that bathroom! Put cover-up on her scratches right now! I said, You can't put cover-up on her scratches. That's not going to work. He said you cover up cuts on your face all the time.

"We went to the bathroom and her eyes were watery and she said it burned. I said, Tabbi, you didn't kill her, did you? She said, I think I did. I said, Well, then, she's not dead, maybe, right? She said, No, she's dead, but I'm not sure if I am the one who did it. I said, What do you mean? She said, Lawrence choked her, because she kicked him in the nuts.

"I said, Was she okay or not? And she goes, No. She, like, laid there after he did that. I said maybe she wasn't dead and she said yes, she was. I said, How do you know that? She said that after Lawrence choked her, she said she stabbed Laurie in the leg and she said Laurie didn't move, she just laid there. She said she didn't even flinch. And I said to her, What do you mean you stabbed her in the leg? She said not really stab her, I kind of just hit her. I said, Did it cut her? And she said yeah. Then I said, Well, you guys didn't really kill her. She said, Yeah, I'm telling you, I think we did. And then I went out to the living room and Lawrence started fighting with Tabbi. He said, You can't go to school like that, you have to make up some story. Your face looks horrible.

"They started fighting. He said, You have to throw away your Dolphins jacket. She said, No, I'm not throwing that away, that's my favorite. Then he said, You have to throw away your sweatshirt. She said, No, I'm going to turn it inside out and wear it to school. He said you have to throw this away, you have to throw that away and she was yelling back at him. He told her to go back and get dressed and she did.

"We took her to school. On the way to school we kind of made up like a start of a story. We said that we were at McDonald's for breakfast and we got in a fight with two Puerto Rican girls and that's where she was going to say she got the scratches from. She said yeah, that sounds good because she had written her mom a note saying she was going to go to McDonald's and she said that sounds good. So we dropped her off at school.

"The second she got out of the car, Lawrence said, I'm going to go to jail. And I just looked at him and he goes, You have to cover up for me, and I said to him, I said, I can't do that. I can't cover up for you like that. He said, Yes, you can. You have to. I'll go to prison for my whole life. I'll get raped. And he said, You are a woman, you are pregnant, you wouldn't get much time. I said, No, Lawrence, I can't do that. I think you should tell what happened. I said if you said that you really couldn't stop Tabbi, like you said, maybe you won't get in much trouble. And he was crying and he was saying, No, no, no, I couldn't stop her. I couldn't do anything about it, but they will never believe it, because they said I raped her and all that stuff. I'll get life in prison. I won't be with you. You won't have any-one to take care of you and the baby. He was crying and everything, really hysterical. He said, I love you. I said okay. I said I'm not going to say that I did what you did, but I wouldn't tell what you did, and he said okay."

They washed the clothes, put them wet into a garbage bag, and then threw them into a Dumpster behind Kmart. Later she threw a bag containing the rope, the knife, two pairs of sunglasses, the hats, and Lawrence's Pony high-top tennis shoes into the Susquehanna River. The bag was weighted down with rocks.

In the parking lot of the Kmart, Lambert looked into the bag, saw red and threw up, she said. Yunkin told her to throw the bag into the river. After protesting that he could throw it farther, she got out and tossed the bag, sending it only about five feet from shore. Yunkin cursed, pulled off his shoes and socks, and headed for the water. "You're going to drown," she cried. He was mad. He had to get the bag into deeper water. But then a truck drove toward them from a nearby marina.

"Get in the car! Get in the car!" he screamed.

"What?" Lambert said.

"Somebody is watching us."

They jumped in the car, sped off, and left the bag about five feet from the water's edge.

Lambert agreed with Yunkin's story that they went back to their house, watched television, and she said he ate, she didn't. She couldn't. They went to get her paycheck, but her story differed slightly from Yunkin's. She contended that he insisted he go in with her.

"I said, You can't go down there, it's employees only. He said, I just don't trust you. I'm afraid you'll call somebody. I said, No, I won't. He said, No, I'm going down with you. And he walked into the employees-only section with me and we went down and got my paycheck. He was holding on to my arm the whole time.

"We came back out, got back in the car, and then he said that we were going to stop on the Lincoln Highway down past the Steamboat Motel, the one that looks like a steamboat. There is a gas station and a pay phone there. It was about a half mile down the road from that, I think, past it. I got out of the car. He said, Call my grandmother, make sure she's home, because we were supposed to be there way before this. I said, Okay. And then he said, Wait a minute! He got out of the car and came with me. He held on to my arm and dialed the number. He said, Talk to my grandmother. I asked her if she was going to be there. She said yes, come on down and all this stuff. I hung up the phone. Then we went down to his grandmother's. We drove down and we got down there and she said, she asked if I wanted anything to eat and I said no. She's always telling me I'm too skinny and I should eat."

"Let me ask you a question. Lawrence testified last week—I don't remember the exact words—but you got an artificial tree then. You had gone for a rope, and if all this was for going tree hunting, why did you get an artificial tree?"

"Because when we got to his grandmother's, he was in a good mood. He acted like nothing was wrong. I told him I was sick, I didn't feel like getting a Christmas tree. His grandmother asked what was wrong. I said I don't feel like going for a Christmas tree. She went into her shed and pulled out an artificial Christmas tree. She said, Why don't you use this? I said, Okay, I don't care anymore, and we put that in the back of the car."

They returned home and Yunkin realized his sweatshirt was not in the clothing bag that had been thrown in the Dumpster. He said they had to throw it out, along with the two other knives that matched the murder weapon. Before they left, their landlord came to the door and said there was an emergency phone call from Yunkin's parents.

"I didn't worry about that, because Lawrence's parents were always trying to find out where we lived," Lambert testified. "They wanted me to get an abortion. They said Lawrence was too young to take care of the baby. We didn't worry about it. We had no intentions of telling them where we lived."

"How did they get your number?"

"I have no idea how they got his number."

Lawrence laughed it off, but went to make a phone call. Lambert said she did not know who he called. When he returned, they left to throw out the other items. They took them to a spot near the river.

"He said, Get out and throw the knives, and I said, Where? There was a bank that went like straight up. I said, I can't throw them way up there. He said, Well, just throw them as good as you can. I threw them and they didn't make it the whole way to the top of the bank, they landed like, I don't know, ten feet down from the top and they slid and then they stopped and caught on a rock and I got back in the car then."

They drove to Buck's house.

"We were sitting—we sat on the couch and Tabbi sat on the chair and we made up this story, like we all added everything to it. I said how about this. Tabbi said how about this. Lawrence said how about this. He kind of made it all together, like into one story."

Buck had already told everyone at school the story about the Puerto Rican girls.

They picked up Buck's check at Weis Market.

"She came out of Weis's and she got in the car and she looked at me and she said, Michelle, I told you she's dead. I said, What are you talking about? She said, There is a girl in there that just showed me the paper. And I said, What do you mean? She goes, It's on the front page. I said, Huh-uh. She said, Yeah, it is. And then she started, her and Lawrence, I think Tabbi started it. But she started singing that song from *The Wizard of Oz* about saying the wicked bitch is dead. Lawrence started singing it and they started laughing hysterically. After they stopped laughing, she said, How about the bitch this morning? She was making all these screwy sounds."

They went to JCPenney at Park City to pick up the leather jacket that Lambert was giving Yunkin for Christmas. She said she noticed they were skittish and would not leave her alone. One of them was always with her.

Then they drove to the bowling alley, twelve miles away. Yunkin got a call there from Vinnie Orsi. Yunkin told Lambert he thought Orsi was drunk.

"I said, What are you talking about? He just said, Don't worry about it, just remember whatever happens, it's me and you. Cover up for me. Me and you can be together, and he said, Fuck Tabbi. That's exactly what he said."

A few minutes later, they were arrested. Lambert acknowledged she lied to police when she told them the story about the Puerto Rican girls. She said she did it to protect the man she loved. She also was scared for herself. She didn't think the police would believe her, because after all she and Laurie did have fights; they couldn't stand each other, Lambert said.

"I lied for myself because I didn't want to go to jail; I was having a baby," she said.

Lambert said she agreed to cover for Yunkin until she heard he had made a deal with the district attorney. She wrote him letters in prison telling him so. She wanted to reassure him that she "wasn't going to chicken out." She said she was also afraid he would implicate her.

"Why would you keep covering up for him?" Shirk asked.

"Because he told me—he said—I told him I wasn't going to say that I did what he did, but I said I would keep my mouth shut about his part in it. He said, Okay, if you cover up for me; he said, I'll tell, you know, I'll tell them what happened, that you didn't do anything to her. He said, I'll tell the truth and we can both get out and be together and raise the baby."

She believed him, she said. She believed him when he said the court would not give her much time because she was pregnant.

In January or February, after she heard about Yunkin's possible deal, she sent him the list of twenty-nine questions, she said.

"Did you change anything on it after you sent it?" Shirk asked her.

"No."

"When it came back to you—I'm not going to go through each line or anything—but did you make any changes on this when it was returned to you?"

"No."

"What did you do with it?"

"I put it in my personal box in the prison, inside of an envelope, and I licked the envelope shut and kept it there."

"Did you keep it there the whole time?"

"No. I took it down and hid it in the law library. There is a little space behind a bookshelf that I hid it down there."

"And, obviously, eventually you gave it to me."

"Yes."

"Do you remember when you gave it to me?"

"About two and a half months ago, maybe three."

"A long time after you had it?"

"Yes."

"There is one thing in there I want to ask you about. I believe there is an indication in there that Lawrence held Tabbi down."

"No, held Laurie down."

"I'm sorry. Lawrence held Laurie down—"

"Yes."

"—while Tabbi cut her."

"Yes."

"Did he tell you that?"

"He said that he choked her; and then he didn't tell me that he held her down, but when they were arguing, she was screaming something about why were you holding her down then? They were yelling really loud."

"So from an argument they were having, you gained that information."

"I kind of figured it out, yeah."

"Lisa, did you go to that apartment to kill her?"

"No."

"Did you go there even to go into the apartment?"

"No."

"Did you have anything to do with stabbing her?"

"No."

"Did you have anything to do with cutting her throat?"

"No."

"No further questions."

Kenneff stood for cross-examination. He began by asking her to retrace her steps after she left the Shows' condominium that morning. She said she couldn't remember exactly; it felt as if she were running all over the place, but she ended up in someone's backyard. She remembered a steep hill. She remembered stepping in a creek. She tripped over a "crunched-down" fence. She was running. Buck was behind her. Yunkin roared up in his car—"spun out," Lambert said—and picked them up.

"Another thing I didn't quite understand," Kenneff said. "When you went in, and Laurie and Tabbi are on the floor inside Mrs. Show's apartment, and you said, 'Stop, Tabbi! Don't hurt her! [We're] still going to cut the hair.' Is that what you were going to do?"

"I didn't say that to her. I put my hand on her arm right here and I said, 'Tabbi, stop it! She's pregnant!' That's when she brought her elbow back."

"But at that point, you thought you could do your prank, cut her hair and get out."

"I wasn't going to cut her hair, once we were there."

"You know now that's second-degree murder if you do something inside the house. If it was your intent to do something inside the house, you know that."

"It was never our intent to do anything inside the house."

"You are saying today it was never your intent to do that inside the house, because today you've been hanging out in the law library, you know that's second-degree murder, don't you? You didn't know it the night you talked to Trooper Solt, did you?" Kenneff pressed.

Lambert did not respond.

"Answer my question," the assistant district attorney demanded. "Did you know the definition of second-degree murder the night you talked to Trooper Solt?"

"No."

"And you know today what an accomplice is, don't you?"

"Yes."

"The night you talked to Trooper Solt, did you know what an accomplice was?"

"No."

"I saw you were crying a little bit, or a few tears in your eyes, as you were talking. Do you feel sorry about what happened to Laurie?"

"Yes."

"When is the first time you recall feeling sorry for what happened to Laurie?"

"When I saw that in the bedroom, even in the hallway, when Tabbi was hitting her and stuff."

"Do you think that's the first time you started crying for Laurie?"

"I wasn't crying while I was in the house, but I was upset the whole day; I couldn't eat."

"So you weren't crying when you were in the house. You described how you came out of the house and sat down on the steps. Is that what you are saying?"

"No."

"I show you Commonwealth Exhibit Number Twenty-six. Why don't you show us in that picture where you were sitting waiting for Tabbi to come back out?"

Lambert took the picture, looked at it, and said, "I was sitting— Right after you go down the first steps, I was sitting right there, like in the corner."

"Were you crying there?"

"I was shaking; I was upset."

"Were you sobbing there?"

"I was just shaking," Lambert said. "I didn't know what was going on, but I thought Lawrence was going to help. When he went in there and everything, I thought everything was going to be all right."

"Now you started to run. Were you crying while you were running?"

"I was afraid of Tabbi. I don't remember if I was crying, I was just running."

"How about when you got in the car? Were you crying when you got in the car?"

"I was crying on the way home. I kept gagging because I kept smelling that smell."

"How about when you went to pick up your paycheck that day, were you crying when you went to pick up your paycheck?"

"No."

"You weren't crying about Laurie then."

"I wasn't sure what had happened. They kept telling me she was dead. Lawrence was with me."

"Were you crying down at Lawrence's grandparents?"

"No, but I couldn't eat, and I didn't want to go get the Christmas tree because I was upset."

"But you weren't crying."

"No."

"You didn't grab Lawrence's grandparents and say something terrible happened and cried."

"No, Lawrence was with me."

"You weren't that concerned about Laurie then."

"I wasn't sure what happened."

"How about when you went to Park City? Were you crying for Laurie while you were walking around Park City, finishing your Christmas shopping?"

"He wasn't doing Christmas shopping. Lawrence said he wanted to get his jacket."

"For Christmas, whatever it was for. But you weren't crying."

"No."

"When you went to the bowling alley and you were with your friends, were you crying there with your friends?"

"No. I wasn't sure what happened. After Tabbi came out of Weis Market and her and Lawrence were joking around about it, I didn't think they did it, because they were joking around about it."

"So you did no crying that day except for a little while coming back in the car from Laurie's. You watched TV, got your paycheck, went out with your friends just like you did most Friday nights, is that right?"

"Yes."

"Let me ask you this question. Who are you crying for today? Are you crying for Laurie or for yourself?"

"Crying for Laurie."

"Sure. You said something interesting. You didn't know Laurie was dead and that's why you weren't as upset on the twentieth, is that right?"

"I wasn't sure."

"Let's see what you did know," Kenneff said, sarcasm barely hidden. "You heard that hissing sound. You knew her lung was punctured, didn't you?"

"I didn't know that's what that was."

"You knew her sweatshirt was soaked with blood, didn't you?"

"Yes."

"You knew that she was so fearful for what was happening to her that she begged you to take her with you."

"Yes."

"You knew, according to your story, when you got back, that Yunkin and Buck both told you that they did horrible things in there to Laurie. You knew she was dead."

"I didn't know she was dead; I wasn't sure."

"Did you go and get a paper that day?"

"No."

"You watched TV that day. Did you turn on the news to see if it was on the news?"

"I watched *Little House on the Prairie* and *Matlock.*"

"Then you got to the Weis Market sometime that night, is that right?"

"Yes."

"And Tabitha Buck comes out and says it's in the paper, Laurie is dead."

"Yes."

"You heard her say that, didn't you?"

"Yes."

"That I guess confirms your fears, is that right?"

"I wasn't sure then, because right after that, that's when she started singing that song about the wicked bitch and they started laughing about it, her and Lawrence both."

"You weren't sure. You knew she was seriously injured; you still weren't sure she was dead."

"No."

"You knew she could hardly breathe when you left."

"Yeah, her face was all red."

"At one time you said she couldn't hardly breathe, is that correct?"

"Yes."

"You knew she had been hit on the head with a knife a number of times, didn't you?"

"I didn't see that, but whenever Tabbi was going at her hair, I wasn't sure, because I couldn't see that very good."

"You knew she was in desperate shape."

"But when Lawrence said he passed Hazel Show, that's what I thought the whole day: Her mom would get home and take care of her."

"Now your story was about a desperate attempt to try to save Laurie's life by pulling her out of that apartment, is that right?"

"I was trying to get her and Tabbi away from each other."

"You were trying to pull Laurie down the hallway of the apartment and out the door of the apartment."

"Yes."

"You would have continued to try to do that if you weren't stopped by Tabbi, isn't that right?"

"I had her by the wrist and I felt her wrestling like this out of my hand."

"You were trying to save her."

"I was trying to get her out of the apartment."

"For what purpose?"

"That was all that was in my head, get her out of the apartment."

"To save her?"

"I was just scared and I wanted to get her away from Tabbi. I tried— Tabbi hit me in the mouth, I was yelling at her. She wouldn't listen to me. The only thing I could think of was get her out of the apartment."

"You went to all those efforts, walked down the steps and sat there on the steps."

"No. I banged into Lawrence and I hit my head on

the wall. He took me down the steps and told me to sit there, and ran back up."

"You didn't knock upon anybody's door in the apartment complex."

"No, because I thought Lawrence was going to help her."

"You ran through that apartment complex. Didn't you knock on any doors?"

"No."

"And at that point, you knew Lawrence wasn't helping her. Everybody is out of the apartment at that point."

"I wasn't sure. I was confused."

"Lawrence is out of the apartment, is that correct?"

"Yes."

"Tabbi is out of the apartment, is that correct?"

"Yes."

"And you are running through the apartment complex, is that correct?"

"Yes."

"Who's upstairs helping Laurie?"

"I thought when Lawrence went in he helped her."

"Who is upstairs at that point helping Laurie?"

"Nobody."

"Tell us how many apartments you ran by."

"I don't know."

"As you went through that apartment complex, estimate for us."

"I don't know which way I went."

"Did you pass any apartments?"

"Just the sides of the buildings."

"Did you knock on any door?"

"No."

"Mr. Fry sees you running down that hill. Did you run up to Mr. Fry and say help a girl that's seriously injured? Her sweatshirt was soaked with blood when I left."

"No; I did not see a person anywhere."

"He saw you."

Lambert just sat there, speechless.

Kenneff asked her about talking with Sergeant Harnish that night. He asked her to recount the day's events.

"What did you think he was asking you those questions for?"

"I thought that Hazel had gotten home and helped Laurie, and I thought that Laurie had said Lawrence and Tabbi did something, or Tabbi did something, and I thought we were getting in trouble for that."

"Did you hear Sergeant Harnish say it looked like a thunderbolt had struck you when they said Laurie was dead?"

"Yes. Yes."

"That was an act, wasn't it?"

"No. I didn't believe she was dead. It was like the whole day it wasn't real. The things they kept telling me, the way they were joking around, they weren't upset about it."

"It didn't sound to me you were very upset about what happened to Laurie."

"The whole day I couldn't even eat."

"You watched TV, got your paycheck, went to Park City, went to the bowling alley."

"Lawrence said where we would go and I went where he said."

The prosecutor asked her about being afraid of Buck because she had the knife. But it was Lambert's knife and Lambert was the one who got rid of it, he said. Lambert considered Buck a "psycho" with a scary laugh, and she was afraid she'd do something to hurt her baby.

"You are at the bowling alley," Kenneff said. "Do you remember Trooper Duby, who testified?"

"Yes."

"Trooper Duby walks up to you and says, 'Are you Lisa?' Do you remember that?"

"Yes."

"And Trooper Duby then turns and sees Tabitha standing there with this big scratch and he said, 'Where did you get that scratch?' And who answers?"

"I did."

"Were you fearful for your baby then?"

"Yes."

"And wasn't that the perfect way to allay the fear for that baby? Say to Trooper Duby, 'Get that psycho away from me!' Wasn't that the way to protect your baby?"

"No, that's not what I said."

"That's not what you said. My question is, wasn't that the way to protect your baby?"

"I'm not sure what you mean."

"You are fearful of this psycho who you've been traveling around with from her house to Weis Market to Park City. You walk around Park City with her. You go to the bowling alley with her. You are fearful of the psycho who is going to kill you and thereby kill your baby. Wasn't that your greatest fear?"

"When Lawrence was with me—"

"Was that your greatest fear?"

"No, because Lawrence was with me. I was not afraid of her when Lawrence was with me, except for when she had the knife, then I was."

"Let me read you this and ask you if this is what you wrote to Mr. Yunkin: 'I was so scared with her laughing in the backseat like she did. I kept thinking, oh my God! She's going to stab us. My baby's going to die. Oh my God! We're going to be stabbed.' "

"Yes, I wrote that."

"And yet you rode around with her in the backseat."

"When she had the knife, that's when I was afraid."

"But you didn't know if she had a knife with her when you picked her up at seven o'clock at her house, did you?"

"I didn't think about that."

"You didn't think about it?"

"No, it never crossed my mind."

"You never thought about your baby's life?"

"It never crossed my mind that she would have a knife again," Lambert said, her cool in tact despite the barrage of questions.

"You thought she was a psycho. Didn't you think a psycho would go and get another knife?"

"I thought Lawrence would protect me."

"Just like he protected Laurie, right?" Kenneff spouted, and looked down at his notes. Lambert did not respond.

He asked her if she had blood on her body when she got into the car.

"I had it right here," she said, indicating her hand, "from when I picked her up, and after Tabbi had stabbed her, it got on my hand; and then I had it right here. And then whenever Lawrence was shaking me, my hands got put together and I had it here, too."

"Do you remember writing this to Lawrence: 'Then you saw the blood when I got in the car. I knew if I told you that she was the only one who hurt Laurie, you would make me turn her in. But I was afraid if I did, that the police would lock me in jail and never let me out because I had blood on my shirt.'? Do you remember writing that to Lawrence?"

"Yes, but that was a lie," she said. "I was telling him what he was supposed to say."

"You were telling him what he was supposed to say?"

"Yes, because I was covering up for him."

"Do you remember writing to him about a conversation that you had in the trailer that day? Do you remember writing to him about that?"

"Yes."

"And do you remember Mr. Yunkin, when he testified, he said that he didn't really know what happened until you got back to the trailer and he confronted you in the trailer and asked you what happened and you told him words to the effect that something happened in there? We didn't know what to do. Tabbi said let's slit her throat and put her out of her misery and we both agreed. Do you remember Mr. Yunkin testifying to that?"

"Yes, I remember him saying that."

"You are telling us that's not the truth, is that correct?"

"Yes, that's not the truth."

"Do you remember writing this to Mr. Yunkin: 'I was so scared that Friday, and I wanted to keep you from being more afraid than you already were of Tabbi; that I don't know what the heck I said to you. I remember you asking me what happened at our house but I can't remember what I said. I didn't tell you what happened, the truth, because I didn't want you to be involved in that horrible mess.'? Do you recall writing that to Mr. Yunkin?"

"Yes."

"I don't quite understand how writing that lie fits into this cover-up. It sounds to me that that fits into Mr. Yunkin's story, that you didn't remember what lie you told him in the trailer that Friday."

"No, I was telling him—I was reassuring him when I wrote him that, and I was also telling him that whatever he wanted to say was fine, because I didn't have any suggestion as to what he could say, 'cause he kept writing and saying he thought he was going to have to testify something."

"How about this letter that you wrote to Mr. Yunkin? Defendant's Five, I think it is. This is kind of a peculiar-looking document, wouldn't you agree?"

"Yes."

"I saw a lot of your letters that you wrote to Mr. Yunkin. Were any of them written in a similar fashion?"

"I'm not sure."

"Do any of them have—written in in black—do any of them have '4 U' squeezed in at the end?"

"When I forget things, I put that little mark and write them overtop."

"And this document starts out: 'Listen to me. I guess I won't tell on you but please answer these questions honestly. There are some things I need to know if I'm supposed to take the blame for what you did.' Is that what it says at the top?"

"Yes."

"So you were asking him for information that you could say in court to take the blame for him, is that correct?"

"I was telling him I needed to know things, if he wanted me to cover up for him, but when I said take the blame, I did not mean I was going to take the blame for what he did, I only meant I was going to cover up."

"There were things you needed to know."

"Yes."

"Look in this letter, the questions that ask for things you need to know to cover up for Mr. Yunkin."

Lambert looked at the questionnaire and said, "Number two, weren't you ever afraid of Tabbi?"

"You knew already he was afraid of Tabbi. You both

said you were terrified of Tabbi with her in the backseat
laughing and having the knife. You already knew that.
You didn't need to know that to cover up for him, did
you?"

Lambert did not respond.

"Did you?" Kenneff pressed.

"I wanted to know if I was supposed to say if he was
afraid of her."

"It wasn't a thing you needed to know because you
already knew it, is that correct?"

"Yes."

"Okay. Where in the letter are the things you needed
to know to cover up for Lawrence?"

She looked down again at the paper.

"Number eleven," she said.

"What's number eleven say?"

"Were your sweatpants and flannel that you got blood
on, did you Dumpster them?"

"You knew that already, didn't you?"

"I wasn't sure."

"Didn't you testify here today that you saw him put
them in the bag in the kitchen where Tabbi's clothes
were?"

"I was confused."

"You weren't confused today, were you?"

"I had already read this letter; that's why I realized
what had happened. I wasn't sure if the clothes went in
the river and the other bag went in the Dumpster. I
wasn't sure which went where."

"What other things did you need to know to cover
up for him?"

"Number seventeen. Do you promise not to beat my
face up anymore if I lie for you? That's why I had said
I hated you. Will you be nice like on our first date?"

"Is that a thing? That's not a thing."

"Yes."

"Is it?"

"I wasn't going to cover up for him if he was going to keep on beating me like that."

"That isn't a thing. The letter starts out, the things I need to know."

"That's something I felt I needed to know."

"That was something you felt you needed to know. That's a thought. What are the physical things, the facts you needed to know?"

Lambert again looked at the pages.

"The second part of twenty-nine. Should I still cover up that you helped Tabbi kill Laurie? Are you absolutely sure?"

"Is that a thing you needed to know?"

"Yes."

"Is that a fact you needed to know?"

"No."

"So you write out thirty questions, and there is only one fact in there that you needed to know, is that correct?"

"Things is a generalization. I did not mean specific facts. I meant things that I needed to know for my feelings."

"There were a lot of things, though, facts that you could've asked him that you needed to know, weren't there?"

"Not really."

"Let's try one. How did the rope get around her neck?"

"He said that he choked her and Tabbi yelled at him, and she told me that back in the bathroom. That's what I figured, choked."

"So you wanted to know exact things you needed to know to cover up for him. You don't know how the rope got around her neck, but you don't ask him about it."

"The police had told me there was a rope around her neck and he said he choked her, so naturally, I made that assumption."

"Didn't you think that was an important fact for you to continue to cover up?"

"I had already assumed that."

"Another fact you didn't know was how her throat got slit, is that correct?"

"Lawrence told me Tabbi hacked her up, and Tabbi said in the bathroom that she killed her."

"You didn't believe that."

"This is after the police told me what had happened."

"Do you think in order to help Mr. Yunkin cover up, a thing you needed to know, a fact you needed to know was how her throat got slit?"

"Tabbi said in the bathroom that she had killed her; she said all Lawrence did was choke her."

"Your answer to my question is, that wasn't a fact you needed to know."

"No."

"How the rope got around her neck wasn't a fact you needed to know."

"No."

"How about where was her body when you left? Is that a fact you needed to know?"

"No, because I had already told him in the car I was not going to say that I did what he did. I was only going to not mention his involvement. I told him I was going to stick to the truth and I was just going to not mention his involvement."

"The statement to Trooper Solt, you said, 'When we walked up, I had on a jergo. It's a straw thing with a hood on it. I have it in my closet.' Was that the truth?"

"Yes, it was in my closet."

"I thought you told us it was thrown away."

"There were two jergos: One was gray and white. Lawrence bought that for him[self], but he shrunk it one time and he had to give it to me, and I had to give him my big blue and green one."

"The jergo you had on wasn't thrown away?"

"It was the little gray and white one that was hanging up in my closet."

"Did you get any blood on that?"

"No."

"You dragged Laurie and you didn't get any blood on the jergo?"

"No, I had her by the wrists."

"A number of people testified here, the Gladfelters, they said a half a dozen times you threatened to kill Laurie. Was their testimony correct?"

"Yes."

"Laura Thomas said you threatened to kill Laurie."

"Yes."

"Mr. Thomas said you threatened to kill Laurie."

"I don't recall ever meeting Mr. Thomas."

"He said he overheard you threatening to kill Laurie. Miss Warner said she heard you threaten to kill Laurie, is that correct?"

"Yes."

"And they all said they heard you say you want to slit her throat, but that's incorrect?"

"They said the conversation was at Laura Thomas's house. I do not recall ever being at her house, and I do not know where her house is."

"So Mr. Thomas isn't telling the truth when he said you were even at the house."

"I'm not saying he isn't telling the truth, I don't recall being there."

Kenneff pressed on, asking her about the confrontation with Laurie at East Towne Mall on November 22 and about Laurie going to the police. He asked her again about the plan hatched the day before Laurie died. She went through each, point by point, not wavering from her original testimony. They were going to take Laurie to the gazebo, tie her hands and feet together, and cut her hair.

"How was that going to help Lawrence with his rape charges?" Kenneff asked.

"He was going to beat up Brad. Once he beat up Brad—he said once he beat up Brad, that Laurie would be scared and Laurie wouldn't say anything, because he was going to beat up Brad really bad."

"You knew Laurie had gone to the police."

"Yes."

"What did you think the police were going to do after you left Laurie tied up at that gazebo with her hair cut?"

"We weren't going to leave her tied up, we were going to untie her hands and feet."

"Then what?"

"Run to the car."

"What did you think the police were going to do when you tied up Laurie, cut her hair?"

"I didn't think about that."

"You knew the police had been involved, you knew that Lawrence was worried about a rape charge; according to Leon Lamparter, you were worried about a charge against you, and you didn't think anything was going to happen?"

"No, because the supposed rape, the rape charges, when she started—"

"I'm not talking about the rape, I'm talking about the assault you were going to commit on her on December twentieth down at the gazebo. You thought everybody was going to let that go away?"

"The fight we had a month ago, nothing happened about that. The supposed rape was six months before that. Nothing happened about that. I just assumed nothing was going to happen."

"You were going to make matters worse and have another assault. Didn't you think people were going to worry about that?"

"No."

"Now you said you are smart enough since you've been arrested to figure out the felony murder rule, you are smart enough to figure out what an accomplice is, and you didn't think anything was going to happen to you if you cut off her hair and tied her up at that gazebo?"

"I didn't think about that, it was just a prank."

He asked about the morning, the course of events as she woke up and went to Buck's house.

"Did you discuss what your opportunity was to do something while Mrs. Show wasn't around?"

"No. All I said to Tabbi was, you need to—you made the call and everything for nothing. She said I can't change it now, it doesn't matter anyway."

"Did you expect other people to be at the bus stop?"

"No. Tabbi said that Laurie was the only one that was there. She rode Laurie's bus and said Laurie got on alone."

"So at this point, now, because the plan has changed, it doesn't matter whether Mrs. Show is home or not."

"No."

"Weren't you concerned that Mrs. Show might come by while you were cutting her [Laurie's] hair and tying her up at the gazebo?"

"No."

"That thought never passed your mind. You told her to go to the high school, junior high, to an appointment that somebody wasn't going to keep, and she's going to have to be coming back. Weren't you concerned that maybe she would see you walking down the street?"

"No, because cutting the hair, we assumed, would only take, like, three to five minutes, and then we were going to untie her and run."

"Weren't you concerned, first of all, that Mrs. Show might come back while you were walking Laurie down the street."

"No, that never crossed my mind."

"What did you think Mrs. Show would've done if she saw you and Lawrence walking down the street with Laurie?"

"Probably get out and ask what the heck was going on."

"You knew Mrs. Show was very upset with you, didn't you?"

"Yes."

"You knew that Mrs. Show wasn't just going to get out of the car and [ask] why are you walking down the road with Laurie?"

"I didn't know what she would've done."

"What do you think Mrs. Show would've done if she saw you down at the gazebo cutting her hair?"

"I have no idea."

"You know exactly what she would've done."

"It never crossed my mind."

"She would have had the police there as quick as she could, wouldn't she?"

"I have no idea."

Kenneff continued pressing for answers. Hazel Show continued locking her eyes on Lambert. She might be Lisa now, Hazel thought, a sweet and innocent girl, but she believed it to be fake. To her, she'd always be Michelle; she'd always lack a soul.

Lambert recounted the morning scene with Yunkin coughing and going to McDonald's. She showed on a map where she thought she walked, through the woods and into the complex.

"What happens when you get to the condominiums?" Kenneff asked.

"We were standing outside. Tabbi was stomping her feet and she said, 'God, it's fuck'n cold out here!' Then she said, 'I'm not standing out here like this. I'm going to go up and see if she is ready to come out yet.' "

"Did you tell that to Trooper Solt?"

"No."

"Why didn't you tell that to Trooper Solt?"

"Because I didn't know how to fit in everything that happened and still cover up for Lawrence."

"How does it help you in covering up for Lawrence to tell a lie about what happened at that moment?"

"Well, when we were standing outside and that, I told him that we were going to go up to the door and talk to her. That's what I told Trooper Solt, that's what I told him."

"Why didn't you tell Trooper Solt that you were waiting outside for her to come out and talk to her?"

"I would have to tell that we were going to walk her down to the gazebo and cut her hair."

"No, you wouldn't have to tell him that."

"Like I told you, we were going there to talk to her when we were standing outside and Tabbi was stomping her feet."

"You could have told that to Trooper Solt without revealing anything about Mr. Yunkin, couldn't you?"

"I wanted a story that would cover up for what he did."

"So you make up a lie to tell Trooper Solt that isn't part of the cover-up."

"I didn't make up a lie before that, I just said everything I could say that was the truth without implicating Lawrence."

"Right, and you could've said without implicating Lawrence that Tabbi and I were standing outside waiting for Laurie to come out to talk to her and Tabbi was stamping her feet saying, oh, boy, it's cold. You could've said that to Trooper Solt, couldn't you?"

"I didn't think about saying that."

"You didn't think about saying the truth, you thought of making up a lie."

"I didn't think about making up a lie, that's what I said."

"You didn't think about making up a lie, you just made it up. Do you do a lot of lying?"

"No."

"Your natural reaction is to—"

"I do a lot of covering up for Lawrence."

"Was it your natural reaction to make a lie up for Trooper Solt?"

"To cover up for Lawrence, yes."

"To change the story from Tabbi standing outside, stomping her feet, waiting to talk to Laurie, to Tabbi going up to knock on the door. You changed that as part of the cover-up, is that what you are saying?"

"I told him that Tabbi and I were cold and that Tabbi went up to the door. I didn't give details about what she said."

"But the time that you talked to Trooper Solt, you didn't know it was important to say you didn't intend to go into the apartment, is that right?"

"We did intend to go in there."

"When you were talking to Trooper Solt, you didn't

know that if you told Trooper Solt you intended to go into the apartment, that was a felony murder, did you?"

"I never told him we intended to go in there."

Buck went up and Lambert heard screaming. She called to Buck, "Tabbi!" No response. "Tabbi!"

"Did you say it in that voice just as you are saying now, or did you yell it?"

"I said it in that voice."

"How could somebody hear you at the top of the stairs?"

"It's not that far."

Lambert recounted the scene inside the Shows' home just as she told it the first time, almost word for word. Hazel Show would say later it seemed as if she had memorized a monologue. When Lambert got interrupted, she had to start from a certain point to regain the story line.

When she finished, Kenneff asked whether Laurie was lying on her back or front when Lambert was dragging her.

"No, she was like—she was walking, but she was stumbling all over the place, like she was dizzy or something."

"And you walked her out this door into the hallway."

"Yes."

"And down this hallway to the front door."

"Yes."

It was already past 5:00 P.M., and Kenneff had many more questions for Lambert. He asked that they adjourn for the day.

Twenty-one

Friday morning, Lambert walked back to the stand. Hazel Show, as usual, watched her every move from the back row. The mother of the slain girl locked eyes with her as soon as Lambert sat down in the brown-leather-upholstered chair.

Kenneff said he wanted to hear her story once more. Solt, the detective who interviewed Lambert the night of the murder, had not been in court the day before, and Kenneff wanted him to hear her testimony. She began with virtually the same words as before. "We were at Kmart. . . ."

Periodically Kenneff stopped her with a question. What's Duane's last name? What does he look like? Where did you hear Laurie was pregnant? Did you walk up the steps or run up the steps? How much noise was everybody making? She answered and kept moving, each time, through her version of events.

Kenneff asked her to act out how she tried to help save Laurie's life by dragging her from the room. He called on Detective Savage to come forward. Savage lay down on the floor and Lambert came down from the witness stand. She reached around the officer's arm and showed how she tried to pick Laurie up. Lambert said she saw blood and let go, and Laurie fell to the floor. Lambert fell to her knees, sort of on top of Laurie.

Kenneff handed her a knife similar to the murder weapon and asked her to show how Buck and Laurie were fighting over the knife. Tears filled Hazel Show's eyes as she watched. She twisted her handkerchief, tighter and tighter. She tried not to make a sound as she glared at Lambert. Kenneff, as Buck, held the knife handle in his fist, blade out; Lambert grabbed the blade with both hands as if to fend off an attack. Lambert said she pulled Laurie into the hallway.

"I looked back at her once and her face was a reddish purple. I think she was dizzy or something, because she was, like, stumbling all over the place."

She went outside and ran into Yunkin, who bolted up the stairs and into the apartment. She sat in the corner of the stairwell. Word for word, the same tale she told before. As hard as he tried to disorient her, Kenneff couldn't make a dent in her story.

She said Yunkin ran down the steps first; then she looked up and Buck was standing at the top of the steps. Her face was twisted and she held the knife in her hand. Lambert said she was scared and backed away, then turned and ran. Yunkin told Buck to get Lambert, and Buck complied. When Buck caught up with her at the steep hill, Buck was no longer carrying the knife, Lambert said.

She provided more detail about what happened at her house after the murder. After Buck showered, she came into the living room, where Lambert and Yunkin were sitting. Yunkin was in his underwear and had blood matted on his knees; Buck wore his robe. Buck said she was sorry and started crying. She tried to hug Lambert, but Lambert pushed her away.

Yunkin rose from the couch and walked to where Buck was sitting on a chair and said, "You stupid bitch. I didn't tell you to kill her. You didn't have to do that."

"You didn't tell me not to," she responded, and then said angrily, "You were holding her down, choking her."

"What the hell?" Yunkin said. "What would you do if someone kicked you in the nuts? It's your fault."

Buck replied, "It's your fault."

Yunkin grabbed Buck and Lambert by their arms and pushed them into the bathroom, demanding Lambert do something to hide the scratches on Buck's face. In the bathroom, Buck told Lambert she thought Laurie was dead, but she wasn't sure if she killed her or if Yunkin did.

Step by step, she recounted washing the clothes, throwing the bags of evidence away. Point by point, Kenneff hammered the lies she told Solt. Was that true? No. Was that a lie? Yes. On and on, for minutes, as Lambert admitted her lies. She said she did it to protect Yunkin, but Kenneff, exasperated, finally said, "You won't give me the answer I'm looking for: You lied to protect you."

His final question: "You don't recall or you never said anything about slitting Laurie Show's throat?"

"I never said anything about that," Lambert responded.

She stepped down from the stand and walked back to her seat.

After a brief recess, the judge and the lawyers moved into the judge's chambers. Shirk asked the judge to declare a mistrial because of prosecutorial misconduct. He claimed the district attorney's office withheld a statement by Yunkin that he wore a pearl earring like that found in Show's condominium and that he told them about his hooded sweatshirt being thrown away. In addition, Shirk claimed, reports of interviews police did with Hazel Show, Richard Kleinhans, and Laura Thomas were not given to the defense and that Kenneff asked two improper questions of forensic scientist Golub. Stengel denied all the motions.

After lunch, Shirk began his closing statement.

"Lisa Michelle Lambert is not guilty of murder," he said, and reviewed her testimony. Her statements since her initial one had remained constant, he said.

"She indicated: We went there, we walked around, we couldn't find the name, couldn't find the right apartment. We finally found it. We went up to it. Tabbi went up to the door. Somehow something happened at the door. Tabbi entered the apartment. I went in. When I went in, there was a struggle. The struggle moved from the hallway area to the bedroom area. I was not involved in the struggle."

No inconsistency, he said.

"Miss Lambert is a teenager, nineteen years old, probably above average intelligence. She has sat here. She hasn't been in a vacuum. She has listened to the testimony here. If she was lying and/or fabricating her testimony, it would've probably fit the evidence a lot better."

He said Lambert's story was the only one that made sense.

"She said we went there to cut hair. An expert, Mr. Golub, came here and said every tuft of hair was cut with a knife. It's consistent with prior attempts to do similar things. She indicated we didn't go there to go in. We were going to wait on her to come out for the school bus and say: Hey, can we walk down to the school bus with you? When we got down to a public area we were going to tie her up, cut her hair and embarrass her. Now the publicness of that area is the fact that the school bus was coming. What would embarrass her is those other teenagers on the school bus seeing her like that."

It was a plan similar to those devised in June and August 1991, he said.

"What would be the embarrassment of a plan to go to Miss Show's apartment, break in or burglarize the apartment, and cut her hair off there? Where is the embarrassment? She's not going to be embarrassed in front of her mother when she comes home. She wouldn't have gone to school that day, and probably either had her hairstyle changed, a wig or something. The same theme: Go to a public place and embarrass her. It makes sense. The story makes sense."

He pointed to the twenty-nine questions. Why would Lambert ask, what did Laurie look like dead? if she knew. And, he contended, why didn't Yunkin answer, what are you talking about? or why did you ask me something like that?—instead of, I remember seeing Laurie dead.

He said the physical evidence supported the defendant's testimony.

"I think it's obvious to anyone in the courtroom today that a very violent struggle took place in that apartment on that morning. Who had the scratches or the cuts or whatever they were? Not my client. Tabbi Buck had the scratches. They did a strip search of my client, found a little bruise—I'm not sure where it was anymore—a little bruise that seemed to be old and not fresh. I think the testimony was they didn't even bother photographing it.

"Interestingly enough, I heard no testimony whether Mr. Yunkin was checked for any scratches, bruises, and so forth. But it's consistent. Lisa says Tabbi did it. Tabbi has the scratches. Anybody who went through that kind of a violent confrontation would most likely have some telltale signs of that confrontation."

He asked Jeffries to come forward and help him show the judge the difference in size between the clothing

Lambert wore to the Shows' house and that which she put on for the rest of the day.

"She was going to spend a lot more time in this," he said, holding up a sweater, "and she had to wear that for comfort a few hours in the morning," holding up Yunkin's sweatpants.

"Mr. Yunkin admitted from the stand he wore those sweatpants to bed. Lisa Lambert, in her testimony, said, interestingly enough, just off the cuff: He got up that morning, had his sweatpants on, threw something on, and away they went. Probably very likely what happened, he was getting up early that morning, just kept on his sweatpants, threw on his red flannel, his jergo, and away they went. It would seem incredible that they got up that time in the morning and he wears these to bed all the time, he took them off to give them to her to put on. Difficult to believe."

The initials "T B" on the wall give Lambert's statement credence, he said. An expert in crime scenes figured out the writing without knowing the names of the defendants.

"They did not get on that wall by themselves," Shirk said. "The only possible way they got on there is that Laurie put them there, and the only possible reason she could've put them there was to name her attacker, her assailant, her killer."

Mrs. Show's testimony that her daughter identified the killer was "one of the two most damaging things," but couldn't Laurie have been referring to Tabitha when she said "Taa, taa, taa."

" 'Michelle did it' might've been, gee, if you get Michelle and talk to her, you will find out what all happened. You will learn who all was here. Because the 'Michelle did it,' if that was intended to mean Michelle actually did this to me, it was inconsistent with what she wrote on the wall. That 'Michelle did it' might've been, if I say that word, Mother will know what group of people the police should talk to to find the perpetrator."

He played down Lambert's statements that she would kill Laurie.

"That's a form of speech," Shirk said. "Sadly, she's right. Anyone that spends any time around a good number of teenagers realizes that. I meant nothing by that. I was angry when I said it in anger. She made a big difference between I said I would kill her and I would slit her throat. She doesn't recall ever saying that."

Court testimony supports her, Shirk said. Kim Warner and Vinnie Orsi said she did not say it.

Shirk questioned the prosecution's assertion that Yunkin was somehow a docile fellow who simply followed Lambert around. He called the idea "impossible to believe."

"He hit her; he indicated on several occasions. He admitted cutting his face, holding her down, and bleeding on her. That is not someone I would characterize as docile. He's a violent individual. Leon Lamparter told us that he wanted to beat up Brad. If you believe what the commonwealth suggests, Miss Lambert talked all of these other people into the June event, talked all of these other people into the August event, talked Tabbi and Lawrence into doing this for her. She planned it so well she got others to do it.

"Somehow, some way, unscientifically proven, fooled two handwriting experts. Cunning. If Miss Lambert has all the talents that the commonwealth gives her, she's a combination incarnate of the Wizard of Oz, Houdini, and Superman. She's a nineteen-year-old girl, a dropout. That's not to say anything about her intelligence, but not a well-educated young girl. She's gotten her GED and we're to believe that she's fooling handwriting experts that have been in the trade, I believe Mr. Gencavage said twenty-seven years."

Shirk said the most damaging evidence was provided by Yunkin. He was the only one who tied Lambert to the murder. The commonwealth offered no physical evidence to support the claim.

"What else about Mr. Yunkin? Probably, Your Honor, there is not a person in Lancaster County who ever believed that he didn't know anything about this event. He's the guy who had a nineteen-year-old girlfriend who was pregnant. Sure, he thought about his child. Do me a favor. They are going to put me away for a long time. You are pregnant, you are a girl. They wouldn't do as much to you. Those are the things we know about Mr. Yunkin."

Yunkin was the one who conspired with Buck, not Lambert, Shirk maintained.

"Now the district attorney is going to argue, I'm sure, that but for Michelle Lambert none of this would've happened. And, Your Honor, there is a certain amount of truth to that. If she hadn't become overly jealous concerning the relationship Mr. Yunkin had with Miss Show, and if she hadn't done some of the things she did throughout that time frame, perhaps a lot of this would have kind of gone by the wayside. However, that doesn't mean she planned premeditated murder or any murder at all."

There were others who could have stopped it: Laura Thomas's father, "an adult, not a teenager, who said he heard something"; Yunkin and Buck, "who actually did the killing"; the police, "who sat on a November twenty-second assault charge and didn't do anything on it for a month."

He said the crime was not murder in the first degree. It was not premeditated.

"Most screwed-up one I have ever seen if it was," he said.

Why was hair all over the place? he asked. Why did they take a rope if they were going to stab her? Why, if she has an aversion to blood, would she kill with a knife?

"The problem in this case from the beginning is that the commonwealth focused into Lisa Michelle Lambert and refused to believe anything other than what fits within that theory; the common perception brought on by whatever, the news, she did it," Shirk said. "Lisa Michelle Lambert is not guilty of first-degree murder. She neither premeditated nor intentionally killed Laurie Show. She did not go there with that intent and she wasn't—there is not one part of the evidence in this trial that indicates that anything different happened than what she said, except maybe the police officers didn't see an egg on her head under her hair. She's not a murderer."

He noted that Pennsylvania law says a person at the scene of a crime who does not participate in the crime is not an accomplice. An accomplice must take part in the crime.

"She didn't have the knowledge it was going to happen. She didn't have the intent to join in and facilitate that activity. Tried to stop it. Maybe not as forcefully as some of us would've liked, but tried to stop it in her own way. There is no evidence that my client committed any felony, there is no evidence my client is guilty of murder in any of these degrees.

"Your Honor, I thank you for your indulgence and I would ask the court as you deliberate over the weekend to return a verdict of not guilty of murder," Shirk said.

Jack Kenneff rose and began summing up his case. He confessed to being a tad uncomfortable. He was used to looking into the faces of twelve people, not just that of a judge.

"I think you have a lot of very, very difficult decisions to make in this case," he told Stengel. "However, I think there is one decision that is very easy. That decision is, whoever killed Laurie is guilty of first-degree murder. The nature of the wounds in this case are such that whoever did that could've had but one intent in their mind when it occurred, and that intent was to kill her.

"Mr. Shirk makes it sound like you need a planned killing for it to be first-degree murder. You do not need a planned killing. Those perpetrators, when they went to that scene, could've been intent on kidnapping, could've been intent on assault, could've been intent on false imprisonment, tying her up and leaving her there in the apartment with her hair cut, embarrassed. But once they drew that knife three times on one wound, twice on another wound, across her throat, there can be no doubt from the evidence, from the testimony of the experts, that this crime is first-degree murder.

"The commonwealth does not have to prove what Miss Lambert's role was in that first-degree murder. We only have to prove that she shared the intent of her co-conspirators. The commonwealth does not have to prove that once that intent was established that Miss Lambert withdrew. The commonwealth doesn't have to prove anything about that withdrawal—when it occurred, under what circumstances it occurred—because under the law if she did withdraw from that house—I'm not suggesting for a moment that the evidence establishes that she did—but if she did withdraw from that house after the intent to kill is formed, she must do two things under the law. She must wholly deprive the conspiracy of its effect, and she must notify the authorities. She did neither."

She didn't knock on the Kleinhanses' door, she didn't call the police, she didn't do anything.

Lambert had to have known what was going to happen, he said. In fact, one look at Tabitha Buck's jacket proved that. A knife and rope could not have fit in her pockets. Yunkin's guilt was not an issue in Lambert's trial, Kenneff said.

"I don't think I held anything back about my feelings about Mr. Yunkin. I said in my opening he's either lying, he's stupid, or he's naive. Perhaps the evidence in this case suggests he's all three."

Moreover, he would not argue that Yunkin was honest in his comments about the twenty-nine questions.

"Did Yunkin participate in the murder of Laurie? My stomach says he did, my heart says he did, my mind says he did. Did he participate in the way that Miss Lambert says? The facts say no.

"Miss Lambert has the motive, she has the means, and she has the opportunity to commit this crime. As the court is well aware, merely because she gets on the stand and tells a story that is consistent with her innocence does not create reasonable doubt. An examination of this case to see if reasonable doubt is present can only occur after you decide what the facts are and apply the facts to the law and in that way determine whether reasonable doubt is present.

"The Lambert motive. Miss Lambert, in asking you to believe her version of what occurred, asked you to forget that she had a motive, that she expressed it, and that she intended to carry it out.

"Show and Yunkin start to date. Show and Yunkin stop dating. It's over. There is no reason for her to continue it. I forget if Mr. Shirk used the word 'obsessed,' but I don't think you can use any other word to describe her feelings about this Yunkin/Show relationship and the ill will that it generated in her toward Laurie. 'Obsessed' is a modest word, a moderate word to describe it."

Two weeks after Yunkin and Show stopped dating, she and others devised a plan to kidnap Laurie. On November 22, Lambert confronted Show in a mall.

"Think of that, of the brazenness of that," Kenneff said incredulously. "Laurie walking in the mall with her mother and brazenly Michelle Lambert comes up and accosts her with the mother present. What does that tell about her state of mind? What does that tell about what type of person she is? Is she the calm, cool, quiet, demure person you saw on the witness stand, or is she something far different?"

On December 18, she told Leon Lamparter she was going to get Laurie. The next night, they purchased rope and hats. No one wore the hats that day, Lambert testified, but they ended up in a Dumpster.

"Why do you throw out two new hats that nobody wore in the commission of this offense, unless you know that there is a good reason to throw them out?" Kenneff asked.

The plan to cut Laurie's hair to embarrass her made no sense, Kenneff claimed. It didn't eliminate a witness to the rape or to the assault.

"That doesn't get Yunkin off the hook. That doesn't get Miss Lambert off the hook. The only way they are off the hook is if Laurie is dead; then there is no witness to the rape. Then there is no victim to the assault, then there is no problem," he said.

He said the physical evidence did not support Lambert's story. If they were going to wait for Show to go to the bus around 7:30 A.M., why didn't they all go get something to drink at McDonald's? They had time. Kleinhans did not hear anything other than the first slam of the

Shows' door. Lambert says she opened the door after Buck went inside, yet Hazel Show testified the door locked automatically when it was closed. A fight ensued on the dining room floor, Lambert alleged, yet nothing was out of place. There was no blood on the floor. Lambert said Buck threw Laurie's cut hair across the room, yet crime scene analysts found some only in one spot.

Lambert said she pulled Laurie, with a punctured lung and other stab wounds, to the front door, yet Laurie refused to go outside.

"Laurie decides, I'll stay here with Tabitha and the knife," Kenneff said mockingly. "That doesn't make any sense."

"And this, to me, is the most amazing series of quiet mayhem mankind has ever known. Laurie, in a desperate fight for her life that goes from the hallway, from the door to the hallway to the dining room, back into her room, on the floor, up, over to another spot on the floor, out in [the] hallway, Laurie isn't screaming. There is no rope around her neck."

In virtually all criminal cases, Kenneff said, the truth rests with piecing the stories together of the people who are merely sitting there minding their own business. Their times won't coincide. They won't be precise. All the facts won't add up neatly. But the truth is the Frys and the Kleinhanses saw two people of equal height leaving the area that day.

"What occurred here fits the motive that Miss Lambert had, fits the motive of ending her relationship with Laurie, ending the threat of the rape charge, ending the threat of the simple assault charge, and that is go to the apartment door, knock; as soon as she opens, hit the door and you are in. Slam the door; the one slam heard by Mr. Kleinhans. Start stabbing away at Laurie. Five cuts in the sweatshirt, only three wounds, indication of movements when the wounds are inflicted. Laurie screams once. What's heard by Mr. Kleinhans? In the bedroom, down on the floor, *thump!* And then the knife is at her throat. Then what are you going to do? The rope was brought along for some reason. And a person, one person is not going to stand there holding a knife at her throat and tie that knot. It's not like it was brought there with a loop already in it. A knot is tied in that rope. Tie that rope snugly around Laurie Show's throat."

What do you do in that situation? Kenneff asked.

"You have to do exactly what they decided to do, exactly what they told Yunkin: You have to slit her throat. And why do you choose slitting of the throat? It's what you discussed sitting at a picnic table, talking about Laurie, eliminating the harder way of doing it by drowning. Kim Warner didn't say—and I suggest the court go back to his notes—Kim Warner didn't say they were talking about this person in general terms, Kim Warner said they were talking about Laurie. Tabitha Buck wasn't there talking about it. No evidence Tabitha Buck had it in her mind. The person who had it in [her] mind sits right over there."

He ended by saying, "I probably had a few things here that I missed, but I think, you know, this really gets down to one or two things and it kind of struck me this way. Miss Lambert wants you to believe that the tormentor became the savior. She wants the villain to become the heroine. That defies belief. Thank you."

After his charge, which normally would have been for a jury's purposes, Stengel adjourned at 5:20 P.M. with the promise to render his verdict on Monday.

Twenty-two

On Monday morning, Judge Lawrence Stengel took the bench and looked out over the crowd. Hazel Show was sitting in the back row, on the opposite side of the courtroom from Lisa Michelle Lambert's parents. Hazel had, as she had so many other weekends, spent both Saturday and Sunday in bed, watching television, ignoring the phones. Hers had become a most insular world since her daughter, her only child, was murdered twenty-seven weeks before.

The Lamberts were there. Joanne Guier, Tabitha Buck's mother, sat by herself, knowing that her daughter would face a similar date just two months hence. Lisa Michelle Lambert sat at the defense table with her lawyers.

Stengel warned the crowd to avoid outbursts. He knew it had been a difficult two weeks for everyone, he said. He wanted to maintain dignity, propriety. He had spent the weekend reviewing the evidence, weighing the facts, considering the credibility of each person who uttered a word.

"I find the defendant guilty of first-degree murder," he said.

Hazel Show wept silently, twisting around and around the handkerchief that was given to her at Laurie's funeral, the one she carried with her through every benchmark in her fight for justice for Laurie. The Lamberts did not respond in any visible way. Guier felt relieved. She believed Lambert was the true killer. Even though her daughter had never spoken to her—or anyone on the advice of her lawyer—about the murder, Guier had complete confidence in her daughter. It was simply not her nature to do what Lambert accused her of doing.

Stengel moved to the punishment phase of the trial that afternoon. He would next decide whether Lambert lived or died. Lambert's uncle, Jeffrey Lambert, was called as her first character witness. The defense wanted to give the court a glimpse of what they considered the real Lisa Michelle Lambert, a young woman with compassion for her family, the elderly, and children. The uncle testified that Lisa had visited him every day he was in the hospital the year before for kidney failure and had in fact offered him one of her kidneys. It was not asked by the prosecution whether she was actually tested as a match or not.

Lambert's mother, Judy, took the stand next to support her daughter's cause. Even though they had been estranged for six months before the murder, Judy Lambert and her daughter had become close in the months since. Judy and Len Lambert were raising Lambert's daughter, Kirsten, who had been born in March. The Lamberts took the baby to the jail three times a week to visit her mother.

Judy Lambert described her daughter as a "sweet" child who took care of her brothers in the years Judy herself was unable to. Headstrong and independent, her daughter became troubled, however, in high school and moved out when she was fifteen. She dropped out of school in the tenth grade. She returned home, but moved out again to live with Yunkin. Judy Lambert de-

scribed Yunkin as a violent sort who beat her daughter
and hit her sons. She had pleaded with Lisa to leave
him. She knew only bad would come from the relationship.

Since the murder, her daughter had matured, she testified.

"I love her," Judy Lambert told the court. "I see her
as a kind, gentle, caring person. I've never seen a violent
side in her. Even during the confrontations we've had
with her, she never once raised her hand at any of us,
at any of our children, and I see her as a kind, loving
mother."

Dr. Gene Cary, a psychiatrist hired by Lambert's lawyers, told the judge that after spending four hours with
her, he had ascertained that she is a "complex young
lady, intelligent, shy" who is preoccupied with emotional
loss.

"This stems from childhood," the doctor said. She
told him she had five brothers, when, in fact, she has
three. She had also lost friends, other relatives, baby-sit-
ters. She was depressed as an adolescent and would
leave the house in the middle of the night and walk for
hours. Her mother thought she was sneaking out for
sex, the doctor testified, but Lambert said that was not
the case.

"I tend to believe her that she was not promiscuous,"
he said.

She was not antisocial, not driven by impulses, but as
she grew older, she became increasingly unhappy. She
had rescue fantasies, the doctor said. She wrote an essay
about an orphan who was rescued by a mythical figure
who then went back and rescued all the other orphans.

Lambert considered her parents emotionally distant,
a fairly typical feeling among adolescents. Their parents
don't understand them. No one understands them. She

had it worse than most and couldn't sleep, couldn't concentrate. Other times she slept all the time. She felt hopeless.

He said she had a most negative self-image and that accounted for getting into what she described as an abusive relationship with Yunkin. She felt she didn't deserve better. She also thought her family did much better when she wasn't around. She carried a lot of guilt because of that, the doctor said.

In addition, the doctor said, she told him she had been gang-raped in her apartment.

"I wasn't supposed to reveal this," the doctor told the judge. "She made me promise not to say anything about it, but I think under the circumstances I think it might shed light on the way she tends to think about things. She broke down and became tearful. She didn't become tearful very often, but she did then."

His diagnosis? Dystemic reaction. Smoldering depression, he said. She was compassionate, too, he said, adding that he found it inconceivable that Lambert could have been involved in mutilating someone.

Kenneff jumped up, "I object to that. It's not a psychiatric conclusion."

"I'll withdraw it," said Alan Goldberg, Lambert's lawyer, who was conducting the interview.

Kenneff asked if the doctor had obtained Lambert's school or hospital records or conducted intelligence tests. No, the doctor answered.

"This gang rape," Kenneff said, "isn't it possible this gang rape is another one of these fantasies?"

"No, I don't believe so," the doctor responded, although he did not base that conclusion on independent interviews.

Kenneff asked him about the diagnosis.

"This disorder is apparently common."

"Yes."

"No further questions."

Goldberg called a series of people to say Lisa Michelle Lambert was a shy, sensitive person. A friend of her mother's from church. A boy who considered her a sister. A nurse who helped her in labor. A girl she knew in the eighth grade. Shy and sensitive. She'd play basketball and hide-and-seek. Go shopping and play dress-up. She was modest around the prison guards when she was in labor. Kind. Even nerdy in junior high. She'd give money to friends and talk them through their deepest, most hurtful problems. She was always there.

Her father, Len, said, "As long as I can remember Lisa, the biggest thing that strikes me with her is her concern for all of us in the family. She's always been very loving toward us. We may not've always understood each other. I think some of that comes in the difficult teen years, but she has never forgotten an occasion for anybody. She always demonstrated her love. She's always been kind and considerate to us. All around, I would say, other than some of the typical problems she ran into, she's been a very special person to have as a daughter."

In what might have seemed like an unusual occurrence to some, Roy Shirk, the man who had just lost his case before Judge Stengel, who had not poked enough holes in the prosecution's case to keep Lisa Michelle Lambert out of jail, took the stand now to save her life. He told the judge it had occurred to him the night before that he probably knew Lambert better than anyone except perhaps her parents at that moment. He had spent untold hours with her since he had been asked by the court to represent her on December 23, 1991.

That day, at the Lancaster County Prison, he was

struck first by her intelligence, he said. She was scared, not hardened. Over the seven months she had been in prison, she had matured into a young woman who was becoming a responsible adult.

Goldberg then called Lambert to the stand. He asked if there was anything she wanted to say to the Show family. John and Hazel Show sat as usual in the back row. Hazel stared intently at Lambert, as she had every time she faced the girl.

"I'd like to say that I'm sorry for my role in Laurie's death, and I did state my role in court and I maintain that was my role, and I'm very sorry that she died; and if I thought anything like that would've happened, December twentieth, I would've never gotten out of bed," she said.

Stengel decided because it was after 4:00 P.M., to conclude the penalty phase the next day. Lisa Michelle Lambert, slightly more than a month shy of her twentieth birthday, mother of a four-month-old baby, would wait another day to hear whether she would live or die.

Twenty-three

Onlookers who happened to see Lisa Michelle Lambert arrive at the Lancaster County Courthouse Tuesday morning were simply stunned by her appearance. For her big day, she chose to make a big impression. Her face still swathed in makeup, blond hair falling to her shoulders, she wore a white ball gown. Some spectators snickered. Others wondered what possessed her to wear such a getup. Hazel Show shook her head in disgust and said, "That's Michelle. Always looking for attention. Always wanting to be the center of everything. She looks ridiculous."

Jack Kenneff was first to offer his closing argument. He knew he had a major challenge before him to convince Stengel to impose the death penalty. Lambert was still a teenager. She was a young mother. She was a female. All worked against him. Lancaster County is a law-and-order community that was clamoring for justice in this case. But death, to many, seemed like too high a price, even with the savageness of the crime.

Kenneff began with a history lesson on the death penalty and teenagers. The most famous case involved two rich teens from suburban Chicago, Leopold, eighteen, and Lobe, nineteen. They wanted to kill for the thrill of it. They convinced fourteen-year-old Bobby Franks to go with them. He went willingly, knowing them and their families. He left his school, got in their car. They put chloroform to his mouth and nose, and after he passed out, they beat him to death. The famed lawyer Clarence Darrow was brought in to represent the boys, who had confessed to the crime under interrogation by the police. To almost everyone's surprise, on the day of the trial, the young men pleaded guilty but asked for a nonjury trial on the penalty phase.

Darrow then spent two days talking about the evils of the death penalty and why it should not be applied to teenagers. But, in modern days, the death penalty is no longer applied in an arbitrary fashion, Kenneff argued. The Pennsylvania legislature spells out specifically when and to whom it can be given. Lisa Michelle Lambert's crimes most certainly fit the description, he said.

He acknowledged that certain factors lessened her crime: her lack of a previous record, her age. But her lawyers failed to paint a portrait of a troubled young woman with psychiatric problems. They did not prove she was a "nice" person who didn't deserve to die. They did not show Lambert as a meek victim of domestic abuse. He called abuse by Yunkin "pure speculation."

"I suggest to you that the defense has not established any connection between the beatings by Yunkin, if it occurred, and the reason this crime happened," he said.

"The baby. I mean that's a real emotional hook for the court. But I think for that to be mitigation, the court would have to say that mothers aren't death-eligible; that because you love and care for your baby, the death penalty doesn't apply to you. That doesn't make sense."

He said remorse is certainly mitigation, but he questioned if Lambert was actually sorry. She said it the day before. But on the day of the crime, she watched television, got her paycheck, went to the bank, did laundry, got a Christmas tree, went shopping and to the bowling alley.

"Please compare the self-serving remorse shown yesterday to the admitted facts of this case," he said.

Kenneff concluded by asking the judge, when he was considering the emotional testimony of the day before by Lambert's family and friends, to remember the pain Hazel Show demonstrated when she testified, to remember her suffering.

Goldberg next summed up the case for the defense by saying Lambert's age and emotional state at the time of the crime should be considered.

"We have a nineteen-year-old girl who is not a city girl, who is not wise beyond her years, and experienced the things that maybe a teenager experienced in the city," Goldberg said. "We have a country girl, less experienced than her chronological age."

He asked the judge to consider that and to consider that Lambert's role was minor.

"Look inside that person," Goldberg said, referring to Lambert's care of an elderly aunt and for her family, her offer of a kidney to an ailing uncle, her pride in not smoking, her refusal to abuse drugs. "Is this a hardened individual? Is this someone who has not redeeming value? Of course not."

He pleaded, "Don't take her away from her family."

Stengel adjourned, saying he would take the matter up in his chambers. He did not know how long it would take. The time was 10:10 A.M. At 1:55 P.M., Stengel rendered his verdict. He said he considered as mitigating factors Lambert's age, no prior record, her character, remorse shown, the fact she had a relationship with her child, the doctor's diagnosis, and her ability to make a contribution to society.

"The court hereby sentences the defendant to life imprisonment," he intoned.

The Lamberts, sitting in the front row behind their daughter, did not react. They smiled at their daughter, waved, and walked out. Lambert returned their smiles as deputies moved in to handcuff her and take her back to prison.

Hazel Show had considered saying something to Lambert. She had wanted her to know the depth of her pain. But when she saw the parents walk out smiling she thought, *What's the point?* Nothing she could say would make a dent in their world.

Twenty-four

Tabitha Buck had continued to be the mystery figure in the Laurie Show murder case. New to the area, Buck was not known among the people of Lancaster or even East Lampeter Township. Born in Alaska but reared most of her life in Oregon, she spent part of her ninth-grade year in Lancaster, moved back to Oregon for tenth grade, and enrolled at Conestoga Valley High for eleventh grade. She was partway through her senior year when the murder took place. Since then, she had been under strict orders from her public defender to say nothing.

Only the barest of details of her life were known. She was seventeen, a juvenile under Pennsylvania law, but she was to be tried as an adult due to the nature of the crime. She had not cooperated with police. She had not testified in Lisa Michelle Lambert's trial. People knew she worked part-time at Weis Market with Jackie Yunkin. They didn't know Buck did not realize Jackie Yunkin was her friend Lawrence's mother until she saw her in the courtroom at her trial. They knew from her booking photo she had irrepressibly wavy hair. They did not know it was a permanent on stick-straight hair. They knew she played in the school band. They did not know she was good enough on the flute to be the first chair. They also knew Lambert had labeled her the true mur-

derer. Few knew she had dreams of being an elementary
school teacher.

When Buck's trial began on September 21, 1992, she
had been in the Lancaster County Prison for exactly
nine months, an excruciating time of first fear and then
resignation for a girl who had never been in trouble
before. The night she arrived, she had been terrified,
filling her head with the images of television prison,
inmates being beaten, raped with broomsticks, gang
fights. After a strip search, she sat on her bed in the
newly built part of the jail and cried. Her whole body
shook. Lambert, on the other hand, was taken to the
area known as the dungeon, the oldest part of the
prison, built in the 1920s, that inmates say has leaking
walls and rats.

Because the publicity after the murder and during
Lambert's trial had been so extensive, Judge Michael J.
Perezous moved the proceedings to the Easton County
Courthouse in Easton, eighty miles away. A jury of six
men and six women were selected in Courtroom 4.

Joanne Guier sat behind her daughter with Alvin
Buck, her ex-husband, Tabbi's father. He had flown in
from Oregon to be with his daughter. Hazel and John
Show sat on the opposite side of the room. Hazel
steeled herself for what she hoped would be the last
time she had to testify, the last time she had to hear
the lurid details of the people who stalked her daughter.
She held in her hand the handkerchief given to her at
her daughter's funeral, the one she carried through
every event in her drive to obtain justice for her only
child.

It would be the last trial, for Lawrence Yunkin had
cut a deal with the prosecution. He would testify in both
cases and be able to plead guilty to a lesser charge.

Buck drew as her attorney James P. Cullen, a public

defender whose political ambition to become a judge was well known around Lancaster County. Many thought the high-profile nature of the Buck case suited his needs. He advised her that the best chance was to remain quiet and put her fate in the hands of the jury. The district attorney's office was not going for the death penalty in her case.

The Bucks were frustrated because Cullen would not include them in setting the strategy for the trial. Alvin Buck suggested several ideas, but was turned away on each one. Cullen seemed to just dismiss them. Plus, he had advised Tabbi against talking to anyone, even her parents, about the murder.

In an opening statement, the prosecutor, Kenneff, related the facts just as he presented them in Lambert's trial: she and Buck went to the Shows' house, killed Laurie, Yunkin was not there. Yunkin's assertion that he did not know what was going to happen was unbelievable, however, the lawyer said.

Cullen quickly cast Yunkin as "a liar, an unmitigated, unrepentant liar" who had literally gotten away with murder. He pointed out that the one person who was not involved in any of Lambert's early schemes to get back at Laurie Show for her involvement with Yunkin was Tabitha Buck. Cullen gave Yunkin a new title. Whenever he referred to him during the opening statement, he called him, "Mr. Yunkin, the liar."

As he recounted the story of Lambert and Show, he told the jury they would hear testimony that Laurie identified her killer. "Michelle did it," she told her mother. She didn't say Tabbi. She never said Tabbi, he pointed out.

Kenneff called as his first witness Robin Weaver, the handsome East Lampeter Township policeman, who was one of the first officers on the scene that morning. Just as he did in Lambert's trial, Weaver began with what he saw when he arrived at 7:44 A.M. on December 20 at The Oaks, finding a clot of people standing outside, ambulances pulled to the curb. The first person he saw as he entered the upstairs dwelling was blood-soaked Hazel Show, clutching a pillow, screaming, "Michelle did it."

He described for the jury his duties as evidence officer, collecting and marking items from the crime scene, drawing sketches of the floor plan. Weaver's testimony filled the afternoon. When Kenneff completed his examination of Weaver shortly before 5:00 P.M., the judge decided to halt the proceedings for the day. He sent the jury members home with the usual admonition to avoid talking about the case to anyone or reading anything about it. He told them to get a good night's sleep, no watching *The Late Show* or *The Tonight Show*. They needed to be alert. He also said he would tell them the next day to eat light lunches so the blood didn't drain from their heads to digest food. It makes people drowsy, he said.

Weaver took the stand again Wednesday morning for cross-examination. Cullen painstakingly took Weaver through the various pieces of evidence he found in Laurie's room and the resulting depiction on his sketches.

Various police officers and doctors testified to the nuts and bolts of the case: the wounds, cause of death, evidence collected from the Susquehanna River and a trash truck, a repeat of the earlier Lambert trial. Kenneff built the facts of his case. The women killed Laurie, Yunkin drove them there. He followed virtually the same order of witnesses as he did at Lambert's trial. This time, though, a jury of everyday folks, not used to the gore of violent death, was looking at crime scene and autopsy photos, not a judge who makes his living arbitrating criminal trials. The men and women of the jury were handed pictures of a bloody rope, the neck wound, among others. Most gave quick glances and handed them on.

A major difference in Buck's trial was that Cullen did not need to cast doubt on whether Laurie could not speak. In fact, for his purposes, it was better if the jury believed she did. Her mother would testify that Laurie never uttered Buck's name. The coroner Penades made no mention of his "research" cut on the leg of another body, nor was he asked.

In the afternoon, Lawrence Stewart Yunkin was called to testify. He gave his address as Lancaster County Prison, his home of nine months. He had been employed for the nine months before his arrest by Denlinger's, where he made roof trusses of wood. In the summer of 1991, he and Lambert lived in the Bridgeport community in East Lampeter Township. They had known each other two years and had lived together for one.

He met Buck in September 1991 on the loop, a place in Lancaster where teens hang out, cruise in cars. He saw her about three times a week.

He met Laurie Show in the summer of 1991. They were involved romantically, even though he was still living with Lambert, for about eight days. They broke off their relationship because "Michelle was interfering," he said.

Kenneff asked, "Did anything in particular happen to Miss Lambert in the summer of 1991?"

Yunkin, looking at Kenneff, responded, "Yes, she got pregnant to me."

Yunkin said whenever Laurie Show's name was uttered, Lambert would "get all fired up; she was mad that I dated her."

He recounted his story of the days leading up to Show's murder. They went to Buck's house that night, to Kmart, buying the rope, black ski hats, on and on. He dropped them off at the Shows', he picked them up; Tabbi said "the bitch scratched her," Michelle said she got kicked in the face.

That afternoon Cullen began examining the man he had called a liar. He began by asking him about his agreement with the prosecution.

"At the time you contemplated this plea agreement, you knew the sentence for murder in the first degree was death or life in prison."

"Yes."

"You had no interest in being a defendant in a capital case, did you?"

"No."

"You didn't want any part of the death penalty, did you?"

"No."

"And you didn't want any part of life imprisonment, did you?"

"No."

"Now you agreed that you would plead guilty to the crime of hindering apprehension, is that correct?"

"Yes."

"And you know the sentence for that, don't you, the maximum sentence?"

"Yes."

"It's three and a half to seven years, isn't it?"

"Yes."

"That's a much better deal than life in prison, isn't it?"

"I know."

"And you knew at the time that you were initially arrested by the police that it was in your best interests to minimize all of your involvement in this accident, didn't you?"

"At the time being, yes."

"And you've known it would still be in your best interest to minimize all your involvement, isn't it?"

"I'm being truthful."

"The question I asked you was, you knew it was in your best interest, and still do, to minimize your involvement, don't you?"

"Yes."

Cullen asked him about the pearl earring Hazel Show found in her home. Yunkin identified it as Lambert's and admitted he had worn it. He asked Yunkin about his relationship with Laurie.

"It terminated as a result of an accusation that you had sexual intercourse with her against her will, isn't that correct?"

"No, it's not."

"It's your testimony that it was an amicable parting?"

"Yes."

"It's your testimony that the two of you agreed to stay friends?"

"Yes."

"Do you recall that this sexual intercourse was reported to the police as having been a forcible rape?"

"Not at the time, no."

"You did at some point learn that was the case, isn't that correct?"

"Yes, it is."

Yunkin said he didn't worry about it, though, because he didn't do anything against her will.

Cullen poked holes in Yunkin's credibility as he asked about how they ended up at the Shows' house, whether

Lambert just simply gave him directions. Did he know where he was? Did he know who lived there? He asked about the summertime plans to embarrass Laurie.

"And you knew that after she was lured out of the apartment, that Michelle and you had, and these other people had, certain plans as to what would be done with Miss Show, didn't you?"

"They were going to talk to her."

"That's what you thought was going to happen?"

"That's what I was told, yes."

"You were a full participant in this talking, too."

"Yes."

"And you knew that Miss Lambert had something similar in mind when you arrived at the condominiums, isn't that correct?"

"No, I did not."

"You thought she was going to the condominiums at approximately six-forty, six-fifty in the morning just to visit?"

"No, I did not."

"What did you understand she was going there for?"

"I mean, I knew who she was going to see, but I thought Laurie's mom was home, so I didn't think twice about it."

"You knew Mrs. Show had no interest at all in seeing Michelle, didn't you?"

"Correct."

Yunkin denied he knew anything about the plan to hurt Laurie or embarrass her. At 5:00 P.M. the judge interrupted Yunkin's testimony and ended the court day.

Yunkin regained the stand first thing Thursday morning. Cullen pressed him about what he knew that morning. Yunkin said he did not know what the girls were going to do to Laurie, but he believed they were going to hurt her.

He asked whether Yunkin dropped them off there, believing Laurie would be hurt, and picked them up afterward.

"Correct."

"And you know that makes you an accomplice to murder, doesn't it?"

"Correct."

"You aren't charged with murder, are you?"

"No, I'm not."

"You have the deal of a lifetime."

"I believe so, yes."

Cullen's point could not have been missed by anyone in the room.

Friday morning. Five days into the trial. Eleven witnesses. Fifty-nine exhibits. Kenneff began with the Kmart employee who testified at Lambert's trial, before calling Buck's mother to the stand. A dietary supervisor at Moravian Manor nursing home, Guier told the jury she picked up her daughter and a friend from school at 4:00 P.M. on the day before the murder. She took the girls to the mall at Park City and went to meet with her pastor. She said she would be there at 9:00 P.M. to pick them up, but was forty minutes late. They were upset; the friend was going to get in trouble for being home late. She was sorry, Guier said. Her appointment took longer than she expected.

She took the friend home and headed to the market for milk and bread. On their way, Buck saw Lambert and Yunkin in a parking lot of their apartment. Guier turned around and Buck talked to them briefly, standing outside their car. Returning, she told her mother everything was fine.

"I didn't think anything about it," Guier testified.

But then sometime after 11:00 P.M., Lambert came to the door. Guier called her daughter into her bedroom and told her she didn't want her visiting with anyone. She needed to go to bed so she could get up for school the next morning.

The next morning, Guier woke sometime before 7:00 A.M. to the sound of the front door closing. She thought it odd her daughter left for school so early. Buck never was one to stand in the cold and freeze as she waited for the bus. Then Guier found a note in the bathroom that said Tabbi was having breakfast with Lambert and Yunkin. They would take her to school.

When she talked to her daughter on the phone in the early evening, she sounded fine, the mother testified. But she did tell her she had been in a fight earlier in the day. The person scratched her face with his keys. Guier said she scolded her daughter for fighting.

The prosecution also provided testimony that placed Yunkin at the McDonald's near the Shows' apartment at about the time of the murder and that the three conspirators were seen leaving the Yunkin-Lambert residence at the time Yunkin said they did. Bits and pieces to bolster Yunkin's story, to establish his credibility.

Witnesses also testified that she seemed "normal" at school on the day of the Show murder, and several remembered her face was scratched and her hands were swollen. Jurors also were shown a videotape of the crime scene, with the Shows' Christmas tree standing innocently in the living room and Laurie's bedroom resembling a set from a horror film.

Stacy Cassione, a friend of Buck's, offered a new glimpse of the stormy relationship between Lambert and Yunkin. The eighteen-year-old said she was on the loop with Buck and heard Lambert "rattle off a string of obscenities" at Yunkin. He replied, "If you don't leave me alone or back off, I'll screw around with Laurie again."

"She just flipped out," Cassione said. "She ran over to him, started pushing him around and yelling at him. He showed no emotion at all. He just stood there."

Cassione said everyone just stood and looked at Lambert. She was making a fool of herself. Buck didn't take part in the discussion and made no threats against Show.

The next week, Lambert asked her to kidnap Laurie as she waited for the bus, take her behind the bushes, tie her up, and cut her hair. Cassione said she was frightened by Lambert. From then on, Cassione said she minimized her contact with Buck because of Lambert.

With a weekend respite, the twelve jurors and two alternates filed back into the courtroom for a new week of testimony on Monday morning. Kenneff began with questioning Robert Catherman, a forensic pathologist who examined photographs of Buck taken after the murder. He identified the marks on her shoulder as having been made by someone scratching her with fingernails through one or two layers of clothing. The scratches on her face were made by a sharp object, probably the ring Laurie was wearing on her right hand, he said.

Cullen pressed him.

"You are not in the position, Doctor, to say whose fingernails made the scrape mark that we have seen on the shoulder."

"No," he responded. He couldn't say if it was a man or a woman, black or white.

Scrapings from under Laurie's fingernails turned up nothing more than her own hair. Nothing from Lambert, Yunkin, or Buck. Type B blood on her class ring matched her own blood and Yunkin's, forensic pathologist Donald Bloser Jr. testified. In fact, all of the blood in the room was Type B, not Buck's Type A or Lambert's Type O.

"It couldn't be Miss Buck's?" Cullen asked.

"That's correct," Bloser said.

Bloser also said the blood on the clothing recovered by police was not a strong presence, and it could have gotten on all the clothing from a single piece.

Laura Thomas, a friend of Lambert's, testified as she did at Lambert's trial about the various plans she and others made to embarrass or hurt Laurie Show. The first took place the last weekend in June 1991. Thomas and Kimona Warner were to lure Laurie Show from her apartment, drive her downtown, take her clothes off, and tie her to a pole. Warner told the court she wouldn't take part.

"I told Laura Thomas it was ridiculous," Warner said. Instead of getting her out of the apartment, Warner and Thomas told Show to stay home, lock the doors, and not to answer the phone. They told Lambert that Laurie's mother wouldn't let her go out.

Cullen asked Warner, "I take it then that she [Buck] wasn't involved in any of this activity you've described for us."

She responded Buck was not.

The week after July 4, Lambert and others talked about yet another attempt at embarrassing Show.

Rick Lentz, a former boyfriend of Laurie Show's, testified he saw Buck slap Show at the Fireman's Expo in October, two months before Show's murder. Buck said, "We're going to get you," Lentz testified. He went to Laurie's defense.

"If you don't leave her alone, I'm going to fucking deck you," he told the girl as he balled his fist.

Buck looked stunned by the testimony. Years later she would continue to deny such a confrontation existed. She believed the young man probably saw someone slap Show, but it wasn't her, she said.

Twenty-five

On Tuesday, what many believed would be the last day of the testimony, Jack Kenneff told the judge that Lisa Michelle Lambert had been brought to the court and was waiting to testify. Kenneff, however, did not want to call her as a witness. She had demanded some sort of consideration from the commonwealth in return for her testimony, which Kenneff did not want to grant.

She told him she would testify as she did in her own trial, but Kenneff said even though that testimony would implicate Buck, he did not believe she was telling the truth. Cullen agreed she did not need to be called and said he would not request that the judge tell the jury about a missing witness.

It would have been the first face-to-face meeting between the women since the day of the murder, when they were in the Garden Spot Bowling Alley together. Even though they had been housed in the same prison, Buck had seen Lambert only through a pane of glass. They were on a rotation the facility called "separation," kept apart at all times. When Buck ate with the other prisoners, Lambert ate in her cell and vice versa. When Lambert came out for medication, Buck went to her cell.

Kenneff resumed his case, calling many of the same witnesses from Lambert's trial, including Ron Savage, the chief investigator for the East Lampeter Police. After he testified to Buck's and Lambert's heights, Kenneff asked the sheriff to bring in Lisa Michelle Lambert. Many in the courtroom seemed startled. Cullen jumped to his feet. "Could we approach the bench?" he asked the judge. "I'd like an offer of proof as to what's going on here."

Kenneff only wanted Savage to identify Lambert and to show how tall she was compared to Buck. The judge allowed it.

Lambert came in and stood by the railing. He asked whether she looked different from the day she was arrested. She was thinner and paler, he said. Thinner because she had delivered her baby; paler because she had been in prison. Kenneff asked Buck to stand. She stood between the sheriff and Lambert's lawyer. Hazel Show glared.

As his last witness, Kenneff called Hazel Show. Hazel mounted the platform and sat in the witness chair. Once more, she thought. For Laurie. She twisted her handkerchief and looked toward Kenneff. She didn't have the same hatred for Buck she felt for Lambert. She didn't try to stare her down. To be sure, Hazel believed Buck was guilty and deserved to go to jail, but she did not hold her as responsible for Laurie's death as she did Lambert. She had never even heard Buck's name until she was arrested.

Hazel told the jury about all the incidents Laurie had had with Lambert; of the strange phone call the day before her daughter was murdered; of finding her on her back on the floor of her bedroom, dying.

"I cradled her in my arms to try to keep her together," Hazel said, weeping. "I said I'm so sorry . . . and she told me Michelle did it."

Hazel also identified a compact, blue mascara, and some lipstick that came from Buck's purse on the night of the murder as having been similar to some missing from Laurie's room.

Cullen stood to cross-examine Hazel. Questioning the mother of a dead girl is always a tricky proposition for a defense attorney. The lawyer must balance compassion and concern with an effort to cast some doubt on the witness's story. He chose only to press her on the makeup. He asked whether she had told police she could not identify the lipstick and the mascara. Yes, she had said that. And there are hundreds of compacts made by Cover Girl, just like the one Buck had? he asked. Yes, she responded.

Cullen called as his first defense witness Hector Feliciano, a coworker of Yunkin's at Denlinger's, who said he asked Yunkin on December 18 whether he planned to go to the company Christmas Party. He responded he would probably be in jail.

"I'm going to kill some bitch," Yunkin told him.

"The person he referred to was someone other than his ole lady?" Cullen asked.

"Yes."

Feliciano also said Yunkin threatened to kill him if he told anyone what he had said.

Next Joanne Guier told the jury her daughter always used Cover Girl products, including the lipstick that was in her purse the day of the murder.

"She had that kind of makeup every day," Guier said.

"Defense rests," Cullen said. Less than an hour of defense. Two witnesses. Alvin Buck was stunned. Where were the character witnesses? Friends and family would have flown in from Oregon. His girl would have been valedictorian at her Oregon high school. Everyone liked her. Why wasn't Tabbi's time card from work subpoenaed to show she could not have been the one who slapped Laurie at the expo?

After lunch Cullen began his closing remarks.

"The last words from Laurie Show were Michelle did it. Michelle, Michelle. I love you. Love you. Love you. You heard her mother repeat it from the witness stand. Laurie

Show, ladies and gentlemen, is the one person to know exactly who it was who assaulted her."

Impartial. Unbiased. No reason to lie. The only one who is, he said.

"She did not name Tabitha Buck," he said.

In addition, he said, police did not find Buck's blood or hair at the scene of the murder. No fingerprints, either, he said. The rope did not belong to Buck, nor did any of the clothes.

"The people who have the opportunity to perpetrate this crime are Yunkin and Lambert," he said. They were the ones who disposed of evidence. Yunkin was in that apartment that day and there was no evidence showing Buck was there with him, Cullen said. Yunkin had a motive to kill Laurie, and he has proven himself a liar.

"I would leave you with one thought," Cullen said. "I would ask you to be fair."

Kenneff agreed that Yunkin's testimony "defied belief," not in that he dropped the women off but in that he did not know what was going to happen. He also pointed out that Buck did nothing to help Show; she did nothing to report Yunkin and Lambert's crime.

Wednesday morning Perezous told the jury about the law and sent them off to deliberate. They had heard seven days of testimony and more than forty witnesses. The jury returned its verdict by 2:25 P.M.: guilty of murder in the second degree. Unanimous.

Perezous said he had been thinking about many aspects of modern-day life during the trial.

"What this case represents is all of our problems," he said. "We must find an answer to the violence that is pervading our lives." A recent FBI report showed a twenty-seven percent increase in crime by juveniles, he said. Since 1965 the arrest rate tripled.

"This case represents a tragedy of monumental proportions," he said. "At least four families will never be

the same as a result. It involves the most extreme consequences of human action, that being the commission of
grievous bodily harm to somebody else. This is not, however, a plan which involved professional, hardened, or
experienced criminals, or unsavory or despicable people,
or even mature or older individuals. Neither was it carried
out by drug or other alcohol or substance abusers."

He went on to point out this crime was planned and
carried out by high school students who came from mid-
dle-class families. Not the inner city. Not deprived.

"They are legally old enough to vote but not old
enough to lawfully drink, old enough to go to war and
to marry and to have children but who apparently do not
have the maturity and experience to be able to consider
the consequences of their conduct," he said.

"I don't have the solution, but I know what we are doing
is not working," the judge said, noting it costs as much to
imprison a child as it does to send him to Harvard.

"We must be willing to spend as much money, and
more, for education and other programs and jobs before
people get into trouble," the judge said. "Not only do
we have children having children, but we also have children killing children and plotting to kill children, doing
other things that would not normally be associated with
being a child."

Fortunately, most children are decent and productive,
he said.

"Let us hope that they will do a better job with their
legacy than has been done for some of them," he said.

Perezous sentenced Buck to life in prison, as required
by the mandatory sentencing guidelines of the state legislature.

Joanne Guier put her head in her hands and wept,
trying to muffle bitter tears. Sitting directly behind her
was Hazel Show. Hazel felt great compassion for the
woman. She had seen her in the bathroom at the court-

house several times, but had not spoken to her. She learned from Lambert's trial not to speak to the families of the defendants or to someone else in their presence. Deputies had asked her to be careful when Lambert's mother overheard her say the Lamberts were making "all nicey-nicey" when just a few weeks earlier they didn't want any part of her.

But here, after all this time, all this testimony and effort, Hazel felt she needed to reach out to this woman. She leaned forward and said, "I'm sorry either of our daughters ever met Michelle Lambert."

Both mothers had lost their daughters. In Pennsylvania a life sentence means life, no parole.

Back at Lancaster County Prison that night, Buck couldn't stop crying. She did not kill Laurie Show, she thought, and now she would spend all the rest of her days separated from her family in a state she hated. She pulled out a piece of paper and wrote to Hazel Show. It was all she could think to do. She had seen Laurie's mother the day before as Hazel testified against her. She had seen her that afternoon as she was escorted out of the courtroom, handcuffed.

"I am sorry for your loss," Buck wrote. "But I did not kill your daughter."

Days later Yunkin pleaded no contest to third-degree murder and was sentenced to ten to twenty years in prison. The prosecution threw out its earlier agreement that allowed him to plead guilty to a charge of hindering apprehension. They said the deal was off. Yunkin did testify against the women, as agreed, but the twenty-nine questions had cast him in a bad light. His credibility had been tarnished.

Part 4: The Appeals

Twenty-six

With the trials over, Hazel Show went back to her condominium and her job as a nurse's aide at the hospital. She didn't know how to pick up the pieces exactly. One day just slipped into the next. John Show found himself in a similar situation. He was back on the job at what was now New Holland North America. He felt particularly close to his coworkers. Many had contributed to a scholarship fund in Laurie's name for a senior at Conestoga Valley High School.

Lambert and Buck were taken to the women's prison in Muncy, about eighty miles north of Harrisburg, the state capital, more than a two-hour drive from Lancaster. Shortly after Buck was convicted, Yunkin wrote to her, "I'm really sorry this happened to you." She cast it aside and never responded. She didn't want to hear that from him.

Muncy, Pennsylvania, population three thousand, sits at the foot of White Deer Mountain along the east bank of the Susquehanna River. Its brick shops and stately colonial homes on Main Street serve as a pleasant entrance to an equally attractive state prison. Were it not for the tall chain-link fence topped with barbed wire, the granite buildings and careful landscaping of Muncy prison would look like a college campus. It was built in 1920 as a training facility for women offenders aged sixteen to thirty, and became a general prison for women in 1953. Until 1993 it was the only women's prison in Pennsylvania. Just over nine hundred women were housed there in early 2000, three on death row, 127 lifers, like Buck.

Lambert had arrived first. She was given a physical and sent to the Diagnostic Classification Center. Buck came two days later and was sent to Restrictive Housing Unit, the hole, housed next door to "Precious," then the only woman on death row.

Buck was terrified. She called her mother, sobbing. Guier felt helpless, but she was making plans to move to Danville to be near her daughter.

Precious saw Buck's despair and wrote poems to her and gave her words of encouragement.

"Stop your crying," Precious said. "You're going to be all right."

It helped Buck settle down. Here was a woman facing death and she was centered, carrying on. Three weeks later, Buck learned she had been sent there to keep her away from Lambert.

After Lambert and Buck switched places, Buck thought the guards were eyeing her suspiciously at first. Soon one told her why. They expected her to act like Lambert.

"You are so totally different from the other one," a guard told her.

Buck didn't want trouble. She worked in the kitchen from 4:00 A.M. to 11:00 A.M. and then went to school. She earned a General Equivalency Diploma, a hollow achievement for a girl who had intended to graduate with honors the previous June. She had wanted to be a teacher, so when the opportunity came, she went to work in the school, tutoring women for the GED exam.

Buck's mother was her faithful visitor, meeting her

two days each week in the airy visiting room. They would sit on the green chairs that fill the room as the children of inmates scurried around. High chairs, snack machines, children's books made the room seem less prisonlike. Stacks of worn paperback editions of the New Testament were piled on a nearby bookcase.

Lambert was transferred to Cambridge Springs on January 13, 1993. The prison, near Erie, had recently been opened. Soon word came back through the prison grapevine that Lambert was having an affair with a guard. Later Lambert accused James Eicher of raping her several times, the first time on her daughter's second birthday in March 1994. She claimed that sometimes he raped her twice in the same day, and had also raped her on her birthday.

Many believed, however, it was a voluntary relationship. A counselor said Lambert referred to Eicher as her "buddy."

"My hormones are up to here," Lambert told the counselor, raising her hand above her head. "All the other women have everybody else out there, outside the fence, and I have what's in here."

She did not claim it was rape until later. Initially, when confronted about the relationship, Lambert denied it.

Although he denied the allegations of rape, charges were brought against Eicher because he was a corrections officer and she was an inmate. Eicher was convicted of aggravated indecent assault, indecent assault, and official oppression in May 1996 and sentenced to a year and a half in prison.

Lambert was transferred to Edna Mahon Correctional Facility in Clinton, New Jersey.

The incident came to light as Lambert began an appeals process that would turn Lancaster County's legal world upside down. Her initial appeals were denied. The first one Stengel denied in July 1994; the next in March 1995. Both rulings were upheld by the higher state courts.

In 1996 Lambert wrote in her almost childlike cursive penmanship a petition to the U.S. district court in Philadelphia, claiming she had been given an unfair trial. She was in solitary confinement when she wrote the petition, which ended up in the hands of Judge Stewart Dalzell, a Republican appointee from a blue-blood Philadelphia law firm. With thinning gray hair on top of his head, which flows into a sort of pageboy sweep, Dalzell cut quite a figure among Pennsylvania judges. He was known as a law-and-order judge with a stern and forceful attitude on the bench. He sent Lambert's petition to one of Philadelphia's most prestigious law firms, Schnader Harrison Segal & Lewis.

A young lawyer with a privileged upbringing in Westfield, New Jersey, responded to an e-mail asking someone to represent Lambert. Christina Rainville had recently won $12.5 million for a small software company in a breach of contract lawsuit against Novell. She was ready for another pro bono case, one of the main reasons she chose Schnader when she graduated from Northwestern University Law School. The firm allows its lawyers to spend ten percent of billable hours on charity work.

Rainville, then in her mid-thirties, felt a drive to help people who have no voice. Her father had been orphaned at seven, yet grew to own a manufacturing company; her mother's family lost everything for helping Jews escape Nazi persecution.

Reading the news accounts on Lambert's case, though, convinced her she was preparing to stand up for a monster, not an underdog. She crafted a list of questions, each one she thought would prove the young killer's guilt. But as soon as she heard Lambert's voice, she knew she was innocent. She sounded meek and mild-tempered.

"I just knew," she would say many years later, trying to describe why she spent so much time, facing such long odds, battling for a new trial for Lambert. Peter S. Greenberg, her husband, nineteen years older and a partner at Schnader, agreed to help. Greenberg and Dalzell both attended the University of Pennsylvania as undergraduates and to earn their law degrees. Although they were the same age, Dalzell was admitted to the bar two years after Greenberg.

Rainville and Greenberg, along with six associates, researched the case for weeks, and by the time they filed a petition alleging false imprisonment on January 13, 1997, they had uncovered ninety-five incidents of prosecutorial misconduct and police wrongdoing. Tampering with evidence, perjured testimony, keeping information helpful to Lambert from her attorneys—the list was stunning. The details of each were astounding. Rainville claimed police framed her client because three of them had raped her in her apartment one summer day in 1991, six months before Laurie Show was killed.

Lancaster County residents were shocked. Hazel Show was aghast. She believed her fight for justice for her daughter had ended in a courthouse in Easton, Pennsylvania, five years earlier. She had begun to put her life back in order, working at Donecker's, an upscale department store in historic Ephrata, just north of Lancaster. She was spending time with friends, rather than sitting in her bedroom ignoring the phone and any knocks on the front door. Now she would have to go again to a courthouse and listen to it all over.

Dalzell set a hearing for March 31, 1997.

"This is a case of manipulated and destroyed evidence," Rainville said as she opened her case in the Philadelphia courtroom packed with spectators and the press. "Every single piece of evidence that was presented at her trial was fabricated and was a lie. Lisa Lambert is an innocent victim." Rainville claimed Lambert had been abused by her boyfriend and was so frightened of him she did not go to police to tell that Yunkin and Buck had killed Laurie Show. Moreover, she found no friends among police officers, because three of them had gang-raped her in her apartment in East Lampeter Township.

Rainville also said she would show Hazel Show was lying as well. Laurie Show could not have talked that day. She would bring experts to say so.

Representing the commonwealth was Joe Madenspacher, the Lancaster district attorney. He refuted Rainville's allegations, saying Lambert was not believable.

"Her entire house of cards will fall down," he said.

Police were perhaps sloppy or careless, but they did not set out to frame Lambert. She was like a chameleon, he said, changing stories to suit her needs.

Rainville called Charles Lason, a professor in speech from her own alma mater, Northwestern, as her first witness. He said Laurie's vocal tract had been destroyed by the knife wound, leaving her unable to speak. Moreover, she would have been rendered unconscious in a matter of seconds. She could not have said anything.

Lason was asked about the local coroner's report indicating Laurie could speak.

"I don't think they were telling the truth," he said, the first testimony in a series offered by Rainville to show how far-reaching the conspiracy against Lambert actually was.

As the days passed in federal court, Rainville brought

forward witnesses to show Lambert had been abused by Yunkin, that she was afraid of him. Michael Pawlikowski, a lifeguard at Town & Country Apartments down the street from the Shows' condominium, said he saw Yunkin at the pool one day with a butterfly knife. He also saw Yunkin grab Lambert and dunk her in the pool. Also, another doctor testified that because of the massive amount of blood lost Laurie could not have lived longer than five minutes after her throat was slashed.

Rainville tried to show police incompetence and deceit when the chief had issued a press release saying they were looking for Yunkin. He changed it, however, to say only Lambert just before Yunkin signed a plea agreement. Moreover, police said they didn't find a pink trash bag at the river, when in fact they had, and a videotape of the river search given to the defense was shorter than the original by at least four minutes. It clearly had been edited, Rainville claimed.

Lambert's signed and sworn statement was "unusual," a former Philadelphia police detective said. Five pages were typewritten; one page was half typed, half handwritten; and one was all handwritten. The writing was done in a ballpoint pen, yet Lambert's handwritten signature over the top of all of the statement was done in red felt-tipped pen.

Rainville went to Boston to find one of the nation's preeminent experts on sexual and physical abuse. Ann Burgess, a psychiatric nurse, said Lambert was overwhelmed by Yunkin's dominance, swinging between being afraid on one end and being in love on the other. He had "total power" over her, Burgess claimed. At one point, Lambert claimed Yunkin had gotten away with a host of villainous acts and she was afraid he would continue to, and most especially that he would hurt her baby.

"The times that are good are good," Burgess said. "She just put up with the beatings." He loved her. He was going to marry her. She had nowhere else to go.

"It is very difficult to understand why women stay in this kind of situation," Burgess said. "But studies show other cases that women stay in the relationship because they feel they have no power to extricate themselves."

The alleged gang rape by the police officers on June 17, 1991, only served to confuse and terrify her even more.

"She is a target," Burgess said.

On the sixth day of the hearing, Lambert took the stand.

She described her early life as one of deep religious involvement and sorrow in losing two brothers who were stillborn. She grew up before her time, taking over her mother's duties during her five pregnancies. A friend Tressa died of a cocaine overdose when she was seventeen. She described meeting Yunkin, their dates and fights, the alleged rape and beatings. She claimed Yunkin's mother told her if she was nicer, Yunkin wouldn't beat her.

"Did you believe that?" Greenberg asked.

"Yes," Lambert responded.

Rainville took over questioning and asked how Lambert knew Robin Weaver, the East Lampeter Township policeman she had accused of raping her. She met him at her parents' house when he came to pick up his son, Kurt, at Lambert's brother's birthday party.

"My mother and I had taken the hose and we filled up balloons with the water so the kids could have a water balloon battle, and we put them in a trash bag. We were all running around chasing each other, and I had on a bathing suit, and I ran around the side of the house to throw a balloon at one of the kids, and I ran into Robin Weaver and broke the balloon all over him, and that was how I met him."

She was fourteen.

The next time she saw him was at the mall several months later. He asked her if she had a boyfriend and she said she didn't.

"He asked me if he could take me somewhere sometime, and I said, 'What do you mean?' He said: 'Well, like a date.' And I said, 'No.' I said, 'You're older— you're as old as my dad.' I was like: 'No.' "

When was the next time she met Robin Weaver?

The next time she saw him, he asked again if he could take her out.

"He said, 'You're older now,' and he said, 'Can I take you somewhere?' I said, 'What do you mean? Like a date again, right?' He said, 'Yeah.' I said, 'No.' He said, 'Like not even to a restaurant?' I said, 'No.' He said, 'Why?' I said, 'Because you're as old as my dad. You're too old.' "

She ran into him several more times as she was walking around. He would stop his car and talk to her, occasionally take her wherever she was going.

Then in 1991, Lambert claimed, Weaver's demeanor changed.

"One night I was with Allen Rudolph, and I hadn't seen Robin probably in two months or three months. We were swimming in the creek and we were skinny-dipping, because we didn't have our bathing suits, and Robin Weaver and two other police cars, this was in the middle of the night, they pulled up to the pines, and I didn't know how they knew we were there, but Robin got out of the car and he went after Allen. He just charged at Allen, and I pushed Allen into the creek and I told him to run. I said [to] get out of here. Run. He didn't want to go, and I started screaming at him. I said

[to] just get out of here, just get out of here. He left. Allen swam and he got on the other side, and then he ran home, and I could hear him crashing through the trees.

"Then Robin got mad and he started screaming at me. He's like, 'He's a kid. What are you messing around with him for? He's a kid. I'm a man. You should be going out with me.' He was just . . . he was enraged. He was furious. The two cops with him are laughing at him. They told him that he better get a grip on himself."

"When you were having this conversation with him, did you have any clothes on?" Rainville asked.

"No," Lambert said. "I had a sheet on me, and Robin kept telling me to drop the sheet and he said, 'I'm a cop.' He said, 'I'm telling you, drop the sheet.' I said, No. I wouldn't drop it. I told him, I said, 'What are you going to do? Shoot me?' Then his—the guys that were with him just laughed. Then they went and they got my clothes and I went in the woods and got dressed and then I came back out."

She walked through the woods to Allen's house. When she left about thirty minutes later, Weaver was waiting for her on the road.

"He told me, 'Get in the car,' and I said, 'No.' He said, 'Get in the car now.' So I got in the car and I told him, I was, like, what do you want? He said, 'I just want to talk to you.' I said, 'All right.' He started telling me that my clothes were too skimpy and that I was going to get raped. And he said, 'You know what you're doing, the way you walk around.' "

He stopped at the stoplight, she said, and they talked for about half an hour.

"I told him everything. He said to me, 'Why don't you leave Lawrence?' He said, 'I'm a nice guy.' I told him, I said, 'You're married and you are too old.' "

After that, Lambert claimed, she saw Weaver sitting outside her house in his patrol car at all hours of the day.

"I went down to get the mail one time, and he started, he started acting like really mean with me. Like telling me, 'Get in the car.' I said, 'No.' He said, 'Get in the car. We're going out.' I said, 'No, we're not.' I wouldn't go with him. He started getting, like, really mean. Then I started getting phone calls telling me that they were going to rape me."

"Did you recognize the voice?"

"No. It was gravelly. At first I thought it was Lawrence being hateful and just playing, I don't know, some kind of mean joke on me, because it would happen when Lawrence was at work."

About the fifth time she saw Weaver sitting outside her house, she called Chief Glick. She told him she was having trouble with Weaver.

"I told him that I knew Robin Weaver and he said, well, what is the problem? Is this a personal thing? I said, I don't think it is. Not now. Because he's in uniform and he's in a police car when he's doing these things, and I don't think it's anything personal anymore."

He said he would look into it. Lambert said the chief also told her not to tell anyone else about it. After that, she didn't see him again until June 17.

She had spent the day at the pool and a friend took her home. She felt drained from a day in the sun and fell asleep on the couch. She awoke to the sound of a car in the parking lot and heard people get out and then footsteps on the stairs. She assumed it was Lawrence.

She opened the door for him, turned, and saw it was Robin Weaver and two other people behind him, one in a police uniform, the other—an older man—not. The man in uniform had short-cropped dark blond hair and was probably in his early- to mid-thirties. The other was over fifty with thin hair on top, a long pointy nose, and a stomach over his pants. She saw his badge on his belt.

She was wearing a bikini.

"Robin Weaver pushed me back, kind of like this," she said, "and I thought he was kind of playing around, and I was, like, what are you doing? I just looked at him like, like he was crazy. He kept pushing me back and he pushed me into the living room and I kept looking at him and I was, like, Robin, what are you doing?"

He pushed her to the floor as the uniformed officer got on her left side and leaned across her chest, pinning her arms. The older man positioned himself above her head and they laid something cold and hard across her throat. They tapped something hard on her head; she couldn't tell what.

"Robin Weaver said [to] show it to her. They showed it to me and it was a black gun."

She said she froze.

"Robin, he yanked my bathing suit bottom down and he—just like my left leg was out and the bottom was still on the side, the leg of it was around my ankle, and he got on me and he pulled, he pulled my legs up, like he put his hand under me here, and he pulled his zipper down and he raped me, and I don't know, all the time he was doing it, I just looked at his badge, I kept seeing it flash, the light kept hitting it from the window, and every time he moved, I kept seeing it just flash.

"Then he said something about sharing to the guy in the uniform and he said: All right. He came down and he did it, and I just watched his badge the whole time, the flash. Then they told the other guy, the older guy, that he had to do it, because he was there, and he came down and then he raped me. Then the guy said, the older guy up here, when he was done, he said, 'I think she needs to have her mouth shut. What are we going to do about this?'

"The guy in uniform said, he pointed to Robin and said, well, he's the boss. Leave it up to him. Robin looked at me and, he looked at me really hard for a minute, he looked down at me like that, and then he was like: nah. We can just leave her here. They all got up and started to leave, and he moved over to the side and let the older guy leave first, and then the guy in the uniform left, and then Robin looked back at me and he looked down at me and he smiled, like this really sick smile, and he said: 'After all, who would believe her?' And he turned around and left."

Asked why she didn't call the police, she said, "Because they were the police."

She got up and called Mike Pawlikowski, but he wasn't home. She tried to call Lawrence, but couldn't find him. She called Hazel Show.

"I asked her where Lawrence was and I was hysterical. I was screaming. She kept telling me to calm down and [saying], Who is this? I kept telling her, 'Where is Lawrence? Where's Lawrence? I know he's there. Where is he?' She kept telling me to calm down and I was freaking out and I was hysterical. And then she ended up hanging up on me, because I don't think she could understand me."

She called many others.

"When Lawrence came back home, did you tell him?" Rainville asked.

"I jumped out of bed and they had left, one of the police officers left a gun in the house, and I don't know how, I found it in the living room when I went back in there, and I thought they came back and I had the gun in my hand, and I jumped up out of the bed and I stuck it in Lawrence's face, because I didn't know it was him, and I thought it was them coming back, and I don't know. It was just—I was sleeping, and I would be up, and somebody was in there and I just panicked. He grabbed it away from me and he threw it on the floor, and he started beating me up and he kicked me in the stomach, and then he left and he left it laying on the floor."

"Did you ever tell Lawrence what had happened?"

"No."

She told no one after that.

The allegations did not come as a surprise to East Lampeter Police. They had heard it when the brief was filed and they had heard her story in detail when she was deposed earlier that year. Lambert identified the uniformed officer as John Bowman while she was giving her deposition in mid-March.

While she was telling her story, John Bowman and other East Lampeter Township police officers were sitting in the hallway playing Scrabble. Bowman and Weaver knew Lambert had accused them of raping her, but they had not been told what day the incident was supposed to have taken place until her deposition.

Someone came outside and told Bowman. It was June 17, he said.

"What?" Bowman exclaimed as he jerked at his wedding ring, slipping it off. He looked inside and smiled.

"I was on my honeymoon!" he said. Bowman had married his longtime sweetheart, Teresa, three days before the alleged rape. He was in Virginia Beach.

But even though he showed motel receipts and phone records, Lambert was still saying the second guy looked like him.

"It's like tilting at windmills," he said. "How much proof do they need?"

Lambert told the court she heard not long after the gang rape that Yunkin had raped Laurie Show, but she didn't pay the rumor much attention. She said she wasn't jealous.

"Did you ever ask Yunkin whether he had raped Laurie Show?"

"Yes. August eighth. Lawrence and I were at the mall, at East Towne Mall, and Laurie came out of work and her father came to pick her up. That was John Show. He came to pick her up. He called Lawrence a rapist and said that Lawrence raped his daughter, and I turned and looked at Lawrence, I was like: What? I had heard rumors, but it never, like, really hit home until that day.

"John Show and Lawrence almost got in a fight, and Laurie was crying and pushing her dad back, and I was trying to pull Lawrence back, and then they didn't fight but they almost—they were going to fistfight."

Later that night, she asked him if he raped Laurie.

"He brought his hands up like this and smashed me in the face. He just looked at me, his head turned like someone hit him that fast. He stopped dead in the middle of his conversation and he—he punched me with the back of his hand in the mouth, and I screamed and I jumped out of the car right before it stopped, and I went to run up the stairs into the apartment, and Lawrence grabbed my leg and he ripped me back down the stairs."

She ran up the stairs, and at the top of the stairs, Yunkin shoved her down and he hit her in the stomach. She darted into the bedroom, but he grabbed her by the throat and punched her in her face, she said.

She screamed as blood poured from her nose and mouth. When Yunkin slipped and fell, she ran out of the house, but he caught up with her and shoved her down the wooden staircase into the parking lot.

Her neighbor Steve Drehoble carried her into his house. He had called the police. They asked if she wanted to prosecute. The officer, not one of the men she accused of raping her, took her upstairs to pack her clothes. He took her to the police station, but she did not want to prosecute.

"He would be out in a week and he would come kill me," she said.

Lambert testified to numerous other beatings at Yunkin's hands. After Yunkin killed her chinchilla, she tried to end her relationship with Mike Pawlikowski. Even though she was still living with Yunkin, she had been dating him. Their relationship started after she got mad at Allen Rudolph for ripping her bathing suit off her at the pool.

But Jackie Yunkin found out Pawlikowski was spending days with Lambert at the house she shared with Yunkin. She told her son about it, Lambert testified. He came home, grabbed a butcher knife, and sliced his face.

" 'If I ever see Mike Pawlikowski again, I will slice his head off,' " Lambert said Yunkin yelled at her. " 'And you can keep his head in the refrigerator.' "

Lambert told Dalzell about the plans to embarrass Laurie Show and of the confrontations they had had. When they moved to the trailer in Pequea, she felt like a prisoner. Yunkin left for work at 5:00 A.M. and didn't return until evening. She was there all day alone with no telephone.

Lambert also said it was Laurie Show who was harassing her, not the other way around. Laurie called her apartment looking for Lawrence regularly, Lambert said. The first shoving incident at the Deb Shop in July was started by Laurie when Lambert asked her to stop calling her house. She was pregnant and sick, and getting up to answer the phone was a problem.

"I thought she was trying to kick me in the stomach," Lambert told the court. "I pushed her by the shoulders, because I didn't want to fight her."

She hit her head on the window.

The incident at Root's Market was started by Hazel Show, Lambert said, as Hazel glared at her from her seat. Hazel could not believe what she was hearing. Lambert had managed to twist every story around to make her seem the victim. That's what years in prison did to people. Too much time to think and connive, Hazel thought.

Lambert said Hazel screamed at Lawrence at the market and called him a rapist.

The incident at East Towne Mall was a misunderstanding. She came up behind Laurie, thinking she was someone else, and pulled her hair. Laurie tried to kick her in the stomach once again. Lambert said she did not hit Laurie, ever.

Yunkin controlled her life completely, she said. He took her paychecks and cashed them and she had to ask him for money. He tortured her cat, Bubbles, which her mother got when she was pregnant with her. By the end, Buck was the only friend he would let her see. And she had told them she had killed someone in Alaska, Lambert claimed.

It was Yunkin's idea to get rope and hats at Kmart the night before Laurie's murder, Lambert claimed. And it was Yunkin and Buck who planned the assault.

"Lawrence was adamant about it," Lambert testified. "He was between being in a rage and being upset. He kept saying he was going to jail. He was pacing back and forth. He kept digging his fingers through his hair."

They told Lambert they were going to beat Laurie badly, but Lambert told them they couldn't, that Laurie was pregnant. She tried to talk them out of it. Finally they agreed to the hair-cutting prank, Lambert said.

She also said her letters to Yunkin, in which she said he had nothing to do with the murders, were actually code to him to stick to the story, that she would protect him. She would not implicate him.

Lambert told Dalzell she refused to let her first attorney, Roy Shirk, bring up the issue of the gang rape, because she was afraid the police would go to her parents' house and hurt her baby. She forbade her second lawyer to bring it up as well, and initially she told Rainville she could not use it. She allowed it only after her parents moved and she felt safer.

"And the other things is," Lambert said, "I'm just so tired and I just don't care anymore. And two, when I heard Robin Weaver said during his deposition that I had raised it in the petition, I couldn't believe it because there is no way he could have ever known about that unless he was there and he did it. It was not raised in the petition."

"Is that true?" Dalzell asked.

"That is true, Your Honor," Rainville answered.

She read him the testimony from his February 26th deposition. He said he told people Lambert was making an allegation against him for stalking and rape.

"I want him here this afternoon," Dalzell demanded, "and I don't want anyone from your office to say a word about what has come up here, but just I want him here. If he resists, please tell me. I will have the marshal arrest him, OK?"

Madenspacher called his office and told them to get a message to Weaver to come to Philadelphia as soon as possible.

"It is imperative, imperative that he get down here today," the judge said, adding twice more that he intended to have Weaver arrested if he didn't show.

Rainville told the judge the district attorney's office had talked with Weaver about the rape allegation the previous week.

"So he's been coached," the judge said.

"It sounds like it to me, Your Honor," Rainville responded.

"I'm going to direct that Mr. Kenneff have no further contact with any witness in this case," the judge said. He also ordered that Kenneff not read anything in the newspapers about the case and advised him to seek counsel from a lawyer.

"God help him if he coached this witness. God help him," Dalzell said.

The judge also ordered no contact between six police officers and any witnesses.

Rainville took Lambert through the document known as the twenty-nine questions, point by point. She said she asked Yunkin whether he had cheated on her with anyone except "those little girls." She explained that she meant an eleven-year-old girl who was in his house. Lambert said he pulled his penis from his pants and told the girl to tie a red ribbon around it. At the pool where he was a lifeguard, he pulled young girls into his lap and pinched their chests, she said.

On cross-examination Madenspacher asked Lambert about letters she wrote to Yunkin while they were in Lancaster County Prison, letters referring to someone as a slut.

Lambert denied she meant Laurie Show.

Madenspacher asked why she didn't go to a rape crisis center after the gang rape.

"I didn't know there was any such thing," Lambert replied.

"Well, why didn't you go to your parents?"

"Because I didn't want—for one thing, they knew Robin Weaver and his son."

She didn't tell Yunkin or the other men she dated. She didn't tell the security guard at a fair she attended not long afterward, Madenspacher said.

He also asked Lambert to go through the murder once again. Her story did not waver.

Weaver showed up for the afternoon session. It was day seven of the hearing. He said he talked with the district attorney's office about the allegation and made some notes about discrepancies in her story. One was that police officers' uniforms in June were silver and were changed later that year to blue.

Rainville asked why Weaver did not put in his report that Laurie identified Lambert as her killer.

"I don't remember it being said," he responded.

The next day, Weaver continued testifying. He admitted he had been suspended from the force in 1988 for five days for using excessive force on a woman and in 1991 for assaulting a mentally retarded man.

"I was exonerated by my department, because I didn't do anything wrong," Weaver said.

"There have been other allegations of excessive force made against you?" Rainville asked.

"Probably, yes."

"You don't know?" she asked, her voice rising.

"No," he responded.

Madenspacher asked whether the allegation was true, and Weaver said it was not. He also said he learned of the allegation on February 20 from Ron Savage, a policeman. Savage told him he didn't know for sure, but he believed she was accusing Weaver.

Lambert's lawyers also called attention to the defense's pathology witness who was expected to say Laurie could not speak, but after a conversation with the prosecution testified that she could. They also cast doubt on the crime scene photos, saying many parts of the Shows' home were not photographed. Various police officers testified about how they did their jobs, searching the river for evidence, getting statements from the defendants. Rainville continued making the point that police were framing Lambert to cover for their pals. Thirty-five times the district attorney's office failed to give Lambert's lawyer information he needed.

Kenneff was asked about the black sweatpants that were Yunkin's but were supposedly worn by Lambert the morning of the murder.

"You're the same person who put Yunkin on as a witness at trial to say they were the very same sweatpants he was wearing and Lisa was wearing?" Greenberg asked.

"Correct," Kenneff answered.

"Now you're saying these sweatpants would look ridiculous on Yunkin and there is no evidence you put on trial that the sweatpants were other than Yunkin's—correct?"

"Correct."

"If you had your way, she would have been executed on that evidence?"

Kenneff did not respond. Dalzell ordered him to answer.

"We have produced these sweatpants," he reluctantly said.

"Is this some kind of bizarre attempt to keep her in jail? You think this is some kind of game?"

"No, I don't, sir."

"You realize there's a human being in jail serving a life sentence based on evidence you put on in front of Judge Stengel and now you're disowning it? Not only are you disowning it, you're committing perjury, sir. Are you sure it's Lisa Lambert that's the dangerous person in this room?"

Madenspacher objected as he bolted from his chair.

Greenberg withdrew the statement.

The Greenberg-Rainville team pressed on: The prosecution had not interviewed Laurie's boyfriend; there were discrepancies in police reports; police did not give the defense information about a woman who said she saw Yunkin leaving the condominium complex.

Ron Savage returned to the stand, and as he spoke, something in Hazel Show's mind began to swirl. She was remembering something from the day her daughter was killed. She had in fact seen Yunkin driving near her home. Dalzell broke for lunch and Hazel stumbled toward the elevator. She was shaking and began to cry. She doesn't remember walking the two blocks back to her hotel room. She could hardly stand. The memory of Yunkin's face in a car etched into her brain.

She called Renee Schuler, who relayed a message that she was under court order not to talk to anyone about the case. Then Hazel called Pam Grosh, the victim advocate. She set in motion a procedure that turned lives upside down, Hazel Show's and dozens more in East Lampeter Township.

A meeting was quickly arranged in Dalzell's chambers. Hazel sat sobbing and shaking. Lambert was escorted in and Dalzell said, "I'm sorry my dog is not here for you to pet."

Hazel told the judge, "As I was sitting there today, then it came back that I was going in—we have an entrance going in and one coming out—and I was going in and about three-quarters of the way in, a car was coming out and I looked at Lawrence. There was recognition on his face and he pushed someone with blond hair down and there was a dark-haired person in the backseat.

"Savage told me that the lady [Bayan] was kind of disturbed anyhow and probably wouldn't be a reliable witness. So we [were] better to go with Oak View Road because everyone had them [Michelle and Tabitha] running in that direction . . . I never thought anymore of it until I was sitting in there [the courtroom] . . . It all just came back."

Hazel showed the judge on an aerial photo where she saw Yunkin. It was the same place Lambert had said. Lambert had testified Yunkin said, "Oh, fuck, I just saw Hazel."

Dalzell told the lawyers and Show that he was going to free Lambert immediately. Savage had perjured himself and should be removed from his post. He ordered U.S. marshals to protect Lambert, Rainville, and Greenberg.

"They are in danger of retaliation," Dalzell said.

Hazel Show broke down, sobbing.

"But Laurie told me she did it," she sputtered. Dalzell was not listening. Hazel was taken into a secretary's office to calm down, and the court called a nurse to check her vital signs. She was in shock. Lambert would be free.

In open court minutes later, Dalzell announced his decision. The new information is "totally consistent with what Miss Lambert has said since 1992," he said.

Rainville and Greenberg took her home to the Central City town house they shared with their young son. Pick up whatever Lambert needed at the store, the judge said. She needn't go back to prison.

Dalzell asked the lawyers "to look for any case in any jurisdiction in the English-speaking world" where misconduct was as severe. It was April 16, a Wednesday. Lambert had not walked the streets freely for more than six years.

Hazel Show, leaning on her brother Butch, caught the next train back home to Lancaster. John Show met them at the train station and took them to his house in Bird-In-Hand. They, along with other family members who had heard the news and rushed over, sat around the living room, a distinct gloom filling the home. It felt as if Laurie Show had died all over again.

Twenty-seven

Dalzell resumed the hearing on Thursday morning. Hazel Show did not return. Madenspacher asked him to reconsider his decision to free Lambert.

"You'd agreed to it," Dalzell replied of the release.

"I agreed to that, and in retrospect I was wrong," the district attorney said.

The district attorney had barely finished when Dalzell said briskly, "OK. That's denied. What's next."

He then asked Dalzell to remove himself from the case. Bemused, Dalzell took off his bifocals and looked at the ceiling. He chewed on the earpiece of the glasses.

Dalzell said he was "punctiliously fair," and he most certainly would be shocked whenever he heard perjury in his court. Motion denied.

Dalzell responded, "We are going to continue this case and hopefully finish it today."

The judge also said he would ask for a federal investigation of the East Lampeter Township Police and the Lancaster County District Attorney's Office.

Dalzell called Savage, now represented by Alvin Lewis at the expense of the Lancaster County commissioner, back to the stand. Lewis said Savage was prepared to continue testifying truthfully.

"We see no evidence of perjury in the courtroom. The charge of perjury has the attempt to chill the proceedings," Lewis said, adding that Lambert had been convicted fairly in Lancaster County Court.

Dalzell did not want to hear it. He told Savage to take the stand.

Savage could not remember when he arrived at the Shows' house, the time of the emergency call to police, or when he let an officer leave the scene.

"You're lying about everything you did that morning?" Rainville asked.

"No, I'm not," he replied. He also denied editing the tape of his interrogation of Yunkin. Rainville said he erased two minutes and thirty-eight seconds.

The next day, Hazel Show returned to the courtroom to testify. Her ex-husband came, too. She was emotional, much more so than any other time she testified. She felt angry that Lambert had been free now for two nights. She also thought Lambert had a smug look on her face.

Yet, she managed to make her way through the story once more, beginning with how angry Lambert was over Laurie's seeing Yunkin. She called and threatened so often, Hazel changed her phone number to an unlisted one.

"We left the phone off the hook when we wanted to go to bed," Hazel said. "If you didn't answer it, it would ring for hours. If you answered it, Michelle would be yelling, screaming, and cursing."

Once again she told of trying to hold her daughter's sliced body together and of her last words, "Michelle did it, Michelle did it."

Her story complete, Dalzell praised her for telling about her recollection.

"I've been in the legal profession for thirty years, and I've never seen a more courageous act by any witness than what you did on Wednesday," Dalzell said.

Hazel replied, "My parents brought me up to tell the truth, and I believe in God. I know one day I'll see my daughter in heaven, so it's up to me to tell the truth."

As she sat back down in the courtroom, she realized she had not been able to make her central point. She would have had to arrive home earlier than she had previously believed if she had seen Yunkin because he testified he saw school bus lights. That means she most certainly heard her daughter's dying words.

In her closing remarks, Rainville said Lambert's 1992 trial was "the worst case of prosecutorial misconduct that there ever was." Police and prosecutors fabricated the evidence. Yunkin and Buck killed Laurie Show.

Lambert should be freed and not retried.

"All the evidence that would allow [her] to prove her innocence has been destroyed. Justice requires that Miss Lambert be released. The truth is out. Lisa Lambert is innocent. Innocent of murder. Innocent of conspiracy. The horror of horrors is that they knew she was innocent all along," Rainville said.

Madenspacher said, "We did provide the information that enabled them to bring forth these allegations."

Police did not alter the crime scene.

"They really did a pretty bad, sloppy job of it" if they did," Madenspacher said.

Dalzell interrupted with these concerns: Why did police and Kenneff not investigate Yunkin's role in the murder more thoroughly? Do you think the commonwealth gave up too early, too much, to make a pact with this devil? Why is Lambert described as wearing different outfits?

"It's just a defect that leaps off the page," Dalzell said.

What about the gap of two minutes and thirty-eight seconds in the tape of Yunkin's statement?

Madenspacher said Lambert admitted being at the Shows' home, making her guilty of something.

Lambert alleged ninety-five counts of prosecutorial misconduct.

"Let's say she has proven twenty of them, how could you have a retrial? How could there be a new trial, because you'd have excluded all poisoned evidence," Dalzell said.

He also wondered about motive. Buck was along for some wild ride. Didn't Yunkin have more reason to kill than Lambert?

Hazel said her daughter identified Lambert, the district attorney said.

"That's your most powerful evidence," Dalzell said.

Dalzell said he would be in court Monday morning at eleven o'clock with a ruling.

Twenty-eight

For the official ruling, Dalzell's opinion filled ninety pages.

Lisa Lambert had claimed she was "actually innocent of the first-degree murder" and that "she was the victim of wholesale prosecutorial misconduct.

"After fourteen days of testimony covering 3,225 pages of transcript, we have now concluded that Ms. Lambert has presented an extraordinary—indeed, it appears, unprecedented—case. We therefore hold that the writ should issue, that Lisa Lambert should be immediately released, and that she should not be retried."

Dalzell said he believed Laurie Show did not say, "Michelle did it." No physical evidence linked Lambert to the murder, and she had no injuries, cuts, or bruises when she was arrested. The blood found on Laurie Show's ring did not match Ms. Lambert's. Experts testified Laurie could not speak.

In addition, Yunkin confessed in the twenty-nine questions, and he lied on the stand.

"A review of these twenty-nine questions, and, most importantly, Yunkin's answers to them, leaves no doubt that Yunkin was the murderer of Laurie Show, and that his accomplice in this enterprise was Tabitha Buck, and not Lisa Lambert," Dalzell wrote.

Lambert was not wearing Yunkin's clothes. The sweat-pants in evidence were too small for Yunkin.

"By far the most damning evidence against Ms. Lambert at trial regarding her animus against Laurie Show was the testimony of Laura Thomas that she heard Ms. Lambert in June or July of 1991 say she intended to 'slit the throat' of Laurie Show. It is now clear that this evidence was a fabrication of Detective Savage," Dalzell wrote.

Three officers interviewed her and none wrote that she had said anything about throat slitting.

"Thomas admitted to the East Lampeter Police that she made up this story, and conceded that she even used an onion to create tears and slapped her face to create redness."

She was charged with making a false report, a misdemeanor, and pleaded guilty to disorderly conduct on March 9, 1992. Thomas paid a fine of $50 and costs of $65.

The evidence corroborates Lambert's account, Dalzell said. Lambert testified she had nothing to do with the rope. A bloodhound on December 23, 1991, found the rope after being presented with Tabitha Buck's scent. Lambert testified blood was in the hallway and on the tile floors outside Laurie Show's bedroom. Three medical personnel confirmed it.

Yunkin exploited Lambert's vulnerability, the judge said. He dominated her and convinced her to cover up for him.

Dalzell said Rainville proved twenty-five of the ninety-five allegations of prosecutorial misconduct, chief among them that witnesses including Hazel Show saw Yunkin in the condominium complex that morning and that the twenty-nine questions were not altered. He found the police tape of the river search had been edited and that crime scene pictures had been altered. The phone cord was wrapped around Laurie's leg, yet no one on the scene saw the cord there. In addition, Dalzell said, police destroyed evidence, including the earring back found in Laurie's hair and the pearl earring found on the floor.

Dalzell said the police altered the crime scene and Lambert's written statement.

"The trial was corrupted from start to finish by wholesale prosecutorial misconduct," the judge said. "Former Detective Savage may have committed perjury before us and obstructed justice in 1992. Other witnesses in the state capital murder trial, including chief county detective Solt, Detective Barley, Lieutenant Renee Schuler, and Officers Weaver, Reed, and Bowman, fabricated and destroyed crucial evidence and likely perjured themselves in the state proceeding. At least six seemed to perjure themselves before us. Agents of the commonwealth intimidated witnesses both in the capital murder trial as well as in this habeas corpus proceeding. The prosecutor who tried the Lambert case and sought Ms. Lambert's execution knowingly used perjured testimony.

"We have found that virtually all of the evidence which the commonwealth used to convict Lisa Lambert of first-degree murder was either perjured, altered, or fabricated. The commonwealth has even attempted to perpetrate a fraud on this court by destroying the men's extra-large black sweatpants it used to convict Lisa Lambert and substituting a much smaller pair in this proceeding, apparently in an attempt to undermine Ms. Lambert's contention that it was Yunkin who wore the black sweatpants.

"This is a case with no shortage of victims. First and foremost among the victims of what happened here is, of course, Lisa Lambert. For her the long nightmare that began in her teens is ending. It will, however, take much more than the granting of her petition to heal the wounds and banish the demons that have for so long hurt and haunted her.

"Another victim is Hazel Show and her family. As a result of this headlong caricature of a prosecution, this courageous and honest mother has been deprived of the finality and closure she so richly deserves after the murder of her only child. Had law enforcement officials merely followed the clear guidelines the Constitution provides, this matter would have ended almost five years ago, and the process of healing would have begun then. These law enforcement officials unquestionably have wounded Hazel Show and her family.

"The people of Lancaster County are also victims at the hands of their own government. The community's proper and good feelings of compassion toward the Shows, and outrage at this horrible crime, were abused here. Just as the Shows have suffered from the lack of closure, so has the community at large. But this same community has a powerful interest in the outcome we have reached here. This case shows how high a price the community pays when its government ignores the Constitution to get instant revenge. This case thus demonstrates the importance of preventing a recurrence of such a grotesque parody of due process.

"Those who have read this sad history may well ask themselves, how could a place idealized in Peter Weir's *Witness* become like the world in David Lynch's *Blue Velvet?* Because it is so important to that community—and indeed to many others—to prevent a recurrence of this nightmare, we offer a few reflections on the record.

"Laurie Show's grandfather Dr. Whitlaw Show was in the 1980s Coroner of Lancaster County. Her mother, Hazel, is, as we saw on April sixteenth, a paragon of morality, and kept and—we are sure—keeps what we saw in the video of her condominium as a picture-perfect home.

"Regrettably, Laurie Show had enough contact with the Lancaster County demimonde to meet the very symbol of that dark world, Lawrence Yunkin. He raped Ms. Show on an early date, as he did to Lisa Lambert on their fourth. Unlike Lisa Lambert, however, Laurie Show eventually complained to her mother about it, who lodged a complaint with the East Lampeter Police Department. Reports of this complaint motivated Yunkin to concoct his plan to intimidate Laurie Show into silence, an idea that ended in her brutal murder at his and Buck's hands.

"The record is clear that East Lampeter Township police chief Glick and his colleagues never considered any other suspects than the now-familiar three. And of this trio, Lisa Lambert was as though delivered from central casting for the part of villainess. By the testimony of those who loved her, Aimee Shearer Bernstein and Michael Pawlikowski, she was at the time literally 'trailer trash.'

"The community thus closed ranks behind the good family Show and exacted instant revenge against this supposed villainess. It is important to stress that this solidarity and compassion for the Shows defines our outsiders' idealization of this community. But then what was and is a social strength was turned inside out into corruption.

"Almost immediately after the snap judgment was made, law enforcement officials uncovered inconvenient facts such as the absence of cuts and bruises on Ms. Lambert—answer, no photographs of her—and many on Tabitha Buck and some on Yunkin—answer, conceal or destroy the mug shots. And as these untidy facts accumulated, Kenneff and Savage discovered a balm for these evidentiary bruises, Lawrence Yunkin.

"Yunkin would say and do anything to obtain what his lawyer rightly described as 'the deal of the century' in the February 7, 1992, plea agreement for 'hindering apprehension,' which would carry a state sentencing guideline's range of zero to twelve months. Thus Lancaster's best made a pact with Lancaster's worst to convict the 'trailer trash' of first-degree murder.

"In making a pact with this devil, Lancaster County made a Faustian bargain. It lost its soul and it almost executed an innocent, abused woman. Its legal edifice now in ashes, we can only hope for a *Witness*-like barn raising of the temple of justice."

Dalzell's decision blew out across the hills of Lancaster County like a summertime tornado. Residents were outraged. A pact with the devil? In their community? John and Hazel Show immediately began collecting signatures on a petition to have Dalzell impeached.

In a jail cell in Lancaster County, Tabbi Buck was lying on her bed when a guard told her she had a visitor. She didn't want a visit, she said. The guard insisted. She needed to see this person. She went out and a former inmate was there. She sat down in a folding chair opposite Buck, took hold of her hands, and looked into her eyes.

"She's out," the woman said.

"What!" Buck exclaimed. "No, this can't be true."

She started crying and hurried back to her cell. She lay down on her bed and sobbed.

"This can't be true. This can't be true," she said. "I saw what she did. No way."

A female guard came in and comforted her.

Her mother, meanwhile, heard the news in a call from a Pennsylvania friend.

"You're kidding me," Guier exclaimed into the receiver. "Well, Tab's just taken the rap. This is a crooked deal. To paint her as a poor innocent thing who got railroaded, that's just ridiculous."

Guier felt helpless, as she had many times before. She was consumed with the thought that if she or her ex-husband had had the money to hire their own lawyer, their daughter would not be spending the rest of her natural life in prison. Anger filled her. Her faith in the system faded away. Justice? For whom?

Jackie Yunkin had just come into her mother-in-law's house in Parkesburg, Pennsylvania, from buying a slip for a dress she intended to wear to her father-in-law's funeral the next day. Her brother-in-law looked at her sadly and said, "I don't know how to tell you this."

Barry Yunkin said, "Just tell her."

"Michelle was released about one this afternoon," he said.

Jackie Yunkin went to her knees. Crying, she blurted, "Lawrence can't come home to bury his grandfather, and this bitch gets to walk away. It's not fair."

As far as the Yunkins knew, it was over. Lambert was permanently free, while their son, who wasn't at the house, who didn't know anything about the plan to kill Laurie, was still behind bars.

Twenty-nine

Lisa Michelle Lambert went home with Greenberg and Rainville on her first night of freedom and stayed for three months. Rainville worked on building Lambert's self-esteem. She taught her how to dress, took her to new types of restaurants. Lambert got a job as a secretary and met new friends. She was especially fond of Greenberg and Rainville's son, Jeremy.

Lambert moved in with a friend in Wilmington in July and then later got her own apartment. Rainville says she and her family were threatened repeatedly. One letter called her a "fuckin Jew bitch." Her son became unnaturally fearful.

Just before the new year in 1997, the third circuit court of appeals overturned Dalzell's ruling. The court said Lambert had not exhausted all of her remedies in state court. A new hearing would be held in Lancaster County and Lisa Michelle Lambert would go back to prison.

Rainville and Greenberg drove Lambert back to Edna Mahon Prison in their blue Honda on February 4, 1998. She'd been free for ten months. Dressed all in black, as was Rainville, the twenty-five-year-old Lambert looked solemn as she went into the New Jersey prison for women. She had said she would never go back to jail. She would kill herself first. She planned to take pills in a hotel room. Her daughter, now six years old, asked her not to hurt herself. Somehow, the little girl had read her mind, Lambert said.

Rainville told reporters gathered outside the prison that she admired Lambert more than anyone in the world.

"She's so brave," Rainville said. "She's very courageous."

The lawyer also called the appeals court ruling an outrage and said, "It's a dark, dark day for American justice."

Judge Lawrence Stengel announced he would hear the postconviction relief appeal in Lancaster in the spring. This time the commonwealth would be represented not by local officials but by the attorney general's office. There was an allegation of conflict of interest, which fit the narrow parameters for the state to take over a local case.

Christy Fawcett, deputy attorney general, would present the state's side at the hearing. Born in Minnesota, Fawcett worked for three years as a newspaper reporter in Muncie, Indiana, after graduating from Purdue. Newspaper work soon soured and she enrolled in law school. But after her first year, she quit to sail a thirty-six-foot wooden ketch in the Caribbean with her husband, Rob, who had just completed his residency as a family doctor. It had long been a dream to float aimlessly across the sea before the demands of real life pressed in on them.

They read and wrote and played Scrabble, sometimes going for days without seeing anyone else. It was solitude at its best. Nine months of sun and water and coming to an understanding of self and others. They sailed along the eastern United States to Long Island and through the Florida Keys. They ate what they caught and jumped over the side of the boat to bathe. They had stocked about $600 worth of canned goods on the boat before setting sail and then spent perhaps $4,000 more during the nine months they acted as vagabonds.

When the time came to head back to civilization, they decided to move to Hanover, Pennsylvania, where Rob's brother lived. He was a veterinarian in Hanover, his wife's hometown. Christy and Rob docked in Miami with no money, a "rude awakening," Christy would say years later. They sold their bicycles for food and the life raft for train tickets to Hanover.

Rob Fawcett started a private practice in family medicine; Christy finished her law degree at Dickinson. By the time she took over the Lambert case, she had worked as an assistant district attorney in York County, Pennsylvania, and the chief deputy prosecutor there, trying a range of cases. She tried several death penalty cases, including that of Mark Spots, known locally as a "natural born killer." He killed three elderly women in four days in three different counties. He was convicted and sentenced to die.

Fawcett joined the attorney general's office in the fall of 1997 in the capital litigation unit. Her role was to help local prosecutors with death penalty cases. She had heard of the Lambert case, of course, and, in fact, was in the federal courthouse in Philadelphia on another matter on the day Dalzell freed Lambert. She remembered the pandemonium of that day. Few could believe Dalzell had freed the young woman. Fawcett and the other attorneys general assigned to the case agreed at the outset they would give the trial record as objective a review as possible and "let the chips fall where they may," she recalled.

"If there was impropriety, we'd deal with it up front," she said years later. She said they found none. She pressed on, preparing for the post conviction relief hearing, over which Judge Stengel would preside.

On a morning in late April 1998, the same cast—defendant and victims, witnesses and the just plain curious—gathered once again in the courtroom where Lambert had been convicted six years earlier. New to the group was the feisty young attorney Christina Rainville met by an equally aggressive opponent, Christy Fawcett.

Rainville stunned courtroom observers and much of East Lampeter Township with her opening argument on April 30, 1998. She said policemen in East Lampeter Township, anxious to pin Laurie's murder on Lambert because three of them had raped her five months earlier, carried Laurie's body back into her condominium the night she died and staged crime scene photographs. The new photos, showing a telephone cord wrapped around Laurie's leg, were designed to make Lambert look like a liar because she had said Buck threw the phone across the room, Rainville said.

None of the prosecution or Show family members had heard that allegation before. Fawcett looked at the other lawyers in the team as if to say, Is she really saying this? Is she really claiming that police, prosecutors, and the coroner conspired to take a dead teenager's body from the morgue, located beneath a busy nursing home, and carried it through the streets of Lancaster and outlying hamlets, and into the second story of a condominium in a complex with dozens of homes?

Rainville pressed her case, one that hinged on showing prosecutorial misconduct. "Everyone makes mistakes, Your Honor, but human beings don't make 120 to 130 mistakes. The prosecution made many mistakes, every one of which hurt Lisa Lambert, every one of which helped the commonwealth fabricate its case," she said. "Prosecutors changed evidence again and again."

Lambert sat silently at the defense table. She wore

light blue pants and a gray sweatshirt. Her hair was brown and long, in a slight wave well past her shoulders. She had been back in prison for about three months. She had been brought from the prison in New Jersey the day before and would be housed at the Lancaster County Prison for the duration of the hearing, which would probably be about two months.

In her opening remarks, Fawcett told the judge, "She stands convicted of first-degree murder because what Lisa Lambert did in 1991 was first-degree murder of Laurie Show."

The lawyers spilled out their cases, much like the testimony had been previously presented. Days turned into weeks. This time the coroner refuted the allegation that the body had been taken from the morgue, as did Renee Schuler, the policewoman who lived across the street from the Shows. The body had been brought to the morgue on that December afternoon. The family viewed it that night. An autopsy began at 8:30 the next morning.

There was also testimony from a new source. Tabitha Buck had agreed to testify for the prosecution. In prison she fought with herself for days on end over whether to do so. Her conscience was telling her to do it. But she was after all a lifer, someone who knows the frustration, the anguish of being locked behind barbed wire–topped fences forever. And that lifer mentality could not wish an interminable jail sentence on anyone, even a woman who had betrayed her. That feeling was forcing her the other way.

Finally one night, she sat up straight in her bed and knew for sure what she was to do. This wasn't about her or Michelle. It was about Laurie and about Hazel Show. Hazel Show deserved to know what happened that morning in her daughter's bedroom before daybreak. She deserved to know the truth.

Buck realized, too, that no matter where she was, she had to be able to look at herself in the mirror.

She wore the blue prison jumpsuit of Lancaster County Prison as she walked into the courtroom in Lancaster. She swore to tell the truth.

Buck said she, Lambert, and Yunkin "hung out" through the fall of 1991. She soon learned that Lambert did not like Laurie Show. Lambert often called Laurie a "bitch." On the evening of December 19, 1991, around 10:30, Lambert came to her house; Yunkin stayed in the car.

"Michelle was very upset and went on and on about wanting to get Laurie back . . ." Buck said. Lambert was "crying and ranting, raving, she was upset."

"I asked her what she was going to do. She said, 'I'll kill her.' "

Lambert asked Buck to go with her to see Laurie the next morning. Buck should "wear [her] hair up, no makeup or fingernail polish." Yunkin and Lambert picked her up the next morning. Yunkin dropped them off on Oak View Road by a field. He went to McDonald's. Lambert told him to come back in fifteen minutes. They walked across the field toward the condominium complex. Lambert was not sure which one was the Shows'. When they found it, Lambert told Buck to go knock on the door and ask for Hazel Show. She did; Laurie answered the door.

Buck said she asked for Hazel, but Laurie said she was not home. Buck knew she wouldn't be there, because Lambert had called and arranged for Hazel to be at a counselor's appointment. Lambert pushed inside.

"Michelle apparently pushed Laurie back some distance," Buck said. "They were, like, in front of the kitchen area or the living room area. And they were holding each other's arms wrestling, like, arguing, yelling. At one point, Laurie, I guess, broke away from Michelle and came toward me and I remember Michelle saying something about don't go, stop or something and—oh, I did have sunglasses on. I failed to mention that. And Laurie grabbed my face, pushed me somehow, and knocked the sunglasses off, and Michelle was behind her and she had a knife and they were in the corner there where the door meets the wall, the hinges of the door, I guess."

"Do you know what Laurie was trying to do when she came toward you?" Fawcett asked.

"My guess is she was probably trying to leave."

"Could she leave?"

"She didn't have a chance."

"And why not?"

"Michelle was on her."

Lambert had a "large kitchen knife." Huddled in a corner near the front door, the two fought over the knife. Laurie grabbed the blade and Lambert pulled it out of her hand. Laurie ran into her bedroom, but Lambert "grabbed her by the back of her hair when she walked through the door and she cut her hair."

Laurie had a phone in her hand, but Buck did not know what happened to it. Laurie was on her knees facing the bed, and Michelle smacked her at least twice, possibly more, in the back of the head with the butt of the knife. Lambert handed Buck the knife and tried to get a rope over Laurie's head.

"Stop struggling," Lambert said. "It would be a lot easier this way." Laurie then reached for a pair of scissors, but Buck moved them beyond Laurie's reach.

"What happened after you moved the scissors out of Laurie's reach?"

"Michelle told me to cut her throat."

"Michelle told you to cut Laurie's throat?"

"Uh-huh."

"What did you say to Michelle?"

"I said no."

"Okay. Did you still have the knife in your hand at that point?"

"Yes."

"What did you do with the knife?"

"Michelle took it back."

"What happened after that?"

"She cut her leg and told her to stop struggling. Michelle told me to grab her feet, make her stop kicking, and I did."

"You did that?"

"Yes."

Buck sat on Laurie's feet, facing away from her, she testified. Laurie's feet stopped moving. Buck moved and looked at Laurie.

"I saw her throat cut," she said. Lambert was sitting next to Laurie, on Laurie's right. The throat was cut so deeply, she could see into Laurie's throat and could hear a "hissing, whooshing sound."

"After you turned around and saw that Laurie's throat was cut and you saw that Michelle was still next to Laurie, did you see that the knife was still in Michelle's hand?"

"Yes."

"What did you see Michelle do then?"

"When I looked at Laurie, I said, 'Is she dead? Did you kill her?' And Michelle said, 'I don't know,' and proceeded to further cut Laurie's throat."

"Can you describe what she did when she further cut Laurie's throat?"

"She held her chin back with her left hand and cut her throat, as though she were cutting bread."

"Okay. Did you see how many times that cut went across Laurie's throat?"

"Several times."

Lambert handed her the tip of the knife, which she put in her coat pocket. Buck picked up her sunglasses, and they left.

Lambert told her to put her hood up as they walked toward the woods. Yunkin picked them up on Oak View Road, north of the condominium entrance.

Yunkin looked at Lambert and said, "Blood?" They drove in silence to the trailer, where the women took showers. Buck tossed the tip of the knife somewhere in a room. She pulled on a pair of Lambert's black stretch legging pants and her white sweatshirt. Then Yunkin drove her to school.

Buck testified she did not answer completely in her April 1997 federal deposition and that she lied to Detective Joseph Geesey when he came to visit her at Muncy in 1997. Left out of her deposition testimony was the fact that she didn't say Lambert put the rope around Laurie's neck, and she didn't talk about Lambert's feelings about Laurie, or her sunglasses. She also left out that she saw Lambert make the cut on the throat and that Lambert told her she had called Mrs. Show the night before. Rather, she suggested that she learned that Mrs. Show would not be in the condominium that morning as they approached the front door.

She didn't tell all she knew because she was scared, she said.

"I was told not to say anything to anybody for a very long time, and I was left under the impression that the more I knew of anything, the worse off it would be for me. And aside from that, I was extremely intimidated that day. And I don't expect many people will understand this other reason. But being a lifer and having been incarcerated a lifer for as long as I have now, I would like to see women doing a life sentence go home,

get out of jail, and I just couldn't see saying certain
things, even against Michelle, if this were going to be a
chance for her to go home."

After the deposition, Buck wrote to her attorney R.
Russell Pugh.

"I have not been completely honest about what happened. Most of what I've told you is the truth but I've
purposely left some things out. Some very important
things. I knew how Michelle felt about Laurie. She
talked about it all the time. She always said how she
wanted to kill her. She would think of different ways to
do it and would ask me my opinion. I would tell her
that her plans would work and she'd laugh. She never
followed through with any of them, so I truly didn't
take her seriously. At first I didn't know who she was
talking about when she said 'Laurie,' but when she told
me her name was Laurie Show and she went to C.V., I
made a point to find out who it was. Laurie rode my
bus and I avoided her. I never spoke to her. I doubt if
she even knew my name.

"When Michelle came to the apartment on the nineteenth, she was upset and wanted to talk. She said she
was going to get Laurie, because the police were after her
for an assault against Laurie. She told me she had called
Ms. Show and pretended to be a counselor from school.
She said that Ms. Show wouldn't be at home in the morning and she wanted me to go with her. I asked her what
she was going to do and she said she was going to kill
her. I didn't believe her and I told her so. Then she said
she was just going to get her back for dating Lawrence
and for calling the police on her. I had never seen
Michelle fight anyone. She was all talk, so I guess I just
figured she was just talking and wasn't really going to hurt
Laurie. I told her I would go with her. She said for me
not to wear any nail polish or makeup and to put my hair

up. She said that way, if anything did happen, there would be no evidence of who was there. Again, I didn't take her seriously.

"The next day, I wore an old pair of blue jeans that were a favorite of mine and my white sweatshirt. When Michelle came, she asked if I had any sunglasses and I said yes. She told me to bring them. I did wear makeup and my hair was down. She didn't say anything about it, so I knew she wasn't serious about what she had said.

"When we got to the apartment, Michelle told me to put the sunglasses on so that Laurie wouldn't recognize me. I told her she didn't know me anyway but she insisted I wear them. Once we were inside the apartment, all hell broke loose. When Laurie tried to run to the door, she grabbed my glasses and threw them in the corner. She may have scratched me then.

"In the bedroom when Laurie was kneeling over the bed, Michelle handed me the knife after hitting Laurie with it. Then she pulled out the rope from under her shirt [jergo] and tried to put it around Laurie's neck. She told Laurie it would look like a suicide, and if Laurie didn't give in, then she [Michelle] would get a group of pagans to sacrifice her.

"Laurie stopped struggling and allowed Michelle to put the rope completely over her head. Then she went for the scissors. When I pushed them away, Michelle told me to cut Laurie's throat. I looked at her like she was crazy and I said 'No!' She told me to give her the knife and I did. Laurie was struggling again and Michelle cut her leg. She told her it would be a lot worse if she didn't cooperate. That's when Laurie started kicking again and Michelle told me to grab her feet. In the process of getting her feet down, she kicked me in my mouth.

"When I got off of Laurie's feet, I saw the neck wound and heard the air escaping. In my mind, I knew that she must be dead, but I asked anyway. I asked Michelle, 'Is she dead? Did you kill her?' She said, 'I don't know.' Then she cut Laurie's neck even deeper. I saw her do it. That's when she said, 'Come on. Let's go.' On my way out, I picked up my sunglasses and we left. At the trailer, we took showers and Michelle gave me a pair of black stretch pants to wear. My jeans had ripped open on one of the legs and there was blood on them.

"Everything else I told you was true. I didn't think she would actually do it and once she did, I was scared half to death. I don't know why I didn't tell you about her calling Ms. Show. I don't know why I didn't tell you about the rope. All I know is that I'm telling you the *whole* truth now. This is very hard for me to do, but I figure—what do I have to lose? I'm already doing Life. I know that I lied under oath at the deposition and I don't know what that will mean now. When I testify in court, I want to tell the truth. I hope that it isn't too late.

"I know I've disappointed you. You believed me and I lied to you. I apologize to you for deceiving you. If you want to wash your hands of my case—I won't blame you. Maybe I'll end up dying in prison, but at least my conscience will be clear. I know that I had no intentions of harming Laurie and I didn't believe Michelle would, either. But maybe I do deserve this life sentence.

"If I'm meant to go home—God will let me go and it won't happen without Him. Again, I am so sorry for lying to you. I'm sorry for lying to everybody, including Detective Geesey. I hope that you won't hate me because of it. I feel like the world has been lifted from my shoulders, but I know it will be hard for me to face you now. I am so sorry."

Buck also testified she received a letter from Rainville, asking for her help in November 1996. Rainville told Buck the federal court had appointed the Schnader law-firm to represent Lambert. She was writing, she said, to tell Buck she believed they had discovered new evidence that may help her as well as Lambert. The new evidence placed Yunkin at the scene and showed he had participated in the murder, the lawyer wrote. She might, in fact, be able to get a new trial, too, Rainville told her.

The lawyer encouraged Buck to tell what she knew about Yunkin's involvement. Even though Lambert was no longer her friend, and despite the bitterness between them, Buck should set that aside and tell about Yunkin's real role. They could help each other. Rainville also provided Buck with her phone number and told her to call collect if she was not represented by a lawyer at the time.

Buck wrote back that whatever new evidence Rainville claimed to have uncovered, it was simply untrue. She said she understood that her law firm was charged with doing whatever was necessary to defend Lambert, but the truth was, Yunkin was not there and did not participate in the crime. Buck said Lambert knew that as well as she did. She said she would not lie or corroborate Lambert's story just to get out of jail. She did not take other people's lives into her own hands, she said.

Buck said she did not know whether Yunkin knew in advance what Lambert intended to do to Laurie, but she did know for sure that he did not kill Laurie Show. She would not lie and cause Yunkin to serve a life sentence for something he didn't do. She knew too well what that felt like, Buck wrote.

Further, Buck said she resented Rainville's assumption that she would jeopardize someone else's life to make her own easier. That's Lambert's character flaw, not hers, Buck said. She ended her letter saying there was only one truth, known by her, Lambert, and God, and she would not help Lambert in any way.

On the day of closing arguments, Lambert's parents issued an astonishing press release. They accused their daughter of lying under oath when she testified that a family member sexually assaulted her ten years earlier.

"It's a total fabrication," Len Lambert said.

His daughter testified the incident was "unwanted sexual contact, not sexual assault." She considered it a "cry for help" from the family member.

"A claim of this nature leaves an indelible mark on a family," Len Lambert said. He felt he needed to take a stand on the matter, because it had never been challenged.

The hearing had taken eight weeks. Stengel had a month to render a decision.

On August 24, 1998, Stengel declared Lambert's petition without merit. Painstakingly in 322 pages, he refuted every one of the claims Lambert had made in federal court and Dalzell upheld.

There was no miscarriage of justice, the commonwealth judge said.

Hazel Show told the truth; the twenty-nine questions did not raise a reasonable doubt about Lambert's guilt; and her diagnosis as a "battered person" had no legal impact.

"We find the issues regarding Laura Thomas's credibility, Lawrence Yunkin's black sweatpants, the video of the river search, the statement taken of Ms. Lambert, the photographs of the crime scene, and the pearl earring to have more sensational appeal than legal merit. The issues have generated more heat than light in this case."

Stengel said it was difficult to decide just which moment of the hearing was the most bizarre.

"One likely contender, however, was the testimony by Dr. Burgess as to the sexually explicit poem dated January 16, 1992, written by Ms. Lambert for Mr. Yunkin."

Written in a childlike cadence, the poem talked about wanting oral sex and then shoving him to the floor for intercourse. She said she wanted him to make her scream until she begged for more, to pull her hair and call her a prostitute, and to ram his penis inside her for hours. Even when he was asleep, she said, she wanted him to have sex with her and to hurt her until she cried.

"The image that Ms. Lambert now tries to market, that she was a demure, dominated, controlled victim, is contrary to so much evidence," Stengel wrote. "From her verbal and physical assaults on Laurie Show, to her planning the abduction in the summer of 1991, from planning the attack on Laurie Show on the morning of December 20, 1991, to her strongly worded letter to Mr. Yunkin in the prison, Ms. Lambert demonstrated a character that is anything but demure and controlled."

He also refuted her assertion that she lived in fear of the police, especially Weaver.

"Ms. Rainville, co-counselor for petitioner, went so far as to suggest throughout the hearing that Ms. Lambert's child, born in March 1992, was the product of this gang rape. Yet, we know better. In one of Ms. Lambert's letters to Mr. Yunkin while in prison, she refers specifically to the baby and to Lawrence as the father."

She wrote she had told her parents they could have the baby. She would not give the baby to Yunkin's parents, because she believed they had raised him inappropriately. His mother "babied" him to the point he couldn't think for himself, she said. Moreover, Lambert wrote that she was dismayed that he was not even happy when she told him she was pregnant. He hit her and cheated on her, and then didn't believe she was pregnant.

Lambert told him that in her mind no one was a father to the baby. She loved him, but she loved the baby more, she said.

The baby's paternity had already been established in a custody hearing. Yunkin acknowledged paternity and DNA testing affirmed it. Lambert, as well as her parents, did not deny the results. The court ruled that the Yunkins had standing to sue for custody.

"Does it appear curious to anyone beside this court that Ms. Lambert will allow her attorney to assert that one of the rapists was the father of her daughter, while choosing not to contest DNA evidence that Lawrence Yunkin was the father of the child by a probability of 99.98 percent?"

Stengel doubted the verity of Lambert's gang rape story.

"To believe this, the court must believe that Officer Weaver, upon entering the Show condominium on December 20, 1991, observed a dying teenage girl and thought first to use the event to frame Ms. Lambert. To believe this, the court must accept that Detective Savage took a grieving mother aside within an hour of her daughter's death and planted in her mind the suggestion that her daughter made a dying declaration. To believe this, the court would have to accept that these police officers were acting first and foremost in an effort to use the murder of Laurie Show to frame a woman who was gang-raped six months earlier by them or by members of their department. This is just not believable.

"Nor does the gang rape explain why Ms. Lambert failed to go to the police on the morning of December 20, 1991. In fact, given every opportunity to explain to the police and at trial why she did not report the murder after she fled from the condominium complex, she never mentioned fear of the police because of a 'gang rape.' She talked about Mr. Yunkin watching her 'like a hawk,' she talked about being afraid of Ms. Buck, and she talked about not having access to a telephone. Yet, she went to collect her paycheck, she went to the local mall, she went to Mr. Yunkin's grandmother's home, she went back to Ms. Buck's residence, and then ultimately to the bowling alley. It strikes this court as unbelievable that Ms. Lambert failed to report this incident to anyone because of fear of the police arising out of the 'gang rape.'

"We know that in the spring, summer, and fall of 1991, Lisa Michelle Lambert demonstrated, time and again, hostility and aggression toward Laurie Show. We know of the many hysterical phone calls, the menacing language, and the relentless, threatening conduct. There is no question that Ms. Lambert contemplated, over an extended time period, the possibility of doing physical harm to Laurie Show. We find that Ms. Lambert discussed killing Laurie Show on at least two occasions."

Witnesses said Lambert tried to get others to kidnap and assault Laurie Show, that Lambert assaulted Laurie Show, that she hated Laurie Show, and that Laurie Show was terrified of her.

Stengel said he believed Buck was telling the truth about the murder. Lambert planned it and carried it out. Lambert didn't turn into a passive observer after getting Buck to help her, buying the materials and planning the attack.

"The crime scene photographs, the autopsy photographs, the condition of the condominium, and the condition of the body of Laurie Show led this court to one inescapable conclusion: Whoever performed these acts did so with a level of rage completely inconsistent with any accidental killing or a death incidental to a 'prank.' We firmly believed in 1992 that Lisa Michelle Lambert drew the knife across the throat of Laurie Show, causing her death. She was the only person with the level of emotion, the focus of purpose, and the clear opportunity to have performed that dreadful act. There is no question that Ms. Lambert is not, and never will be, 'innocent' of this crime."

Part 5: Epilogue

Thirty

Sometimes when Tabbi Buck thinks too long and too hard, when a certain sound or smell comes her way, a long-ago winter day in Lancaster, Pennsylvania, rushes into her mind. She sees the image of a dying girl as clearly as if it were still December 20, 1991. She didn't mean to be where she is, in a state prison at Muncy. The dawn of a new millennium came to her there in an open cell block surrounded by ninety other women. She was twenty-five. She had lost all of the chubbiness of her youth, cutting a sleek figure with hair still long and permed to nearly curly. Dark mascara and gray-brown eye shadow were her favorites. No more blues for her.

In her teenage dreams, she expected to be married by then. Most certainly, she would have been a teacher. But the laws of the Commonwealth of Pennsylvania prevented her from getting a college degree or even taking college courses. She was a lifer. No hope for parole unless something truly extraordinary happens. Lawmakers say a college education is wasted on such a girl.

She measures her life in the "before Michelle happened to me" and the after. Self-evaluation is the one constant in her life as sure as the unending litany of rules within the prison world. She wonders how she could have been so blind as not to see the true Lisa

Michelle Lambert. She didn't even know her real name was Lisa.

"She was my ride," Buck said. "We were not confidantes."

Yet, they were codefendants. They stayed in the same prison for more than a year, but came face-to-face only twice, both times in a courtroom. Buck felt the wrenching pain of betrayal. Lambert called Buck the murderer. With Yunkin, Buck plotted an especially heinous way to kill a sixteen-year-old girl, Lambert had said. She also told a courtroom full of people and the thousands of others who read newspapers that Buck had killed someone in Alaska. Buck was not yet four when her family moved from there, and she has not been back since. Lambert talked about Buck's boyfriends and how one used her for sex. She said Yunkin called Buck a "dyke."

"I don't believe anything she says," Buck said as she sat in the expansive visiting room at Muncy prison. As an elementary-school-age child visiting his mother counted the green chairs lined in straight rows, Buck talked about how much she misses the girl she used to be.

"I was naive, very friendly, happy," she said. "I smiled all the time. Since Michelle happened to me, I always look for the ulterior motive in other people."

She keeps people at arm's length. She had one close friend in the prison, a fellow lifer nicknamed "Snowy." They were roommates for five years, but they had a fight and stopped speaking. That's when Buck asked to be moved to the other side of Bethune Unit, the open side, where the bunks are separated not by walls and locked doors but by partitions. Not as much privacy, but not as confining, either.

When Buck arrived at Muncy, she expected all manner of difficulties, but life has not been horrid. She worked in the kitchen for a time, then in activities, be-

fore transferring into the school to tutor women in
math. She lost her privileges, though, for having three
jewelry violations. The rule is an inmate can have jewelry if she comes in with it. Buck did not. Once she
had a ring, the other times earrings.

"Apparently you don't listen," the hearing officer said
to her and dispatched her to RHU, the hole, for thirty
days. That was in 1994. Since then, she's worked in the
commissary and as a plumber. Finally she made it back
to the school, where she is the real teacher, not a
helper. She's gotten over the shyness that kept her from
being the leader before. She gets paid 24¢ an hour, one
of the highest wages in prison work.

She takes a fitness class and, in season, plays volleyball
and softball. Her volleyball team had a 17-4 record recently.

She tries not to think about how long she might be
in Muncy. Her lawyer, Russell Pugh, is working on getting her relief.

"I know I very well may be here the rest of my life,"
she said. "I try not to go there. To me, that's like hurting myself."

She's found peace in it and in herself.

"I am a good person," she said. She dreams not for
herself but for her family members, especially her
nieces. That doesn't mean she has given up on herself.
Facing reality seems to her a better way of saying it.

Buck said testifying against Lambert was difficult, but
it was right. Pugh said it wasn't without great sacrifice
that she did it. She admitted to being an accomplice in
a murder and she got no deal from the commonwealth
for implicating Lambert. Yunkin did. Long before either
woman stood trial he worked out a deal for ten to
twenty years. His parole hearing will be sometime in July
2001. She has no such date. It's unclear whether she

has any real hope for a reduced sentence. So much depends on what happens with Lambert, who in early 2000 was still appealing her conviction.

Pugh has a dream that one day he'll make the two-hour drive to Muncy, and instead of pulling out metal from his pockets and walking through a metal detector and then locked doors to see her, she will come strolling out the gate. She'll get in his car and he'll take her to the airport and put her on a plane bound for Oregon, where her mother and father live. Lawyers don't usually talk that way about convicted murderers.

Buck wonders about Lambert and how she's managed to drag out her case for so long, how she got a brilliant, aggressive Philadelphia lawyer to literally stake out a crusade for her. She wonders how Lambert convinced a well-respected federal judge to let her go. Even if it was for just ten months.

"How does she convince these people that what she's saying is true?" Buck asked. "How important is Michelle? Why would you believe all this crap?"

Many people have asked that of Christina Rainville, Lambert's attorney who in large measure staked her career on Lambert. Some people say she became obsessed with Lambert's case. She sees it as righting a wrong. Many years ago, in what seems like another lifetime to her, she was joined to a controlling man. She wore too much makeup and tried to please him with skimpy skirts. In addition, when she was twelve, she was molested by a teacher. She knows what it's like to feel powerless. She knows what it's like to be Lisa Michelle Lambert.

Rainville believes completely in Lambert. Her husband is the only man Lambert trusts. One or the other of them talks to Lambert every day, a routine they've kept since they met her three years ago. People tell them they are too emotionally involved. But to them,

Lambert is family. Rainville gave birth to a daughter in
1999, completing the family she always wanted.

Lambert's parents, meanwhile, moved to Maryland
several years ago and are raising their daughter's child.
The threats and abuse in the community had become
unbearable, they said. They went through a messy custody battle with the Yunkins, but the Lamberts eventually won out.

The Yunkins sued for custody, then dropped the suit
to seek visitation rights. They felt it was in the girl's best
interest, because by the time the case was to be heard,
she was two and the Lamberts were the only parents
she had known. The court did allow them supervised
visitation for a time. They met at Busy Barn. Kirsten, at
nearly two, was shy and frightened. Jackie Yunkin had
seen her one other time—fleetingly—when she was
dropping money off for her son at Lancaster County
Prison. Judy Lambert had the month-old baby in the
visiting room with her daughter. Jackie Yunkin said that
as soon as Lambert saw her, Lambert threw a blanket
over the baby's head.

The court ordered a DNA test to establish paternity.
It took three weeks for the results.

"I was doing flips," Jackie said. "I'm screaming. It's
Lawrence's. It's Lawrence's."

Eventually, though, the court stripped him of his pa-
rental rights. A sad state for the Yunkins.

On a visit to her son in the prison at Dallas, Pennsylvania, Jackie Yunkin showed him a picture of Kirsten.
He looked at the photo and said, "Mom, is this my
daughter? Oh my God, look at her blond hair and blue
eyes. She's beautiful, Mom."

He talks to his parents on the phone on Wednesdays,
and they make the three-hour drive to see him on Sat-
urdays. Jackie Yunkin is still pulling down two jobs, Weis

Market and the bowling alley, while her husband is driving a truck. They had a son, B.J., in 1993.

"I think God gave us him," Jackie said. "When Lawrence went to prison, we went into a shell. We shut the world out. You don't understand why things happen. You think OK, we're bad parents. It's like God is saying here's your second chance."

She said the trials were tough, especially hearing her son characterized as an abuser, a rapist, a murderer. She had not heard that Laurie Show accused Yunkin of rape until one day in the courtroom during Lambert's trial. He looked pleadingly at her as if to say it's all right.

"The whole time you're thinking, that's OK as long as I know the truth and God knows the truth," she said.

Yunkin has learned sign language in prison. His job is making bread in the kitchen, but he would rather do something outside such as lawn maintenance or farm work. He plays on the baseball team, traveling to other prisons. He's been a good prisoner, in trouble once for gambling. Jackie hopes he'll be paroled on his first try next year. Most think he'll serve about eleven years.

For quite some time, Jackie Yunkin felt much anger toward Lambert, but then she realized she was only hurting herself.

"A lot of times, I wanted to kill her myself, but that's not my nature," Jackie said. "I could beat her up maybe."

Her son told her he will always love Lambert. She gave him a child.

The Lancaster County District Attorney's Office and the East Lampeter Police Department emerged battered but unfazed from a civil rights investigation ordered by Dalzell. The police department, especially, was wracked with turmoil for some time. Officers could not speak with one another. Everyone was interviewed. Suspicion hovered over them. Residents would call and say, "Send one

of your perverts around." Others stood with them. The
U.S. Justice Department found no improprieties. Kenneff
ran for D.A. but lost; Madenspacher became a judge.
Renee and Jere Schuler divorced. She was promoted to
lieutenant, second in command of the East Lampeter
Township Police Department, which has added a second
floor and eleven officers since the Laurie Show murder
investigation.

Schuler said it was difficult for the department and
most especially for Weaver, Bowman, and her to get over
the charges leveled against them through Lambert and
Rainville.

"We all here started feeling victimized," she said. "I
had to get to the place where I realized I'm a survivor,
not a victim. They're not going to affect my day, my
life. They're not going to control my life."

Hazel Show steadily rebuilt her life, and as she did, a
bit of Laurie slipped away. For sure, her daughter will
always be with her. She feels her presence all the time.
She feels her love. No one can take that. Laurie's friends
used to come around every now and then, but they
stopped years ago. Laurie would have been twenty-five on
her last birthday. Her friends are married with children
of their own.

Hazel was planning to be married herself in September 2000 to a man she met while visiting a friend. He
has helped her emerge from the shell she wrapped
around herself for so long after Laurie died. The marriage seems like a step away from Laurie, too. She will
no longer have the same name.

She has spent untold hours in courtrooms and hotel
rooms in her quest for justice for her daughter. She has
spent money she couldn't afford and lost wages from
days off from work. And she expects there will be more

loss. But she has an ease about it now that she didn't have before.

"What the system doesn't take care of, God will," she said.

Still, she resents the intrusion in her life. She resents people calling her a liar. She resents someone putting the image in her mind of police dragging her daughter's body back into her house, putting blood and dirt on her face so they can frame an innocent girl. Lisa Michelle Lambert is no innocent to Hazel. She looks in her eyes and sees emptiness. She looks in her eyes and sees evil.

"It just compounds everything that has happened," she said of the Rainville conspiracy theory.

Christy Fawcett, the assistant attorney general who represented the commonwealth in the successful 1998 postconviction relief hearing, decried the idea as ludicrous. She counted forty-six people who would have to be disbelieved in order to believe Lambert's story. Since the hearing, Lambert has added two more to the list of conspirators: Fawcett and her investigator.

"You can't even get two people to keep their mouths shut about anything, especially something that bizarre," Hazel said.

She and her ex-husband submitted petitions bearing forty thousand names on it to the court administration claiming Dalzell acted improperly and should be impeached, but the review board declined to act. They had better luck lobbying for a law making stalking illegal. Acting Governor Mark Single signed it in 1994 as Hazel and John stood by. No longer does someone have to wait for an act of violence before a warrant can be issued.

John Show lessens his pain by reaching out to others. He attends a monthly support group for parents who have lost children to violence. Through it he speaks with parents of murdered children all over the country. He knows how they feel. It takes a parent who has been through it to understand. Others can only imagine, and what they imagine is just not as bad as it is. He feels Laurie's presence often and thinks of her and her sweet smile every single day.

Each year Show brings forth a candlelight ceremony celebrating lives lost. It is held on the weekend before Christmas. The first was held the year after Laurie died. Some three hundred people joined him at his church, Mellingers Mennonite, to stand before a six-foot-tall cross emblazoned with three hundred lit candles to remember Laurie and others. Hazel went that year and the next, but the strain of the emotion is too great for her to bear. John cries talking about it; it is so powerful an event. In 1999 bagpipers played. In 2000 he was planning on bell ringers.

When he retires in 2001, he plans to become a full-time victim's advocate, along the lines of John Walsh and Fred Goldman.

"There are so many laws that need to be passed," Show said. Laws that help victims not criminals. Sometimes he fantasizes about having his own prison. Television, weight lifting, and most especially law libraries would be banned.

"It would be like the old chain gangs," he said.

He also has not given up pressing for an investigation of Stewart Dalzell, the federal judge who released Michelle Lambert in 1997.

"We need something done," he said.

Joanne Guier, who married in 2000 and changed her last name to McKinney, has her own action plan. She wants to see her daughter Tabbi released. In early 2000, Tabbi had served nine years. That seemed close to enough for being an accomplice to murder.

"She should serve her debt to society, but she does

not deserve to have the same sentence as the one who did the murder," McKinney said. "Tab has always befriended the underdog. She became a pawn in a plan. There's nothing I can do about it. I'm the mom, I'm supposed to be able to do something, but I'm helpless."

McKinney said she doesn't make excuses for her daughter's behavior, for running with the wrong crowd, and for going out that night to the bowling alley as if nothing had happened.

Tabbi Buck said she went because Lambert and Yunkin showed up at her door and she was afraid. It is the same reason she didn't go to the police. She had seen what Lambert was capable of and it scared her.

"Right before they came over, I was watching television and was overwhelmed with grief. Everything hit me about what had happened and I thought, oh my God. I wanted to call the police and they [Lambert and Yunkin] came, and then in that moment, I went along with the story. I don't understand it and I know many people don't understand it, but I'd probably do the same again. It is survival instinct."

Now, she says, she looks in the mirror and she likes what she sees.

"If I die here, at least I'll know I'm a good person," she said.

Lisa Michelle Lambert, meanwhile, passes her days at Edna Mahon Prison in New Jersey. She refuses interviews. Recent ones didn't turn out as she had hoped. She thinks she was not treated fairly. She is still a beautiful young woman, but with brown hair and eyes and a touch of carefully applied makeup. Gone is the thick foundation, the black-rimmed eyes. In a televised interview in the late 1990s, she said, "One day we're just teenagers. It's just a mess."

The Lancaster County judicial system is so corrupt

"nobody knows how deep it is," she told ABC's Forrest Sawyer on *20/20* in 1999.

She looks blankly at him and says, "It's very sad." Her voice straggles out in a flat monotone. "I'm very sorry about what happened, but I wasn't the cause of it."

ACKNOWLEDGMENTS

Some years ago, when I was writing newspaper stories about the young mother who drowned her two sons in a Union, S.C. lake, the woman's mother said something I have never forgotten. "Why has one family's tragedy become a nation's entertainment?" she asked. I had no answer. Her words come back to me with great regularity as I write more newspaper stories and as I write books about crime. The question makes me think of respect for the dead, but most especially for the living.

I heard those words clearly as I sat in the living room of Hazel Show's home in East Lampeter Township, Pennsylvania, just steps from the spot where her daughter was slain, as she recounted that day and the days that followed. She told me stories she had told no one before. For that I am grateful and feel much responsibility.

I feel deep gratitude as well for John Show, Laurie's father, who was willing to share his sorrow yet again so his daughter will not be forgotten. To the members of the East Lampeter Township Police, especially Lt. Renee Schuler, much thanks. They were swept up in nothing less than a tidal wave of criticism for the way they did their jobs, a tumult that caused deep hurt and worry. And yet, they were willing to go back to their memories for the sake of truth. Tabbi Buck was most helpful as were many members of her family. And the Yunkins, Barry and Jackie, provided invaluable insight into the lives of their son and his former girlfriend.

Thanks, too, to my agent Frank Weimann and my editor at Pinnacle, Karen Haas. They are the most patient people on the planet.

To my friend, fellow writer, and best critic, Jamie Jones, deep respect and appreciation. And to my children, Josh, Lauren, and Colin, unending and unconditional love.

Hazel and John Show have taken life's worst shot, the unnatural course that unfolds when a child precedes parents in death. They placed one foot in front of another and somehow got through the days of the past decade. It has not been easy. They are heroes, deserving a telling of their lives that is honest and true, one that shows respect, not sensationalism. I hope this meets that test.

Simpsonville, South Carolina
September 12, 2000